CHAPTER 1:

Having established the foundational aspects of Nim, it is essential to delve into the practical applications and the language's real-world capabilities, which underscore its distinctive features and benefits. In this exploration, I will focus on how Nim's design choices translate into tangible advantages for software development and system programming.

One of the most compelling aspects of Nim is its ability to produce highly optimized, efficient code while retaining a high level of abstraction. This duality is achieved through its sophisticated compilation process, which includes multiple stages of optimization. When a Nim program is compiled, it goes through an extensive series of transformations that refine and enhance the generated machine code. This process includes inlining functions, eliminating dead code, and applying various algorithmic optimizations. Such optimizations ensure that the final executable is not only performant but also compact, which is crucial for systems programming where resource constraints are a significant consideration.

Nim's compilation process is further augmented by its support for multiple backends. It can generate code for various platforms, including C, C++, and JavaScript, which allows developers to target different environments without modifying the core logic of their programs. This cross-compilation capability extends Nim's utility beyond traditional systems programming to web development and other application domains. For instance, by compiling to JavaScript, developers can leverage Nim's features to create web applications that benefit from its performance characteristics while maintaining the language's ease of use.

Another significant advantage of Nim is its advanced type system, which enhances both safety and expressiveness. Nim employs a strong, static type system that allows for early detection of type-related errors during compilation. This static typing is complemented by Nim's type inference mechanism, which can automatically deduce the types of expressions, reducing the need for explicit type annotations and thereby simplifying the code. However, when explicit type definitions are necessary, Nim supports complex type constructs, such as generics and custom types, which empower developers to create robust and reusable components. This combination of strong typing and type inference balances safety with flexibility, contributing to Nim's effectiveness in systems programming where precise type management is often critical.

Moreover, Nim's support for multiple programming paradigms—imperative, functional, and object-oriented—enables developers to choose the most appropriate approach for their specific needs. This versatility is particularly advantageous in systems programming, where different problems might require different programming strategies. For instance, an imperative approach might be preferred for low-level memory manipulation, while functional programming can be beneficial for handling complex data transformations. Nim's object-oriented features, such as classes and inheritance, provide additional tools for structuring and organizing code, making it easier to manage large codebases and complex systems.

The language also includes an innovative approach to error handling and resource management. Nim incorporates both traditional exception handling mechanisms and a unique system of compile-time checks that ensure code correctness. For example, Nim's ownership and borrowing model can prevent common issues such as dangling pointers and memory leaks. This model enforces rules about how data is accessed and modified, which is particularly useful in systems programming where manual memory management is often a source of bugs and vulnerabilities.

Nim's robust standard library is another crucial aspect of its practical utility. The library provides a comprehensive set of modules and functions that facilitate common programming tasks, from data manipulation and file handling to network communication and concurrency. This extensive standard library reduces the need for external dependencies and accelerates development by offering well-tested and optimized components. Additionally, Nim's support for creating and managing packages through its package manager, Nimble, streamlines the process of integrating third-party libraries and tools into projects.

The language's emphasis on metaprogramming and compile-time evaluation enhances its adaptability and power. Nim's macro system allows for the creation of custom language constructs and domain-specific languages, which can simplify complex problems and improve code clarity. By enabling developers to generate code dynamically based on compile-time information, Nim facilitates advanced programming techniques that can lead to more efficient and expressive solutions.

Furthermore, Nim's growing community and ecosystem contribute to its viability and support. The community provides valuable resources, including documentation, tutorials, and forums, where developers can seek assistance and share their experiences. The active development of the language and its ecosystem ensures that Nim continues to evolve, incorporating new features and improvements based on user feedback and technological advancements.

In summary, Nim's design and features offer a compelling proposition for modern software development, particularly in the realm of systems programming. Its ability to generate optimized code, combined with a versatile type system, support for multiple programming paradigms, and robust standard library, makes it a powerful tool for developers. The language's unique attributes, such as metaprogramming capabilities and cross-compilation support, further enhance its appeal by providing flexibility and efficiency in various application domains. As we continue to explore Nim's capabilities, it becomes increasingly evident that this language stands as a significant advancement in the landscape of programming languages, merging performance with ease of use in a manner that is both innovative and practical.

To fully appreciate Nim's role in contemporary software development, it is crucial to examine its integration with modern development practices and the practical considerations that arise from its unique features. Nim's design not only impacts the efficiency and versatility of the code but also influences the overall development workflow and ecosystem.

One notable aspect of Nim's integration with development practices is its support for incremental compilation. This feature significantly enhances the development cycle by allowing developers to compile only the parts of the code that have changed, rather than the entire project. This incremental approach accelerates the feedback loop, making it easier to test and refine code iteratively. In systems programming, where debugging and fine-tuning are often time-consuming, Nim's incremental compilation can lead to considerable time savings and improved productivity.

Another important consideration is Nim's approach

to concurrency and parallelism. In modern software development, effectively managing concurrent tasks and utilizing multi-core processors are essential for optimizing performance. Nim provides several constructs for handling concurrency, including lightweight threads known as "async" and "await" for asynchronous programming. These constructs simplify the development of non-blocking operations, allowing developers to write code that is both efficient and easy to understand. The language's design also includes support for channels, which facilitate safe communication between concurrent tasks, thus reducing the likelihood of race conditions and deadlocks.

Nim's performance profiling and debugging tools further enhance its practicality in real-world applications. The language includes built-in support for performance profiling, which allows developers to analyze the execution of their programs and identify bottlenecks. Profiling is critical in systems programming, where performance is often a primary concern. Nim's profiling tools provide detailed insights into code execution, enabling developers to make informed decisions about optimizations and improvements. Additionally, Nim's debugging facilities support a range of debugging techniques, including interactive debugging and the use of assertions to validate code behavior during development.

Nim's cross-platform capabilities also play a significant role in its practicality. The language's ability to target multiple platforms, including Windows, macOS, and Linux, facilitates the development of portable applications. This cross-platform support is achieved through the use of platform-specific backends, which ensure that code can be compiled and run on different operating systems without modification. This feature is particularly valuable in systems programming, where applications often need to operate across various environments. Nim's cross-platform nature reduces the need for platform-specific code and simplifies the deployment process.

Furthermore, Nim's ecosystem is bolstered by its package management system, Nimble, which simplifies the integration of external libraries and tools. Nimble allows developers to manage dependencies, install third-party packages, and maintain project configurations with ease. The availability of a diverse set of packages through Nimble extends the language's functionality and provides developers with additional resources to accelerate development. The active development and maintenance of these packages contribute to the robustness and versatility of Nim's ecosystem.

Security considerations are also integral to the discussion of Nim's practical applications. In systems programming, security is paramount, and Nim addresses this with features that enhance code safety. For example, Nim's strong type system and compile-time checks help prevent common security vulnerabilities, such as buffer overflows and null pointer dereferences. The language's emphasis on memory management and error handling further contributes to its security posture. By reducing the likelihood of common programming errors and providing mechanisms for safe resource management, Nim supports the development of secure and reliable systems.

As we examine the broader impact of Nim on software development practices, it becomes evident that its design choices offer substantial benefits. The language's blend of performance and ease of use, coupled with its support for modern development practices such as concurrency, profiling, and cross-platform development, positions it as a valuable tool for a wide range of applications. Nim's ecosystem, including its package management system and community support, further enhances its appeal and utility.

In conclusion, Nim's integration with contemporary development practices, combined with its unique features and capabilities, underscores its significance in the modern programming landscape. Its ability to produce efficient code, support concurrency, facilitate debugging and profiling, and offer cross-platform compatibility makes it a powerful and versatile language. As developers continue to seek tools that balance performance with productivity, Nim stands out as a compelling choice, offering a comprehensive solution for both systems programming and high-level application development. The exploration of Nim's practical applications reveals its potential to address a variety of programming challenges, providing a valuable asset for developers in diverse domains.

CHAPTER 2:

The next critical aspect of configuring your development environment involves the integration of various tools and practices that streamline your coding process and enhance productivity. After establishing the basic setup with the Nim compiler and Nimble package manager, attention must turn to optimizing how you work with code on a daily basis. This encompasses the effective use of version control systems, setting up testing frameworks, and customizing development environments to match your workflow.

Version control is a fundamental practice in modern software development, providing a mechanism for managing changes to your codebase and collaborating with others. Git, the most widely used version control system, integrates seamlessly with Nim and offers robust features for tracking changes, branching, and merging. To begin, you should initialize a Git repository in your project directory. This can be accomplished by executing the command `git init` within your project's root folder. Following initialization, you can begin tracking files by using `git add` to stage changes and `git commit` to save those changes to the repository. For more comprehensive version control management, you might connect your local repository to a remote repository on platforms such as GitHub, GitLab, or Bitbucket. This setup not only provides a backup of your code but also facilitates collaboration with other developers.

Next, incorporating a testing framework into your development process is essential for ensuring the reliability and correctness of your code. Nim includes a built-in testing module known as `unittest`, which is designed to facilitate the writing and execution of unit tests. By writing tests for your code, you can systematically verify its functionality and catch potential bugs early in the development cycle. The `unittest` module allows you to define test cases and assertions, which can be executed to confirm that your code behaves as expected. Running these tests regularly as part of your development workflow helps maintain high code quality and reduces the risk of introducing errors.

To enhance testing practices further, you might consider integrating Continuous Integration (CI) tools into your workflow. CI systems automate the process of running tests and building your project every time changes are made. Tools such as Travis CI, GitHub Actions, or GitLab CI can be configured to automatically run your Nim tests upon code commits or pull requests. This automation ensures that any issues are identified promptly, allowing for quicker resolution and consistent code quality.

Customizing your development environment to suit your specific needs is another crucial step. Integrated Development Environments (IDEs) and text editors offer various configurations and extensions that can be tailored to improve your coding experience. For instance, in Visual Studio Code, you can customize settings such as code formatting, linting, and build tasks to align with your preferences and project requirements. Extensions like Nim Language Server or NimLSP provide additional features such as code completion, error highlighting, and go-to-definition capabilities, further enhancing your productivity.

In addition to IDE customization, integrating debugging tools can significantly streamline the development process. Nim supports various debugging techniques, including setting breakpoints, stepping through code, and inspecting variables.

Many IDEs, such as VS Code and CLion, offer built-in debugging support for Nim, allowing you to debug your applications directly within the editor. By utilizing these debugging tools, you can identify and resolve issues more efficiently, leading to a more effective development workflow.

As you work with Nim, adopting coding standards and practices that promote code readability and maintainability is essential. Nim's built-in code formatter, `nim pretty`, helps enforce consistent code style by automatically formatting your code according to predefined rules. Consistent code formatting improves readability and helps ensure that your code adheres to best practices, making it easier for both you and others to understand and maintain.

Another consideration is setting up a project structure that supports scalability and organization. For larger projects, organizing your code into modules and packages can improve manageability and facilitate collaboration. Nim's module system allows you to define and organize code into separate files, which can be imported and used across different parts of your project. This modular approach promotes code reuse and makes it easier to navigate and maintain complex codebases.

Finally, documentation is a critical aspect of any development process, particularly for collaborative projects. Writing clear and concise documentation for your code helps other developers understand its functionality and usage. Nim provides support for documentation generation through comments and annotations within your code. By documenting your code effectively, you contribute to the overall quality and maintainability of your project.

In summary, setting up a development environment for Nim involves more than just installing the compiler and package manager. It requires integrating various tools and practices that enhance your coding efficiency and project management.

By incorporating version control, testing frameworks, CI tools, IDE customizations, debugging capabilities, coding standards, and documentation practices, you create a robust and effective development environment. These steps ensure that you can work with Nim effectively, maintain high code quality, and manage your projects efficiently.

When setting up your development environment for Nim, it is also important to consider the integration of additional tools and practices that will further refine and enhance your workflow. Beyond the initial setup of the Nim compiler and Nimble package manager, focusing on the nuances of environment configuration and project management can significantly impact your development efficiency and project success.

One crucial aspect of configuring your environment is the use of environment variables and configuration files. These settings allow you to tailor your development environment to specific needs and preferences. For example, environment variables can be used to specify paths to dependencies, configure compiler options, or manage project-specific settings. In Nim, the `nim.cfg` configuration file is particularly important as it allows you to customize compiler flags, set library paths, and define project-wide settings. By editing this file, you can streamline the build process and ensure that your projects adhere to specific configurations, such as enabling debugging information or optimizing for performance.

Another consideration is the management of external dependencies and libraries. Nim's package manager, Nimble, plays a vital role in this process by facilitating the installation and management of third-party packages. When working on a project, you might need to integrate various libraries or modules to extend the functionality of your application. Using Nimble, you can easily add these dependencies to your project by specifying them in the `nimble` file or installing them directly using the `nimble install` command. This capability ensures that your project remains modular and that all necessary dependencies are properly managed and updated.

In addition to dependency management, establishing a consistent build process is essential for maintaining project stability and reproducibility. Nimble allows you to define custom build commands and scripts within your `nimble` file, enabling you to automate common tasks such as compiling, testing, and packaging. By defining these tasks, you can ensure that the build process is consistent across different environments and that all necessary steps are executed automatically. This automation helps reduce human error and streamlines the development workflow, making it easier to manage complex projects and ensure reliable builds.

Moreover, incorporating continuous integration and continuous deployment (CI/CD) practices into your development workflow can greatly enhance the efficiency and quality of your projects. CI/CD tools automate the process of building, testing, and deploying code, providing rapid feedback and ensuring that your codebase remains in a deployable state. By configuring a CI/CD pipeline, you can automatically run tests, build your project, and deploy updates to various environments whenever changes are made. This practice helps catch issues early, maintain code quality, and accelerate the delivery of new features and improvements.

In the context of debugging and performance optimization, utilizing profiling tools and performance analysis techniques is essential. Nim provides several tools for profiling and analyzing code performance, such as the built-in `profile` module. This module allows you to measure the execution time of different parts of your code and identify performance bottlenecks. By analyzing these performance metrics, you can make informed decisions about optimizations and improvements, ensuring that your application runs efficiently and effectively.

Furthermore, it is beneficial to explore and adopt best practices for project organization and code management. Structuring your projects in a modular and organized manner facilitates easier navigation and maintenance. Nim's module system allows you to break your code into smaller, manageable units, each with its own set of responsibilities. By organizing your code into well-defined modules, you promote code reuse, enhance readability, and simplify the process of managing dependencies and interactions between different parts of your application.

In addition to modular code organization, implementing a systematic approach to documentation and code comments is crucial for maintaining a clear and understandable codebase. Writing comprehensive documentation for your code and using descriptive comments helps others (and yourself) understand the purpose and functionality of different components. This practice not only aids in collaboration and code review but also serves as a valuable reference for future development and maintenance.

Lastly, as you continue to develop with Nim, staying engaged with the community and keeping abreast of updates and new developments in the Nim ecosystem is important. The Nim community offers valuable resources, including forums, mailing lists, and online discussions, where you can seek advice, share experiences, and learn from others. Additionally, following updates and changes to the Nim language and its libraries ensures that you are aware of new features, improvements, and best practices that can enhance your development process.

In conclusion, setting up a development environment for Nim involves more than just installing the necessary tools; it requires a thoughtful approach to configuration, dependency management, build processes, and best practices. By incorporating environment variables, automating build tasks, integrating CI/CD practices, utilizing profiling tools, organizing your code effectively, and staying connected with the community, you create a robust and efficient development environment. These considerations ensure that your projects are well-managed, maintain high quality, and can be developed and deployed with confidence.

CHAPTER 3:

Building on the fundamentals of variable declarations, data types, and control structures, it is essential to delve deeper into some of the more nuanced aspects of Nim's syntax that enhance code clarity and functionality. This exploration includes the use of functions, procedures, and their respective features such as default parameters and overloading. Moreover, understanding Nim's approach to error handling and its approach to modular programming will further solidify your grasp of the language.

Functions in Nim are a cornerstone of programming, providing a way to encapsulate reusable blocks of code. The syntax for defining a function is both simple and expressive. A basic function in Nim is declared using the `proc` keyword followed by the function name, parameters, and return type. For example, a function that computes the factorial of a number can be defined as follows:

```nim
proc factorial(n: int): int
 if n < 1:
  return 1
 else:
  return n factorial(n - 1)
```

In this example, `factorial` is a procedure that takes an integer `n` as an argument and returns an integer. The `if` statement inside the function checks if `n` is less than or equal to 1, in which case it returns 1; otherwise, it performs a recursive call to compute the factorial.

Nim also supports default parameters in functions, which allow you to provide default values for parameters that are not explicitly passed by the caller. This feature can simplify function calls and make your code more flexible. For instance:

```nim
proc greet(name: string "World")
  echo "Hello, ", name
```

In this case, if `greet` is called without arguments, it defaults to "World". This default value feature helps avoid the need for overloading functions or manually checking for missing arguments.

Overloading is another powerful feature in Nim that allows you to define multiple procedures with the same name but different parameter types or counts. This capability can be leveraged to create more flexible and intuitive APIs. Here's an example of function overloading in Nim:

```nim
proc add(a: int, b: int): int
  return a + b

proc add(a: float, b: float): float
  return a + b
```

Here, the `add` procedure is defined twice with different parameter types. Depending on the arguments passed, Nim will automatically select the appropriate procedure to execute. This feature enhances code clarity by allowing functions with similar purposes but different input types to share the same name.

Error handling in Nim is managed through exceptions,

which are used to signal and handle error conditions. Nim provides a straightforward mechanism for raising and catching exceptions using the `raise` and `try` constructs, respectively. Here's an example illustrating how to handle exceptions in Nim:

```nim
proc divide(x, y: int): int
 if y 0:
  raise newException(ValueError, "Division by zero")
 return x div y

try:
 echo divide(10, 0)
except ValueError as e:
 echo "Error: ", e.msg
```

In this example, the `divide` procedure raises a `ValueError` exception if an attempt is made to divide by zero. The `try` block executes the code that might throw an exception, while the `except` block catches the exception and handles it, displaying an error message.

Modular programming in Nim is facilitated through the use of modules and import statements. Modules allow you to encapsulate code into separate files, making it easier to manage and organize your project. To define a module, you simply create a new file with a `.nim` extension and include the desired procedures, functions, and variables. For example, you might have a file named `math_utils.nim` containing:

```nim
proc add(a, b: int): int
 return a + b
```

To use this module in another file, you would import it using the `import` statement:

```nim
import math_utils

echo add(2, 3)
```

This approach helps keep your codebase clean and modular, allowing for better organization and separation of concerns.

Nim's syntax also supports powerful features such as templates and macros, which can be used to create more dynamic and flexible code. Templates in Nim are similar to macros in other languages, allowing you to generate code at compile time based on templates. This feature can be useful for creating reusable code patterns and reducing redundancy.

For instance, a simple template might look like this:

```nim
template printTwice(x)
  echo x
  echo x
```

When used, this template generates code that prints the argument `x` twice:

```nim
printTwice("Hello")
```

This results in:

```
Hello
Hello
```

Templates enhance code reusability and maintainability by

allowing you to define common patterns and behaviors that can be reused across different parts of your application.

In summary, understanding and utilizing Nim's functions, procedures, default parameters, overloading, error handling, modular programming, and advanced features such as templates and macros will enable you to write more effective and organized code. These elements of Nim's syntax provide the tools necessary for both simple and complex programming tasks, allowing for both clean and powerful code development.

Nim's approach to object-oriented programming (OOP) and its support for functional programming paradigms are vital components of its versatile syntax. Exploring these aspects will enhance your understanding of how to leverage Nim's full potential for various programming tasks. By examining how Nim implements OOP principles, manages state, and integrates functional programming features, you will gain insights into writing more sophisticated and adaptable code.

Nim's object-oriented capabilities are implemented through the use of objects and object-oriented constructs such as inheritance and polymorphism. An object in Nim is defined using the `object` keyword and allows for encapsulating data and methods within a single entity. For example, to define a basic class-like structure for a `Person`, you might write:

```nim
type
  Person object
    name: string
    age: int

proc introduce(p: Person)
  echo "Hi, I am ", p.name, " and I am ", p.age, " years old."
```

In this snippet, `Person` is an object type with two fields:

`name` and `age`. The `introduce` procedure is a method that operates on an instance of `Person`, demonstrating how to encapsulate behavior alongside data.

Inheritance in Nim allows you to create more specialized versions of existing objects by extending them with additional fields or methods. This is achieved by using the `object` keyword to create a new type that inherits from a base type. For instance, to create a `Student` type that inherits from `Person`, you might use:

```nim
type
  Student object of Person
    studentId: int

proc introduce(s: Student)
  echo "Hi, I am ", s.name, ", my student ID is ", s.studentId, " and I am ", s.age, " years old."
```

Here, `Student` extends `Person` by adding a new field, `studentId`. The `introduce` method for `Student` is overridden to include the additional information.

Polymorphism is supported in Nim through the use of object types and method overriding. By defining methods with the same name in derived types, you can achieve polymorphic behavior where the method invoked depends on the actual type of the object at runtime. For instance, you might define different `introduce` methods for `Person` and `Student`, and the appropriate method will be called based on the object's type.

Nim also supports functional programming constructs, which offer a different approach to problem-solving compared to traditional OOP methods. Functional programming in Nim is facilitated through the use of first-class functions, higher-order functions, and immutable data structures. First-class functions mean that functions can be passed as arguments to other functions, returned as values, and assigned to variables.

A higher-order function is one that takes one or more functions as arguments or returns a function as its result. For example, you might define a function that takes another function as an argument to apply a transformation:

```nim
proc applyTransform(f: proc (int): int, x: int): int
  result f(x)

proc square(x: int): int
  return x x

echo applyTransform(square, 5)
```

In this example, `applyTransform` is a higher-order function that applies the `square` function to its argument. The result is the square of the number, demonstrating how functions can be used flexibly within other functions.

Immutable data structures in Nim support functional programming by ensuring that data cannot be modified after creation. This immutability provides safety and predictability in concurrent programming environments. For example, sequences in Nim can be immutable, meaning that once a sequence is created, its elements cannot be changed, which avoids potential side effects and makes reasoning about code easier.

Another important feature in Nim related to functional programming is the support for closures. Closures are functions that capture the environment in which they were defined, allowing them to access variables from that environment even after the function has been called. This can be useful for creating functions with customized behavior:

```nim
proc makeMultiplier(factor: int): proc (x: int): int
  result proc (x: int): int
    return x factor

let double makeMultiplier(2)
echo double(5)
```

In this code, `makeMultiplier` returns a closure that multiplies its argument by a specified `factor`. The `double` function is a closure that captures the `factor` of 2, effectively doubling the input value.

Nim's support for concurrency and parallelism is also worth noting as it complements its syntactic features and enhances its capability for handling complex tasks. The language provides constructs such as `async` and `await` for asynchronous programming, allowing you to write non-blocking code that can handle multiple tasks concurrently. For instance, you can define an asynchronous procedure and await its result:

```nim
import asyncdispatch

proc doWork() {.async.}
  await sleepAsync(1000)
  echo "Work done"

asyncMain doWork()
```

In this example, `doWork` is an asynchronous procedure that performs some work after sleeping for a second. The `asyncMain` procedure runs the asynchronous task, allowing you to manage concurrent operations efficiently.

In conclusion, mastering Nim's object-oriented and functional programming features will significantly enhance your ability to write sophisticated and flexible code. By understanding how to leverage objects, inheritance, polymorphism, first-class functions, higher-order functions, immutability, closures, and concurrency constructs, you can create robust and maintainable programs. These advanced features of Nim complement its foundational syntax and control structures, making it a powerful tool for a wide range of programming tasks.

CHAPTER 4:

To further deepen our understanding of Nim's data structures, it is crucial to examine the more advanced features and capabilities that the language offers. This includes exploring the use of `tables`, which are essentially hash maps or dictionaries in Nim, and understanding the nuances of working with `optionals` and `ref` types for more sophisticated data management. These structures extend Nim's flexibility and efficiency in handling diverse programming scenarios.

Tables in Nim, implemented using the `Table` type from the `tables` module, provide an efficient way to store key-value pairs where each key maps to a specific value. This data structure is invaluable for scenarios requiring quick lookups, insertions, and deletions based on keys. The `Table` type in Nim supports various hash functions and allows for flexible key and value types, which can be customized according to the needs of your application. Here is an example demonstrating the use of `Table` to manage a collection of string-integer pairs:

```nim
import tables

var phonebook: Table[string, int] initTable[string, int]()
phonebook["Alice"] 123456789
phonebook["Bob"] 987654321

echo "Alice's phone number: ", phonebook["Alice"]
```

In this snippet, a `Table` named `phonebook` is created to store phone numbers associated with names. The `initTable` procedure initializes the table, and key-value pairs are added and retrieved efficiently. This structure allows for constant time complexity for lookups, making it suitable for performance-critical applications.

Nim's optionals, represented by the `Option[T]` type, provide a mechanism for dealing with values that may or may not be present. An `Option` can either hold a value of type `T` or be `none`, making it a powerful tool for handling scenarios where a value might be absent without resorting to null references. Here's how you can use `Option` to manage optional values:

```nim
import options

var maybeValue: Option[int] some(10)
if maybeValue.isSome:
  echo "Value is ", maybeValue.get()
else:
  echo "No value present"

maybeValue none(int)
if maybeValue.isNone:
  echo "No value present"
```

In this example, `maybeValue` is initially set to an integer value wrapped in `some`. The `isSome` method checks if a value is present, and `get` retrieves the value if it exists. After setting `maybeValue` to `none`, the `isNone` method confirms the absence of a value. This approach avoids null pointer exceptions and improves code safety.

Ref types in Nim, defined using the `ref` keyword, enable the creation of reference types, which are essential for managing objects that need to be manipulated or shared across different parts of the program. Unlike regular value types, reference types are managed through pointers, allowing for dynamic allocation and garbage collection. This feature is particularly useful when working with complex data structures or managing large datasets. Here's a basic example of using `ref` types:

```nim
type
 Node ref object
  value: int
  next: Node

var head: Node Node(value: 1, next: nil)
head.next Node(value: 2, next: nil)

proc printList(node: Node)
 while node ! nil:
  echo node.value
  node node.next

printList(head)
```

In this example, `Node` is a reference type with two fields: `value` and `next`. The `head` variable points to the first node in a linked list, and the `printList` procedure traverses the list, printing each value. Using `ref` types allows for the creation of complex, mutable data structures such as linked lists, trees, and graphs.

Additionally, Nim's approach to data structures is complemented by its support for generics and templates, which enhance the flexibility and reusability of data structures. Generics allow you to define data structures and algorithms that work with various types without code duplication. For example, you can create a generic stack data structure as follows:

```nim
type
  Stack[T] object
    items: seq[T]

proc push[T](stack: var Stack[T], item: T)
  stack.items.add(item)

proc pop[T](stack: var Stack[T]): T
  result stack.items.pop()
```

In this generic `Stack` type, `T` represents the type of elements stored in the stack. The `push` and `pop` procedures are defined generically, allowing the stack to handle any type of element. This demonstrates how generics can be used to create versatile and type-safe data structures.

In summary, the advanced data structures in Nim, including `Table`, `Option`, `ref` types, and generics, provide powerful tools for organizing and managing data. By mastering these structures, you can enhance your ability to handle complex programming tasks, optimize performance, and ensure code safety and flexibility. Understanding and effectively utilizing these features will enable you to write more efficient, maintainable, and robust Nim code.

As we continue exploring Nim's rich set of data structures, it is important to consider the practical applications and performance characteristics of these constructs. Nim's approach to data structures not only facilitates efficient data manipulation but also integrates seamlessly with the language's system-level capabilities. Here, we will examine how different data structures can be leveraged in various programming scenarios, focusing on their performance implications and best practices for usage.

Starting with arrays, while their fixed size can be seen as a limitation, this characteristic actually contributes to their efficiency. Arrays in Nim are stored contiguously in memory, which allows for quick index-based access. This memory locality is advantageous for cache performance and reduces overhead associated with dynamic resizing. Arrays are ideal for scenarios where the data set size is known beforehand, such as in mathematical computations or fixed-size buffers. However, when dealing with situations where the number of elements can vary, arrays might not be the most suitable choice.

Sequences, as discussed previously, offer dynamic resizing capabilities, which are crucial for managing data whose size is not predetermined. The ability to grow or shrink sequences at runtime comes with a trade-off in terms of memory management and potential resizing overhead. Nim's sequences are implemented with amortized constant-time complexity for appending elements, but frequent resizing operations can impact performance. For this reason, sequences are best suited for scenarios where the size of the data set can fluctuate, such as managing user inputs or processing streams of data. To mitigate the impact of resizing, it is often beneficial to preallocate a reasonable size for sequences when possible.

Sets, being unordered collections of unique elements, excel in scenarios that require fast membership testing or when dealing with collections of items where duplicates are not allowed. The underlying implementation of sets in Nim typically involves hashing, which provides average constant-time complexity for insertion, deletion, and lookup operations. Sets are particularly useful for tasks such as filtering unique items from a collection or performing set operations like unions and intersections. The performance benefits of using sets are particularly noticeable when working with large datasets, where efficient membership checks are crucial.

Moving on to tuples, their immutability and fixed size make them suitable for situations where a small, fixed number of related values need to be grouped together. The immutability of tuples ensures that their data remains consistent throughout their usage, which can prevent unintended side effects and simplify reasoning about code. Tuples are often used for returning multiple values from a function or representing structured data that does not require modification. However, due to their fixed size and lack of mutability, tuples are not well-suited for scenarios where the data needs to be frequently updated or extended.

The `ref` type in Nim introduces a level of complexity that is both powerful and flexible. By using reference types, you can create complex data structures such as linked lists, trees, and graphs, where elements are dynamically allocated and managed. The use of `ref` types allows for efficient manipulation of these structures, as objects can be modified in place without the need for copying. However, working with reference types also requires careful management of memory and pointers to avoid issues such as memory leaks or dangling references. Nim's garbage collector helps mitigate these concerns by automatically managing memory, but understanding how to use `ref` types effectively remains important for writing efficient and reliable code.

Generics in Nim further enhance the language's data structure capabilities by allowing you to define data structures and algorithms that work with a variety of types. The use of generics promotes code reuse and type safety, reducing the need for redundant code and minimizing the risk of type errors. For example, a generic stack or queue can be implemented once and used with different types, ensuring that the same data structure can handle various kinds of data without modification. While generics provide significant flexibility, they can also introduce complexity in terms of understanding and debugging code, especially when dealing with complex generic constraints or interactions.

In addition to these core data structures, Nim's standard library and third-party packages offer a wealth of additional structures and utilities. For example, the `sequtils` module provides a variety of operations for manipulating sequences, such as sorting and searching, while the `collections` module includes specialized structures like deques and priority queues. Leveraging these additional tools can help address specific needs and improve the efficiency of your code.

In conclusion, Nim's data structures provide a robust set of tools for managing and manipulating data, each with its own strengths and considerations. Arrays, sequences, sets, tuples, and `ref` types offer different capabilities that can be applied to various programming challenges. By understanding the performance characteristics and best practices associated with each data structure, you can make informed decisions that optimize your code's efficiency and maintainability. As you continue to work with Nim, consider how these data structures can be utilized to meet the specific needs of your applications, and explore the additional resources available in Nim's ecosystem to further enhance your programming experience.

CHAPTER 5:

When delving deeper into functions and procedures, it is essential to understand not only their definitions but also how they interact with the broader programming paradigms in Nim. Beyond basic syntax and usage, the nuances of function and procedure design can greatly influence code clarity, maintainability, and performance.

One of the notable features in Nim is its support for function overloading. Function overloading allows multiple functions with the same name but different parameter lists to coexist. This feature can be particularly useful for creating intuitive and flexible APIs. For instance, you can define several versions of a `print` function that handle different types of input:

```nim
proc print(value: int)
  echo "Integer: ", value

proc print(value: string)
  echo "String: ", value

proc print(value: float)
  echo "Float: ", value
```

In this example, the `print` function is overloaded to handle integers, strings, and floating-point numbers, making it easier to print different types of data without requiring separate function names. The correct version of `print` is selected based on the type of the argument passed.

Another important concept in function design is the use of `result` for returning values. In Nim, functions and procedures use the `result` variable to hold the return value. This approach is somewhat different from many other languages where explicit return statements are common. While `result` simplifies returning values, it's crucial to understand that it is implicitly available within the function body. For instance:

```nim
proc sum(a: int, b: int): int
  result a + b
```

In this `sum` function, `result` holds the value of `a + b` and is returned automatically when the function completes.

Closures in Nim extend the functional programming capabilities of the language. A closure is a function that retains access to variables from its enclosing scope, even after that scope has finished executing. This feature is invaluable for creating callbacks or functions with persistent state. For example:

```nim
proc makeCounter(start: int)
  var count start
  proc increment()
    count + 1
    result count
  return increment

let counter makeCounter(10)
echo counter()  Output will be 11
echo counter()  Output will be 12
```

Here, `makeCounter` creates a closure `increment` that

has access to the `count` variable. Each call to `counter()` updates and returns the value of `count`, demonstrating how closures can maintain state across multiple invocations.

Handling errors and exceptions within functions and procedures is also an important aspect of robust programming. Nim provides mechanisms for error handling using the `try`, `except`, and `finally` constructs, which allow you to manage exceptions gracefully. For instance:

```nim
proc divide(a: int, b: int): int
 try:
  result  a div b
 except ZeroDivisionError:
  echo "Error: Division by zero"
  result  0
 finally:
  echo "Division operation completed"
```

In this `divide` procedure, a division operation is attempted, and if a `ZeroDivisionError` occurs, an error message is displayed, and the result is set to zero. The `finally` block ensures that a message is printed regardless of whether an exception occurred.

Performance considerations are crucial when designing functions and procedures, particularly in performance-sensitive applications. One aspect to consider is the overhead of function calls. While Nim's function calls are generally efficient, excessive function calls or deep recursion can impact performance. In such cases, optimizing functions for better performance or using inline functions might be beneficial. Nim allows functions to be marked as `inline`, which can improve performance by reducing the overhead of function calls:

```nim
proc multiply(x: int, y: int): int {.inline.}
  x y
```

An `inline` function in Nim suggests to the compiler that the function's body should be directly inserted at each call site, rather than performing a traditional function call. This can result in performance gains, particularly in computationally intensive scenarios.

In addition to `inline`, Nim also supports `template` programming, which provides even greater flexibility. Templates in Nim are similar to macros in other languages, allowing you to generate code based on parameters or conditions. They are evaluated at compile time and can be used to implement domain-specific languages or to perform metaprogramming tasks. For example:

```nim
template square(x: expr)
  x x

let num 5
echo square(num)  Output will be 25
```

The `square` template generates code that computes the square of its argument at compile time, showcasing how templates can be used for code generation and optimization.

Understanding these advanced aspects of functions and procedures will enhance your ability to write efficient, maintainable, and flexible Nim code. Whether you are leveraging overloading, closures, or templates, each feature contributes to Nim's versatility and power as a programming language. By mastering these concepts, you can create more sophisticated and robust software solutions tailored to your specific needs and programming goals.

In exploring further intricacies of functions and procedures, it's vital to understand the subtleties of parameter passing and variable scoping in Nim. Nim allows for both value and reference passing, which can significantly affect how data is managed and manipulated within your functions.

When a parameter is passed by value, Nim creates a copy of the argument, and any modifications to this parameter within the function do not affect the original argument. This method ensures that the original data remains unchanged, which can be useful when working with immutable data. However, copying large data structures can be inefficient. For instance, consider the following function that takes an integer by value:

```nim
proc incrementByValue(n: int)
  n + 1
  echo "Inside function: ", n

var x  5
incrementByValue(x)
echo "Outside function: ", x   x remains 5
```

In this example, `x` remains unchanged outside the function because `incrementByValue` operates on a copy of `x`.

On the other hand, when parameters are passed by reference, Nim does not create a copy. Instead, it allows the function to modify the original data directly. This is often achieved by using pointers or mutable types. For instance, if you use `var` parameters in Nim, you are effectively passing by reference:

```nim
proc incrementByReference(var n: int)
  n + 1
  echo "Inside function: ", n
```

```
var x 5
incrementByReference(x)
echo "Outside function: ", x  x is now 6
` ` `
```

Here, `incrementByReference` modifies the original `x`, demonstrating how changes within the function affect the argument outside it.

Understanding scoping rules is also crucial. Nim utilizes lexical scoping, where the scope of a variable is determined by its position in the source code. Variables declared within a procedure are local to that procedure and cannot be accessed from outside it. This principle ensures that data encapsulation is maintained, reducing potential side effects and increasing code modularity. For example:

```nim
proc outerProcedure()
 var x 10
 proc innerProcedure()
   echo "Inner x: ", x  x is accessible here
 innerProcedure()
 echo "Outer x: ", x

outerProcedure()
```

In this code, `innerProcedure` can access the variable `x` defined in `outerProcedure` due to lexical scoping, but `x` is not accessible outside `outerProcedure`.

Nim also supports parameterized procedures and functions, allowing for flexible and reusable code. These procedures can accept parameters of various types, including custom types and tuples. This capability is instrumental in creating generic and adaptable code structures. Consider the following example:

```nim
proc printDetails[T](value: T)
  echo "Value: ", value

printDetails(123)      Prints an integer
printDetails("Hello")   Prints a string
```

The `printDetails` procedure is generic and can handle different types of input due to its parameterized nature, demonstrating Nim's support for generic programming.

Furthermore, the concept of higher-order functions in Nim allows functions to be passed as arguments, returned as values, and assigned to variables. Higher-order functions enhance the flexibility and power of functional programming within Nim. For example, you can pass a function as an argument to another function:

```nim
proc applyFunction[T](x: T, f: proc (T): T): T
  result  f(x)

proc double(x: int): int  x 2

let value  5
echo applyFunction(value, double)  Output will be 10
```

In this example, `applyFunction` takes a value and a function `f` as parameters. The function `f` is applied to the value, showcasing how higher-order functions can be used to create versatile and reusable code components.

Nim also provides support for lambda expressions, which are anonymous functions that can be defined inline. Lambda expressions are particularly useful for short-lived operations that do not require a full procedure definition:

```nim
let increment proc (x: int): int  x + 1
echo increment(10)  Output will be 11
```

Here, `increment` is a lambda expression that increases its input by one, demonstrating how to create quick, concise functions on the fly.

When working with functional programming techniques, it is essential to grasp the immutability and purity concepts that Nim supports. Functions in Nim can be written to avoid side effects and operate on immutable data, which aligns with functional programming principles. For instance:

```nim
proc pureFunction(x: int): int
 x 2

let result  pureFunction(5)
echo result  Output will be 10
```

`pureFunction` operates solely on its input and returns a result without modifying external state, illustrating a functional approach.

Overall, mastering functions and procedures in Nim involves understanding the details of parameter passing, scoping, and advanced programming paradigms like higher-order functions and functional programming techniques. By leveraging these concepts, you can write more efficient, flexible, and maintainable code in Nim, taking full advantage of its powerful and versatile capabilities.

CHAPTER 6:

In exploring Nim's approach to error handling and exceptions, it is essential to understand the nuances of its exception model and how it integrates with the language's design principles. Nim's exception handling is designed to offer flexibility and control, allowing developers to handle errors effectively while maintaining the clarity and efficiency of their code.

One of the critical aspects of Nim's exception system is the ability to define custom exceptions that can encapsulate specific error conditions. By creating custom exception types, developers can provide more context and detail about the nature of the error, which can be crucial for debugging and error management. Custom exceptions are defined as objects inheriting from the base `Exception` type, and they can include additional fields and methods to represent error details comprehensively. For example, a custom exception might include an error code or additional diagnostic information:

```nim
type
  NetworkError object of Exception
    errorCode: int
    errorMessage: string

proc handleNetworkError(e: NetworkError)
  echo "Network error occurred. Code: ", e.errorCode, ", Message: ", e.errorMessage
```

This approach allows for precise and informative error handling, as you can access and utilize these additional details in your exception handlers.

When raising exceptions, Nim's `raise` statement is a fundamental tool. This statement interrupts the normal flow of execution and passes control to the nearest exception handler. Nim's ability to raise exceptions with detailed messages or additional context is particularly valuable for diagnosing issues and understanding their origins. For instance, consider the following code where an exception is raised with a custom message:

```nim
proc divide(a, b: int)
 if b 0:
  raise newException(DivideByZeroError, "Attempted to divide by zero")
 echo a / b
```

In this example, attempting to divide by zero raises a `DivideByZeroError` with a descriptive message, making it clear what went wrong.

Exception handling in Nim is managed through `try`, `except`, and `finally` constructs. The `try` block encloses code that may throw an exception, while the `except` block specifies the type of exceptions to catch and handle. The `finally` block ensures that code is executed regardless of whether an exception occurred, which is useful for resource cleanup or other finalization tasks. Here is an example demonstrating this mechanism:

```nim
try:
 divide(10, 0)
```

```nim
except DivideByZeroError as e:
  echo "Caught exception: ", e.msg
finally:
  echo "This will always be executed"
```

In this code snippet, if a `DivideByZeroError` is raised, it is caught and handled by the `except` block, while the `finally` block ensures that the message "This will always be executed" is printed regardless of the exception.

A significant feature of Nim's exception handling system is its support for higher-order functions in exception handling. Higher-order functions can be employed to create reusable error-handling logic, which can be particularly useful in scenarios where multiple operations require similar error handling. By passing exception-handling functions as arguments or returning them from other functions, you can maintain clean and modular code:

```nim
proc handleException(handler: proc(e: Exception))
  try:
    Code that may raise exceptions
  except Exception as e:
    handler(e)

proc customHandler(e: Exception)
  echo "Custom handler: ", e.msg

handleException(customHandler)
```

In this example, `handleException` takes a `handler` procedure as an argument and uses it to manage exceptions. This allows for flexible and centralized error handling strategies.

It is also worth noting that Nim provides mechanisms

for creating exception hierarchies and handling groups of related exceptions. By deriving new exception types from existing ones, you can establish a hierarchy that reflects the relationships between different error conditions. This hierarchy allows for more general exception handling, where a parent exception type can catch multiple related exceptions:

```nim
type
  FileError  object of Exception
  FileNotFoundError  object of FileError
  FilePermissionError  object of FileError

try:
  Code that may raise exceptions
except FileError as e:
  echo "File error occurred: ", e.msg
```

In this structure, the `FileError` type serves as a base class for more specific file-related exceptions, allowing the `FileError` handler to catch any exceptions derived from it.

In summary, Nim's exception handling system offers a comprehensive and flexible approach to managing errors in your programs. By defining custom exceptions, raising exceptions with detailed messages, and utilizing structured exception handling constructs, you can build robust error management strategies. The ability to employ higher-order functions for exception handling and create exception hierarchies further enhances the power and flexibility of Nim's error handling capabilities. This detailed understanding of Nim's exception handling will enable you to write more resilient and maintainable code, ensuring that your programs can handle unexpected situations gracefully and efficiently.

In continuing the exploration of error handling and exceptions in Nim, it is important to delve into the nuances of exception propagation and the implications for program flow. Exception propagation refers to the process by which an exception, once raised, travels up the call stack until it encounters a suitable handler or reaches the top of the stack, resulting in the termination of the program if unhandled.

When an exception is raised, Nim attempts to locate an appropriate `except` block in the current scope. If no handler is found, the search continues in the calling functions. This behavior underscores the importance of understanding the scope of exception handling and how it interacts with different levels of your program. To illustrate, consider the following example where an exception is raised in a deeply nested function and caught at a higher level:

```nim
proc deepFunction()
    raise newException(ValueError, "An error occurred in deepFunction")

proc intermediateFunction()
 deepFunction()

proc outerFunction()
 try:
  intermediateFunction()
 except ValueError as e:
  echo "Caught exception in outerFunction: ", e.msg

outerFunction()
```

In this case, `deepFunction` raises an exception, which is then propagated through `intermediateFunction` until it is caught by the `except` block in `outerFunction`. This demonstrates how exceptions can be managed effectively even in complex program structures.

Furthermore, Nim's exception handling mechanism supports

the concept of exception chaining, where one exception can be raised in response to another. This is particularly useful for creating higher-level error abstractions or for adding additional context to errors. By using the `raise` statement within an `except` block, you can propagate a new exception while preserving the original one. For example:

```nim
proc processFile(filename: string)
 try:
   Code that might raise an IOError
 except IOError as e:
    raise newException(FileProcessingError, "Failed to process file: " & filename).withCause(e)
```

In this example, if an `IOError` occurs during file processing, a `FileProcessingError` is raised with additional context, while the original `IOError` is preserved. This approach maintains a clear error chain, which can be valuable for debugging and error analysis.

When it comes to best practices for error handling, Nim encourages a careful balance between catching exceptions and allowing them to propagate. Overly broad exception handlers can obscure the source of errors and make debugging more difficult. Instead, it is advisable to catch only those exceptions that you can handle effectively, and to let others propagate up the call stack. This approach ensures that errors are managed where they can be most appropriately addressed, while still allowing for higher-level handling when necessary.

In addition to handling exceptions, resource management plays a critical role in ensuring that your program operates reliably. In Nim, the `finally` block provides a mechanism for ensuring that resources are cleaned up regardless of whether an exception was raised. This is particularly important for managing resources such as file handles, network connections, or memory allocations. By using the `finally` block, you can guarantee that cleanup code is executed, which helps to avoid resource leaks and maintain program stability:

```nim
proc readFile(filename: string)
 var file: File
 try:
  file.open(filename, fmRead)
  Code to read from the file
 finally:
   file.close()   Ensures the file is always closed, even if an exception is raised
```

In this example, the `file.close()` call within the `finally` block ensures that the file is closed properly, regardless of whether an exception occurred during file operations.

Error handling and exceptions also interact with Nim's system of garbage collection and memory management. While Nim's garbage collector automatically manages memory for many cases, careful consideration is needed for situations involving explicit memory allocation or resource management. Combining exception handling with resource management techniques ensures that resources are properly cleaned up and that memory is efficiently utilized.

Lastly, Nim's support for domain-specific error handling patterns can be leveraged to create more robust and user-friendly programs. For example, in applications that involve user input, it is common to validate input and provide informative error messages. By integrating exception handling with input validation, you can enhance the user experience and improve the reliability of your program:

```nim
```

```
proc getUserInput()
 try:
  var input: string
  echo "Enter a number: "
  readLine(stdin, input)
  let number  parseInt(input)
  echo "You entered: ", number
 except ValueError as e:
  echo "Invalid input. Please enter a valid number."

getUserInput()
```
` ` `

In this case, user input is validated and parsed, with exceptions caught and handled to guide the user toward correct input.

In summary, effective error handling in Nim involves a comprehensive understanding of exception propagation, chaining, and resource management. By defining custom exceptions, utilizing structured exception handling constructs, and adhering to best practices, you can build resilient and maintainable programs. Nim's rich exception handling features provide the tools necessary to manage errors gracefully, ensuring that your programs can handle unexpected situations robustly and recover from them efficiently.

CHAPTER 7:

Memory management is integral to systems programming, and Nim provides a flexible approach to managing memory through both automatic and manual methods. Building on the foundational concepts of garbage collection and pointer manipulation, I will delve deeper into advanced techniques for efficient memory management and explore some nuances of Nim's memory handling capabilities.

Nim's garbage collection mechanism, while simplifying memory management, does come with its own set of considerations. The garbage collector in Nim operates primarily through reference counting, which keeps track of the number of references to an object. When the reference count drops to zero, the object is automatically deallocated. This process is straightforward for most use cases, but there are scenarios where reference counting alone may not suffice, particularly when dealing with cyclic references.

Cyclic references occur when two or more objects reference each other, creating a cycle that prevents their reference counts from reaching zero. In Nim, such cycles are managed by the cycle collector, which periodically identifies and collects objects involved in cyclic references. While this mechanism addresses many issues associated with cyclic dependencies, it is not without its drawbacks. The cycle collector introduces overhead, as it must traverse and analyze object graphs to detect cycles. In performance-critical applications, the additional processing time required for cycle collection may impact overall efficiency.

To mitigate the performance impact of cyclic garbage collection, it is advisable to minimize the use of cyclic references wherever possible. This can be achieved by designing object relationships that avoid cycles or by employing alternative patterns, such as weak references, to break potential cycles. Weak references allow objects to be referenced without affecting their reference counts, thus helping to avoid situations where objects are retained solely due to cyclical dependencies.

While automatic garbage collection simplifies many aspects of memory management, manual memory management remains a critical tool, especially in performance-sensitive applications. Nim supports manual memory management through its pointer types, which provide direct access to memory and allow for explicit allocation and deallocation.

Understanding and using pointers effectively involves several key concepts. Pointers in Nim can be categorized into several types, including `ptr`, `ref`, and `addr`. Each type serves different purposes and offers various levels of abstraction for memory management. The `ptr` type is a fundamental pointer type used to reference any data type. It is crucial for dynamically allocated memory and interoperability with external libraries. Here is a deeper look at how to work with `ptr` types:

```nim
type
 MyData object
  value: int

var data: ptr MyData new(MyData)
data[].value 100
echo data[].value  Output: 100
dispose(data)
```

In this example, `data` is a pointer to an instance of `MyData`. The `new` procedure allocates memory for `MyData`, and `dispose` deallocates it. Proper usage of `dispose` is essential to prevent memory leaks.

Nim also provides the `ref` type, which offers automatic reference counting and is suitable for managing the lifetime of objects. This type is especially useful when objects need to be shared across different parts of a program. The `ref` type helps manage memory without the need for explicit deallocation. Consider the following example:

```nim
type
 MyRefObject ref object
   value: int

var obj: MyRefObject MyRefObject(value: 200)
echo obj.value  Output: 200
```

Here, `MyRefObject` is a reference-counted object. The memory associated with `obj` will be automatically reclaimed once all references to it are gone. This simplifies memory management, though it is important to be aware of the overhead associated with reference counting.

Manual memory management requires careful attention to avoid common pitfalls, such as memory leaks and dangling pointers. Memory leaks occur when allocated memory is not properly released, leading to wasted resources. To avoid memory leaks, ensure that every call to `new` is paired with a corresponding call to `dispose`. Additionally, consider using memory profiling tools to identify and address potential leaks.

Dangling pointers represent another critical issue. A dangling pointer occurs when a pointer continues to reference memory that has already been deallocated. Accessing or modifying such memory can lead to undefined behavior and crashes. To mitigate this risk, always set pointers to `nil` after deallocating the memory they reference, and avoid using pointers after the associated memory has been released.

Another aspect of manual memory management is dealing with memory fragmentation, which arises when frequent allocation and deallocation lead to fragmented memory. Fragmentation can impact performance by causing inefficient memory usage and increased allocation times. To address fragmentation, consider using custom memory allocators or memory pooling strategies. These techniques involve managing memory in larger blocks or pools, which can reduce fragmentation and improve allocation efficiency.

Custom memory allocators allow for fine-grained control over how memory is allocated and deallocated. By implementing a custom allocator, you can tailor memory management to the specific needs of your application, optimizing for factors such as allocation size, frequency, and lifespan.

In summary, Nim's approach to memory management offers a blend of automatic garbage collection and manual control, providing flexibility for various programming needs. While garbage collection simplifies most memory management tasks, manual techniques using pointers offer the control necessary for performance-critical applications. By understanding and effectively utilizing Nim's memory management features, including garbage collection, pointers, and custom allocators, developers can achieve efficient and reliable memory usage, while mitigating common pitfalls such as memory leaks, dangling pointers, and fragmentation.

When delving deeper into memory management in Nim, it is essential to address some advanced aspects of working with pointers and memory allocation that are crucial for optimizing performance and ensuring reliability.

Pointers in Nim are powerful tools for direct memory manipulation, but their effective use requires a strong understanding of memory layout and allocation. One advanced technique involves pointer arithmetic, which allows manipulation of pointer values to traverse arrays or data structures. This capability is particularly useful in low-level programming where performance is critical. However, pointer arithmetic must be handled with care to avoid errors such as buffer overflows or invalid memory access. Here is an example of pointer arithmetic in Nim:

```nim
var arr: array[3, int] [10, 20, 30]
var ptr: ptr int  addr arr[0]

for i in 0..2:
  echo (ptr + i)[]  Output: 10, 20, 30
```

In this snippet, `ptr` is a pointer to the first element of the array `arr`. By adding an offset `i` to `ptr`, we access successive elements of the array. This method can be efficient but requires a thorough understanding of the memory layout to ensure correct access.

Another significant area in manual memory management is memory alignment, which affects how data is stored in memory and accessed by the CPU. Proper alignment ensures that data structures are laid out in memory in a way that optimizes access speed and prevents potential alignment faults. In Nim, you can specify alignment requirements using the `align` pragma. For example:

```nim
type
  AlignedData object
    a: int
```

```
  b: int

  Ensure that AlignedData is aligned to 16 bytes
  pragma align(16, AlignedData)
` ` `
```

This code snippet uses the `pragma align` directive to ensure that instances of `AlignedData` are aligned to a 16-byte boundary. Proper alignment can improve performance, especially in systems programming where low-level optimizations are critical.

When managing memory manually, developers often encounter the need to handle different memory allocation strategies. One such strategy is the use of memory pools. A memory pool is a pre-allocated block of memory divided into smaller chunks that can be used for allocating objects of a fixed size. Memory pools reduce fragmentation and improve allocation speed. Nim supports memory pools through its `memPool` module, which provides functionality for creating and managing memory pools.

Here is an example of using a memory pool in Nim:

```nim
` ` `nim
import memPool

const
 poolSize 1024 1024  1 MB pool

var pool  newMemPool(poolSize)

proc allocateFromPool(size: int): ptr byte
 pool.alloc(size)

proc deallocateToPool(ptr: ptr byte)
 pool.dealloc(ptr)

Allocate memory from the pool
var block: ptr byte allocateFromPool(256)
```

Use the allocated memory
Deallocate memory back to the pool
deallocateToPool(block)
` ` `

In this example, `newMemPool` creates a memory pool of 1 MB. The `allocateFromPool` and `deallocateToPool` procedures manage memory allocation and deallocation within the pool, ensuring efficient memory use.

In addition to memory pools, custom allocators offer another way to manage memory with specific performance characteristics. Custom allocators are designed to handle specific allocation patterns or requirements. For instance, an allocator might be tailored for high-frequency, small-size allocations, reducing the overhead associated with general-purpose memory allocation.

Custom memory allocators can be implemented in Nim by defining a procedure that manages the allocation and deallocation of memory. For example:

```nim
type
 CustomAllocator object
  pool: seq[ptr byte]

proc initAllocator(): CustomAllocator
 result.pool @[]

proc allocate(allocator: var CustomAllocator, size: int): ptr byte
 let block  cast[ptr byte](alloc(size))
 allocator.pool.add(block)
 result  block

proc deallocate(allocator: var CustomAllocator, ptr: ptr byte)
 dealloc(ptr)
 allocator.pool.remove(allocator.pool.find(ptr))
```

```
Example usage
var allocator  initAllocator()
var block: ptr byte  allocate(allocator, 128)
Use the allocated memory
deallocate(allocator, block)
` ` `
```

In this code, `CustomAllocator` is an object that manages a pool of allocated memory blocks. The `allocate` and `deallocate` procedures handle memory management for this custom allocator.

Finally, handling memory alignment, fragmentation, and custom allocation strategies requires a thorough understanding of the application's memory needs and performance constraints. By employing these advanced techniques, developers can optimize memory usage and enhance the performance of systems programs.

In conclusion, mastering advanced memory management in Nim involves a deep understanding of pointers, alignment, and allocation strategies. With proper use of these techniques, developers can achieve fine-grained control over memory, leading to more efficient and reliable systems programming. Through careful design and implementation, the challenges of manual memory management can be addressed effectively, ensuring robust and high-performance applications.

CHAPTER 8:

When working with modules and packages in Nim, understanding how to effectively structure and manage code is crucial for maintaining clarity and scalability in larger projects. Modules allow for logical separation of code, facilitating modular design and enhancing code reusability. Packages, in turn, offer a higher level of abstraction, enabling the grouping of multiple modules along with their associated metadata, dependencies, and configurations.

One fundamental aspect of using modules is understanding their scope and visibility. In Nim, the visibility of procedures, types, and variables is controlled by the module in which they are defined. By default, anything declared in a module is private to that module. To make elements accessible to other modules, you use the `export` keyword. This keyword allows for controlled exposure of module contents, which is essential for creating a clean and manageable API.

Consider the following example where we have a module `math_operations.nim`:

```nim
math_operations.nim
proc multiply(a, b: int): int {.export.}
 result a b

proc divide(a, b: int): float {.export.}
 if b ! 0:
  result a / b
 else:
```

```
  raise newException(ValueError, "Division by zero")
` ` `
```

In this module, both `multiply` and `divide` procedures are made public with the `export` keyword. This allows them to be accessed from other modules that import `math_operations`. For instance, in another module, you can use these procedures as follows:

```nim
import math_operations

echo multiply(4, 5)  Output: 20
echo divide(10, 2)   Output: 5.0
```

This encapsulation and controlled exposure of module contents enable developers to build libraries and frameworks where the internal workings are hidden, while only the necessary interfaces are exposed.

When it comes to organizing code into packages, a primary consideration is the logical grouping of related modules. A well-structured package should encapsulate a coherent set of functionalities or related components. The organization within a package typically follows a directory structure that reflects the modular hierarchy and separation of concerns.

In Nim, a package is more than just a collection of modules; it also includes a `nimble` file that provides metadata about the package, such as its version, dependencies, and description. The `nimble` file is crucial for package management, as it helps Nimble understand how to handle the package and its dependencies.

Here's a brief overview of a `nimble` file for a hypothetical package named `data_analysis`:

```nim
```

```
data_analysis.nimble
version "0.1.0"
description "A package for data analysis utilities"
author "Your Name"
license "MIT"
srcDir "src"
binDir "bin"
testDir "tests"
` ` `
```

The `version` field specifies the current version of the package, which is important for dependency resolution and version management. The `description` provides a brief overview of what the package does, while `author` and `license` fields offer information about the package creator and its licensing terms. The `srcDir`, `binDir`, and `testDir` fields indicate where to find the source code, binaries, and tests, respectively.

When developing a package, it's common to include a set of unit tests to ensure that the package functions as expected. These tests are placed in the `testDir` directory and can be run using Nimble's built-in test support. By placing tests in a dedicated directory, you maintain a clean separation between the implementation code and its verification, which is vital for maintaining code quality.

In addition to the core modules, packages can also include examples and documentation to help users understand how to utilize the package effectively. Providing clear examples and comprehensive documentation is crucial for user adoption and satisfaction.

Nimble, as the package manager for Nim, simplifies the process of managing dependencies and building projects. When developing a project that relies on external packages, you can specify the required packages and their versions in the `nimble` file of your project. Nimble will then handle downloading, installing, and managing these dependencies.

For example, suppose you have a project that depends on the `data_analysis` package. You would include the following in your project's `nimble` file:

```nim
my_project.nimble
version "0.1.0"
description "A project that uses data_analysis package"
author "Your Name"
license "MIT"
srcDir "src"
testDir "tests"
deps @["data_analysis > 0.1.0"]
```

The `deps` field specifies that your project depends on version 0.1.0 or later of the `data_analysis` package. When you run `nimble build` or `nimble test`, Nimble ensures that all specified dependencies are correctly installed and available for your project.

Lastly, understanding how to manage and structure packages effectively extends to versioning and release management. As your package evolves, you'll need to increment the version number according to semantic versioning principles. This practice helps users of your package understand the nature of changes and ensures compatibility with other dependencies.

By mastering the use of modules and packages in Nim, you can create well-organized, maintainable, and scalable software projects. This organization not only improves code clarity and reusability but also supports robust development practices that can adapt to evolving project requirements.

In Nim, managing dependencies within a project often

involves using packages from external sources. This process is greatly streamlined by Nimble, the package manager that integrates seamlessly with the Nim ecosystem. Nimble not only facilitates the installation and updating of packages but also manages project-specific dependencies and configurations. Understanding how to utilize Nimble effectively is crucial for maintaining a robust development environment.

When starting with a new project or integrating an external package, the `nimble` file plays a pivotal role. This file contains metadata about the project, including its dependencies, versioning information, and build instructions. For instance, if you're incorporating an external package into your project, you would specify this in the `nimble` file under the `deps` field. The syntax for declaring dependencies is straightforward and allows you to define version constraints to ensure compatibility.

Consider a scenario where your project requires the `httpbeast` package, a popular HTTP server library. To include this dependency, your `nimble` file might look like this:

```nim
my_project.nimble
version "0.1.0"
description "A project utilizing the httpbeast library"
author "Your Name"
license "MIT"
srcDir "src"
testDir "tests"
deps @["httpbeast > 1.0.0"]
```

Here, the `deps` field specifies that your project depends on version 1.0.0 or later of the `httpbeast` package. When you run `nimble install`, Nimble will fetch the `httpbeast` package, along with its own dependencies, and make it available for your project. This automation reduces the manual overhead involved in managing third-party libraries.

In addition to handling dependencies, Nimble also supports creating and managing projects with a clear structure. By convention, Nim projects are organized into a directory hierarchy that separates source code, tests, and documentation. The `srcDir` and `testDir` fields in the `nimble` file help Nimble locate your source files and test cases, respectively.

For example, a typical project directory structure might look like this:

```
my_project/
 src/
  main.nim
  utils.nim
 tests/
  test_main.nim
 my_project.nimble
```

In this setup, `main.nim` contains the primary application logic, while `utils.nim` includes utility functions. The `tests` directory holds test cases that validate the functionality of the code. This separation of concerns aids in maintaining a clean and organized codebase.

When creating a new project, Nimble provides a command-line utility to scaffold the project structure automatically. By running `nimble init my_project`, Nimble generates a basic project layout, complete with a default `nimble` file and directories for source code and tests. This convenience allows you to quickly set up a project with a standardized structure.

For projects that evolve over time, managing versions becomes increasingly important. Semantic versioning is a common practice that helps communicate changes and maintain compatibility. Semantic versioning involves specifying version numbers in the format `major.minor.patch`. Incrementing the major version indicates breaking changes, while the minor version is updated for backward-compatible features. The patch version is incremented for backward-compatible bug fixes.

When you release a new version of a package, it's essential to update the version number in the `nimble` file and ensure that the changes are documented. This practice helps users of your package understand the nature of updates and make informed decisions about upgrading.

Effective versioning also involves maintaining a changelog, which records significant changes, improvements, and bug fixes in each version. Including a changelog in your project helps users track the evolution of your code and provides transparency about what each release contains.

Another aspect of package management in Nim is the use of `import` statements to include modules from external packages. When using packages managed by Nimble, you import them into your code just like you would with local modules. For instance, if you're using the `httpbeast` package, you might write:

```nim
import httpbeast, logging

proc handleRequest(req: Request)
  echo "Received request: ", req.url

let server  newAsyncHttpServer(handleRequest)
server.serve(Port(8080))
```

In this example, `httpbeast` is imported to create a basic HTTP server that listens on port 8080. The `import` statement allows you to leverage the functionality provided by external packages seamlessly, integrating them into your codebase with minimal effort.

In summary, mastering the use of modules and packages in Nim is essential for effective code management and project organization. By leveraging Nimble for dependency management and following best practices for project structure and versioning, you can build scalable and maintainable applications. The ability to modularize code, manage dependencies, and handle versioning efficiently will contribute significantly to the overall quality and maintainability of your software projects.

CHAPTER 9:

In the pursuit of building responsive and efficient systems, leveraging concurrency and parallelism effectively is paramount. Nim provides a rich set of tools for managing concurrent tasks, and understanding these tools is essential for developing high-performance applications. Building on the foundational concepts of threads and asynchronous programming, I will delve deeper into advanced topics in Nim's concurrency model, focusing on practical strategies for achieving optimal performance.

When dealing with concurrency in Nim, it's crucial to understand how to manage multiple threads efficiently. One key aspect of this is thread coordination and communication. Threads often need to exchange information or coordinate actions. Nim supports various mechanisms for inter-thread communication, including channels and atomic operations.

Channels provide a way for threads to send messages to each other in a thread-safe manner. Nim's `channels` module offers a simple interface for creating and using channels. Here's an example of how channels can be used for communication between threads:

```nim
import threads, channels

let channel  newChannel[int]()

proc producer()
 for i in 1..10:
  channel.send(i)
```

```
  sleep(100)  Simulate work
proc consumer()
 for _ in 1..10:
  let value  channel.recv()
  echo "Received value: ", value

Spawn producer and consumer threads
spawn producer()
spawn consumer()

Wait for threads to finish
sleep(2000)
` ` `
```

In this example, a `producer` thread sends integers through a channel, while a `consumer` thread receives and processes these integers. The `send` and `recv` operations are thread-safe, ensuring that data is transferred correctly between threads without requiring explicit synchronization mechanisms.

Atomic operations are another fundamental aspect of managing concurrency. They provide a way to perform operations on shared variables in a thread-safe manner without using locks. Nim's `atomics` module offers support for atomic variables and operations. For example, atomic counters can be used to track the number of occurrences of a particular event across multiple threads:

```nim
import atomics, threads

var counter: AtomicInt  initAtomicInt(0)

proc incrementCounter()
 for _ in 1..1000:
  counter.inc()
```

Spawn multiple threads to increment the counter

```nim
for _ in 1..4:
  spawn incrementCounter
```

Wait for threads to finish
```nim
sleep(2000)
```

```nim
echo "Counter value: ", counter.load()
```
```

In this code, the `AtomicInt` type is used for the `counter` variable. The `inc` method is an atomic operation that increments the counter safely across multiple threads. This approach avoids the overhead of locks while ensuring that the counter is updated correctly.

While threads and atomic operations are essential for concurrent programming, asynchronous programming introduces a different paradigm that is particularly useful for I/O-bound tasks. Nim's asynchronous programming model is based on event-driven principles, allowing you to write non-blocking code that can handle multiple I/O operations concurrently.

A key component of Nim's asynchronous programming is the event loop, which manages and schedules asynchronous tasks. The `asyncdispatch` module provides the necessary infrastructure for working with asynchronous operations. Here's a more detailed example of how you might use async programming for handling multiple I/O operations:

```nim
import asyncdispatch, httpbeast

proc fetchContent(url: string) {.async.}
  try:
    let response  await httpGet(url)
    echo "Content fetched from ", url, ": ", response.body
  except HttpRequestError as e:
    echo "Failed to fetch content from ", url, ": ", e.msg
```
```

```
proc main() {.async.}
 let urls [
  "https://www.example.com",
  "https://www.example.org"
 ]

 for url in urls:
  asyncFetch fetchContent(url)

Run the asynchronous main procedure
asyncMain main()
```
` ` `

In this example, the `fetchContent` procedure is marked with the `{.async.}` pragma, indicating that it is asynchronous. The `await` keyword is used to wait for the completion of the HTTP request without blocking the event loop. The `main` procedure schedules multiple asynchronous fetch operations, demonstrating how to handle multiple concurrent I/O requests efficiently.

In addition to basic asynchronous tasks, Nim also supports more advanced patterns such as asynchronous streams and futures. Futures represent the result of an asynchronous operation that will be available at some point in the future. The `asyncdispatch` module provides the `Future` type, which can be used to work with the results of asynchronous tasks in a non-blocking manner.

To further illustrate these concepts, consider the following example, where we perform multiple asynchronous computations and aggregate their results:

` ` `nim
```
import asyncdispatch, futures

proc computeValue(x: int): Future[int] {.async.}
 await sleepAsync(100)  Simulate computation delay
```

```
return x  x

proc main() {.async.}
 let values  [1, 2, 3, 4, 5]
 var futures  newSeq[Future[int]](values.len)

 for i, value in values:
  futures[i]  asyncFetch computeValue(value)

 var results: seq[int]  @[]
 for future in futures:
  results.add(await future)

 echo "Computed values: ", results

Run the asynchronous main procedure
asyncMain main()
` ` `
```

In this code, the `computeValue` procedure performs an asynchronous computation, and the results of multiple computations are aggregated using futures. The `results.add(await future)` line collects the results of the asynchronous computations, demonstrating how to handle multiple concurrent tasks and aggregate their results efficiently.

By mastering the techniques of threading, atomic operations, and asynchronous programming, you can build highly responsive and efficient systems in Nim. Each approach has its strengths and best-use scenarios, and understanding these allows you to choose the right tool for the job, ensuring optimal performance and scalability in your applications.

As we continue our exploration of concurrency and parallelism in Nim, it's essential to delve deeper into the intricacies of synchronization mechanisms and advanced concurrency patterns. These elements are pivotal for managing more complex scenarios where multiple threads or asynchronous tasks interact in nuanced ways.

Synchronization is a key concept when dealing with concurrency, as it ensures that multiple threads or asynchronous tasks coordinate properly without stepping on each other's toes. One of the primary synchronization mechanisms in Nim is the mutex. A mutex, short for mutual exclusion, is used to protect shared resources from concurrent access, ensuring that only one thread or task can access the resource at a time. Nim provides robust support for mutexes through the `locks` module.

Consider the following example, where multiple threads increment a shared counter. Without proper synchronization, this could lead to race conditions and incorrect results. By using a mutex, we ensure that the increments are performed atomically:

```nim
import threads, locks

var counter  0
let mutex  newMutex()

proc incrementCounter()
 for _ in 1..1000:
  lock(mutex):
   inc(counter)

Spawn multiple threads to increment the counter
for _ in 1..4:
 spawn incrementCounter

Wait for threads to finish
sleep(2000)
```

```nim
echo "Counter value: ", counter
```

In this example, the `lock(mutex)` block ensures that only one thread can execute the code within the block at any given time. This prevents race conditions and guarantees that the shared `counter` variable is updated correctly. It's important to note that proper use of mutexes is crucial for avoiding deadlocks, which occur when two or more threads are waiting indefinitely for resources held by each other.

Another synchronization mechanism available in Nim is the semaphore. Semaphores are more flexible than mutexes and can be used to control access to a certain number of resources. The `semaphores` module in Nim provides the necessary tools for working with semaphores. Here's an example that demonstrates the use of a semaphore to limit access to a shared resource:

```nim
import threads, semaphores

const maxConcurrent 3
let semaphore newSemaphore(maxConcurrent)

proc accessResource(id: int)
  echo "Thread ", id, " is waiting for access."
  semaphore.wait()
  echo "Thread ", id, " has access."
  sleep(1000)  Simulate work
  semaphore.signal()
  echo "Thread ", id, " has released access."

Spawn multiple threads to access the resource
for i in 1..10:
  spawn accessResource(i)

Wait for threads to finish
```

```
sleep(5000)
` ` `
```

In this code, the semaphore limits the number of threads that can access the resource concurrently to three. Each thread must wait for the semaphore before proceeding and signal the semaphore when done. This approach effectively manages concurrent access and prevents resource contention.

Moving beyond basic synchronization, advanced concurrency patterns such as producer-consumer and fork-join paradigms offer more sophisticated ways to handle parallel tasks. The producer-consumer pattern involves two types of threads: producers that generate data and consumers that process it. The challenge is to ensure that producers and consumers operate efficiently and without conflicts.

In Nim, the producer-consumer pattern can be implemented using channels for communication between producers and consumers. Here's an illustrative example:

```nim
import threads, channels

let buffer  newChannel[int]()
const bufferSize  10

proc producer()
 for i in 1..100:
  buffer.send(i)
  echo "Produced: ", i
  sleep(100)  Simulate production time

proc consumer()
 while true:
  let item  buffer.recv()
  echo "Consumed: ", item
  sleep(200)  Simulate consumption time
```

```
Spawn producer and consumer threads
spawn producer()
spawn consumer()

Run for a while and then stop
sleep(5000)
```
` ` `

In this example, the `producer` thread sends data to the `buffer` channel, while the `consumer` thread receives and processes this data. The channel acts as a buffer, allowing producers and consumers to operate asynchronously.

The fork-join model, another powerful concurrency pattern, involves splitting a task into multiple subtasks (forking) and then combining the results of these subtasks (joining). Nim's support for parallel tasks and futures makes implementing the fork-join model straightforward. Here's an example where we parallelize a computation and then aggregate the results:

` ` `nim
```
import asyncdispatch, futures

proc computePart(start, end: int): Future[int] {.async.}
 var sum 0
 for i in start..end:
  sum + i
 return sum

proc main() {.async.}
 let numParts 4
 let range 1..100
 let partSize (range.high - range.low + 1) div numParts


 var futures newSeq[Future[int]](numParts)
 for i in 0..<numParts:
  let start range.low + i partSize
```

```
    let end if i numParts - 1: range.high else: start + partSize - 1
    futures[i] asyncFetch computePart(start, end)


  var totalSum  0
 for future in futures:
  totalSum + await future

  echo "Total sum: ", totalSum

Run the asynchronous main procedure
asyncMain main()
` ` `
```

In this code, the task of summing numbers is divided into multiple subtasks, each computed in parallel. After all subtasks are complete, their results are aggregated to produce the final sum. This approach leverages parallelism to speed up computations that can be broken down into independent subtasks.

By mastering these advanced concurrency patterns and synchronization mechanisms, you can build robust and high-performance applications that efficiently manage multiple concurrent operations. Whether you're dealing with simple tasks or complex systems, understanding and applying these concepts will help you design systems that are not only efficient but also resilient to the challenges of concurrent execution.

CHAPTER 10:

When delving deeper into file I/O operations in Nim, it is essential to understand not only how to read and write files but also how to handle errors and manage file access efficiently. Errors in file operations can arise due to various reasons, such as missing files, permission issues, or hardware failures. Nim provides mechanisms to handle these exceptions gracefully, ensuring that your programs can manage errors without crashing.

The `os` module in Nim includes procedures and types designed for robust error handling. For example, when opening a file, one should always check whether the file was opened successfully. The `openFile` procedure can be used to open a file and handle exceptions that might occur during this process. By wrapping file operations in a try-except block, you can capture and handle exceptions such as `OSError`, which is raised if an error occurs while opening or manipulating the file.

Here is an example of handling file-related errors:

```nim
import os, strutils

proc safeReadFile(filename: string): string
 try:
  let content  readFile(filename)
  result  content
 except OSError as e:
  echo "Error reading file: ", e.msg
```

```
  result ""
proc safeWriteFile(filename: string, content: string)
 try:
  writeFile(filename, content)
  echo "File written successfully."
 except OSError as e:
  echo "Error writing file: ", e.msg

Using the procedures
let content  safeReadFile("example.txt")
safeWriteFile("output.txt", "New Content")
` ` `
```

In this example, if an error occurs while reading or writing files, the exception is caught, and an appropriate message is displayed, allowing the program to continue running without abrupt termination. This approach is crucial for creating resilient applications that can handle unexpected file system issues gracefully.

Managing file access also involves considerations such as file locking, especially in environments where multiple processes or threads may access the same file concurrently. While Nim does not provide built-in file locking mechanisms, you can implement basic file locking using platform-specific features or external libraries. For instance, on Unix-like systems, you can use file locks through the `fcntl` system call, while on Windows, you might use the Windows API for file locking.

When it comes to serialization, the process of converting data structures into a format suitable for storage or transmission is pivotal. Serialization not only allows for data persistence but also facilitates communication between different systems. In addition to JSON and XML, Nim supports other serialization formats, such as YAML, through external libraries.

For more complex data structures or those requiring custom

serialization formats, you might need to manually implement serialization and deserialization logic. Nim's powerful type system and macros can assist in creating flexible and efficient serialization solutions.

Let's explore a more advanced example of custom serialization using Nim's type system. Suppose you have a custom data structure that needs to be serialized to a specific format. You can define procedures to handle the conversion of your data structure to and from this format.

Consider a custom data structure that represents a user profile with nested elements. Here's how you might serialize and deserialize this structure:

```nim
import json, tables, sequtils

type
 UserProfile object
  username: string
  age: int
  address: object
   street: string
   city: string
   postalCode: string

proc serializeUserProfile(profile: UserProfile): string
    var jsonObj   %{ "username": profile.username, "age": profile.age,
          "address": %{ "street": profile.address.street,
                "city": profile.address.city,
                "postalCode": profile.address.postalCode } }
  result jsonObj.toJson()

proc deserializeUserProfile(jsonString: string): UserProfile
  let jsonObj parseJson(jsonString)
  result.username jsonObj["username"].getStr()
```

```
result.age jsonObj["age"].getInt()
result.address.street jsonObj["address"]["street"].getStr()
result.address.city jsonObj["address"]["city"].getStr()
       result.address.postalCode          jsonObj["address"]
["postalCode"].getStr()
```

Example usage
```
let profile UserProfile(username: "JohnDoe", age: 30,
             address: (street: "123 Elm St", city: "Springfield",
postalCode: "12345"))
```

```
let jsonProfile serializeUserProfile(profile)
echo "Serialized profile: ", jsonProfile
```

```
let deserializedProfile deserializeUserProfile(jsonProfile)
echo "Deserialized profile: ", deserializedProfile.username, ",
Age: ", deserializedProfile.age
` ` `
```

In this example, `serializeUserProfile` converts a `UserProfile` object into a JSON string, while `deserializeUserProfile` reconstructs the object from the JSON string. This demonstrates how to handle nested objects and custom data structures with JSON serialization and deserialization.

The process of serialization and deserialization extends beyond JSON and XML to other formats such as binary serialization. For binary formats, you might need to implement serialization procedures that handle byte-level manipulation, ensuring efficient and compact storage of data. Nim's standard library and third-party packages offer support for various serialization techniques, allowing you to choose the most suitable format for your needs.

Understanding file I/O and serialization in Nim equips you with the tools needed to manage data efficiently, whether for storage, transmission, or interaction with external systems.

Mastering these concepts will enhance your ability to develop applications that can handle data reliably and efficiently.

When managing file I/O and serialization, it is crucial to consider data integrity and efficiency, especially when dealing with large datasets or performing complex operations. In Nim, while the built-in file handling mechanisms provide a robust foundation, performance and data integrity can be further optimized through careful design and best practices.

One important aspect of file I/O is ensuring that file operations are atomic where necessary. Atomic operations are those that are completed in a single step from the perspective of other processes. This can be particularly important when updating files where you want to avoid partial writes that might corrupt the file. In practice, ensuring atomicity often involves using temporary files during write operations and renaming them once the write is complete. Nim does not provide built-in atomic file operations directly, but this approach can be implemented manually.

For instance, when updating a configuration file, you might first write the new configuration to a temporary file and then replace the original file with the temporary file. This ensures that if an error occurs during the write process, the original file remains intact. Here's a simplified example of how you might implement this strategy:

```nim
import os, strutils

proc atomicWrite(filename: string, content: string)
  let tempFilename  filename & ".tmp"
  try:
    writeFile(tempFilename, content)
    renameFile(tempFilename, filename)
  except OSError as e:
    echo "Error during atomic write: ", e.msg
```

```
  removeFile(tempFilename)
` ` `
```

This `atomicWrite` procedure writes content to a temporary file and then renames the file to replace the original file. If an error occurs, it cleans up the temporary file to avoid leaving behind unnecessary files.

Another consideration for file operations is handling large files efficiently. When dealing with large files, reading or writing in chunks can help manage memory usage and performance. Nim's `os` module provides functions for handling file streams, allowing for more controlled access to file content. For example, you can use `open` with `read` to process files in chunks:

```nim
import os, strutils

proc processLargeFile(filename: string)
  var fileStream  open(filename, fmRead)
  var buffer: array[1024, char]
  while not fileStream.eof:
   fileStream.read(buffer)
    Process buffer here
   echo buffer
  fileStream.close()
```

In this example, the file is opened in read mode, and content is read into a buffer in chunks. This approach helps to avoid loading the entire file into memory, which is crucial for handling large files.

For data serialization and deserialization, it is beneficial to understand various formats and their implications on performance and compatibility. JSON and XML are widely used formats with different trade-offs. JSON is often preferred for its simplicity and efficiency, particularly when dealing with modern web applications. XML, on the other hand, is verbose and has a more complex structure, but it is still widely used in legacy systems and for its support of schema validation.

When working with JSON in Nim, the `json` module provides straightforward methods for encoding and decoding JSON data. Here's an example of how to work with JSON data in Nim:

```nim
import json, tables

type
  Person object
    name: string
    age: int

proc encodePerson(person: Person): JsonNode
  %{ "name": person.name, "age": person.age }

proc decodePerson(json: JsonNode): Person
  result.name json["name"].getStr()
  result.age json["age"].getInt()

let person Person(name: "Alice", age: 30)
let jsonStr encodePerson(person).toJson()
echo "Encoded JSON: ", jsonStr

let decodedPerson decodePerson(parseJson(jsonStr))
echo "Decoded Person: ", decodedPerson.name, ", Age: ", decodedPerson.age
```

This example demonstrates how to encode a `Person` object to JSON and decode it back. The `encodePerson` function converts a `Person` object into a JSON node, and `decodePerson` reconstructs the object from a JSON node. This method ensures that data can be easily serialized and deserialized while preserving its structure.

For XML serialization, you might need to use third-party libraries as Nim's standard library does not include comprehensive XML support. Libraries like `nimxml` provide XML parsing and generation capabilities. Handling XML might involve working with nodes and attributes in a hierarchical manner, which requires a different approach compared to JSON.

Here is a brief example using `nimxml` to work with XML data:

```nim
import xmltree, strutils

proc encodePersonToXml(person: Person): XmlNode
  let root  XmlNode("Person")
  root.addChild(XmlNode("Name", person.name))
  root.addChild(XmlNode("Age", $person.age))
  result root

proc decodePersonFromXml(node: XmlNode): Person
  result.name  node.getChild("Name").text
  result.age  parseInt(node.getChild("Age").text)

let person  Person(name: "Bob", age: 40)
let xmlNode  encodePersonToXml(person)
let xmlStr  xmlNode.toXml()
echo "Encoded XML: ", xmlStr

let parsedXml  parseXml(xmlStr)
let decodedPerson  decodePersonFromXml(parsedXml)
echo "Decoded Person: ", decodedPerson.name, ", Age: ", decodedPerson.age
```

In this example, `encodePersonToXml` creates an XML representation of the `Person` object, while `decodePersonFromXml` parses XML back into a `Person` object. This approach illustrates how to handle XML serialization and deserialization effectively.

Understanding and implementing file I/O and serialization effectively ensures that your programs can handle data reliably and efficiently, supporting a wide range of applications and use cases. Whether you are working with simple text files, complex binary formats, or structured data formats like JSON and XML, Nim provides the tools and flexibility needed to manage these tasks proficiently.

CHAPTER 11:

In addition to the fundamental aspects of socket programming and HTTP requests, more advanced networking scenarios in Nim involve dealing with various communication protocols and ensuring efficient and reliable data exchange. These aspects are crucial for developing applications that need to operate over complex or unreliable networks.

One key concept to understand in this context is asynchronous I/O. Asynchronous operations allow a program to handle multiple tasks concurrently without blocking the main execution thread. This is particularly useful in network programming where operations such as reading from or writing to a socket can be time-consuming and might block the execution if handled synchronously.

Nim provides support for asynchronous operations through its `async` module, which allows for the efficient handling of I/O operations. To illustrate, consider an example of an asynchronous TCP server. This server will handle multiple connections concurrently by utilizing asynchronous I/O:

```nim
import asyncdispatch, net, strutils, logging

proc handleClient(client: Socket) {.async.}
  try:
    var buffer: array[1024, char]
    let bytesRead  await client.recv(buffer)
    if bytesRead > 0:
      echo "Received: ", buffer[0..bytesRead-1]
```

```nim
   await client.send("Hello from async server!")
 except IOError as e:
  echo "IOError: ", e.msg
 finally:
  await client.close()

proc startAsyncServer(port: Port) {.async.}
 let server  newAsyncSocket()
 await server.bind(Port(port))
 await server.listen()
 echo "Async Server listening on port ", port


 while true:
  let client  await server.accept()
  asyncHandleClient(client)

asyncMain startAsyncServer(8082)
```

In this example, `handleClient` is an asynchronous procedure that handles incoming data from clients and sends responses. The `asyncMain` procedure is used to start the asynchronous server, allowing it to handle multiple clients concurrently without blocking.

For applications that need to interact with web services or APIs, understanding how to handle various HTTP methods is essential. While GET and POST are the most commonly used methods, other HTTP methods such as PUT, DELETE, and PATCH are also frequently utilized for different types of operations. The `httpclient` module in Nim supports these methods, enabling flexible interactions with web services. For instance, performing a POST request to submit data can be done as follows:

```nim
import httpclient, json
```

```
proc postData(url: string, data: JsonNode)
 let client  newHttpClient()
 let response  client.post(url, data.toPretty())
 if response.statusCode  200:
  echo "Response: ", response.body
 else:
  echo "Failed to post data. Status code: ", response.statusCode

let data  % {
 "name": "John Doe",
 "age": 30
}
postData("http://example.com/api/submit", data)
` ` `
```

This example shows how to send a JSON object to a web service using a POST request. The `toPretty` method of the `JsonNode` converts the data into a formatted JSON string suitable for submission. Handling responses from such requests involves checking status codes and processing the response body as needed.

When dealing with communication protocols, it is also important to consider security aspects such as encryption. Secure communication over networks often involves protocols like TLS (Transport Layer Security) to encrypt data exchanged between clients and servers. Nim provides support for TLS through the `httpclient` and `openssl` modules, allowing secure interactions with web services. Configuring a secure client connection requires specifying the appropriate TLS settings, such as certificate paths and verification options.

Moreover, for efficient data exchange in distributed systems, understanding and implementing serialization and deserialization techniques are essential. Data serialization involves converting data structures or objects into a format that can be easily stored or transmitted. Nim supports various serialization formats, including JSON, XML, and binary formats. For instance, serializing data to JSON format and then deserializing it back to a Nim object can be accomplished as follows:

```nim
import json

proc serializeToJson(data: JsonNode): string
  return data.toPretty()

proc deserializeFromJson(jsonStr: string): JsonNode
  return parseJson(jsonStr)

let data % {
  "username": "alice",
  "email": "alice@example.com"
}
let jsonStr serializeToJson(data)
echo "Serialized JSON: ", jsonStr

let parsedData deserializeFromJson(jsonStr)
echo "Deserialized Data: ", parsedData
```

In this example, `serializeToJson` converts a `JsonNode` into a pretty-printed JSON string, while `deserializeFromJson` parses a JSON string back into a `JsonNode`. These functions facilitate the easy exchange of structured data between systems.

In addition to these techniques, optimizing network performance and reliability involves strategies such as connection pooling, load balancing, and caching. Connection pooling involves reusing existing connections to reduce the overhead of establishing new ones. Load balancing distributes network traffic across multiple servers to ensure efficient resource utilization and prevent overload on any single server. Caching stores frequently accessed data to reduce the need for repeated data retrieval and improve response times.

Effective use of these strategies can significantly enhance the performance and scalability of networked applications. Understanding the interplay between various networking concepts and techniques allows developers to build robust, efficient, and secure networked systems capable of meeting diverse application needs.

The implementation of networking and communication features in applications often involves dealing with various complexities and challenges, particularly when scaling to handle increased loads or integrating with external services. One advanced aspect of network programming is dealing with the challenges of scaling applications, which often necessitates using techniques such as load balancing and implementing microservices.

Load balancing distributes incoming network traffic across multiple servers, ensuring that no single server becomes overwhelmed with requests. This distribution enhances the application's ability to handle high traffic volumes and improves reliability by providing redundancy. In a Nim context, while the `httpclient` module helps with making HTTP requests, handling load balancing typically involves configuring infrastructure components rather than code directly. For instance, you might use a load balancer service or hardware that distributes requests based on various algorithms such as round-robin, least connections, or IP hashing.

When building microservices, the application is divided into smaller, self-contained services that communicate with each other over the network. Each microservice typically handles a specific piece of functionality and can be developed, deployed, and scaled independently. In Nim, the `httpbeast` library is useful for implementing microservices by handling HTTP requests and responses efficiently. For example, you can set up a microservice that handles user authentication:

```nim
import httpbeast, logging, json

proc authenticateUser(req: Request) {.async.}
 let userData  await req.body.readAll()
 let data  parseJson(userData)
 let username  data["username"].getStr()
 let password  data["password"].getStr()


 if username "admin" and password "password":
  await req.respond(Http200, "Authenticated successfully!")
 else:
  await req.respond(Http401, "Unauthorized")

proc startAuthService(port: Port) {.async.}
 let server  newAsyncHttpServer(authenticateUser)
 await server.serve(Port(port))
 echo "Authentication service running on port ", port

asyncMain startAuthService(8083)
```

This example illustrates a simple authentication service using the `httpbeast` library. The `authenticateUser` procedure processes incoming requests, validates user credentials, and responds accordingly. This setup is scalable and can be integrated into a larger system of microservices, each responsible for different functionalities.

Another critical aspect of network programming is dealing with asynchronous communication, especially in systems where tasks need to be performed concurrently. Nim's `asyncdispatch` module facilitates this by allowing asynchronous execution of code. This is particularly useful for network operations that might otherwise block the main thread of execution.

For example, when performing multiple asynchronous HTTP requests, the `asyncdispatch` module can help coordinate these operations effectively:

```nim
import asyncdispatch, httpclient, strutils

proc fetchContent(url: string): Future[string] {.async.}
 let client  newHttpClient()
 let response  await client.get(url)
 return response.body

proc fetchMultipleUrls(urls: seq[string]) {.async.}
 var futures: seq[Future[string]] @[]
 for url in urls:
  futures.add(fetchContent(url))


 for future in futures:
  let content  await future
   echo "Fetched content: ", content[0..100]   Display first 100 characters

asyncMain          fetchMultipleUrls(@["http://example.com", "http://example.org"])
```

In this example, the `fetchContent` procedure fetches content from a URL asynchronously. The `fetchMultipleUrls` procedure handles multiple URLs concurrently, demonstrating how asynchronous programming can be utilized to perform non-blocking I/O operations.

When it comes to serialization, ensuring compatibility and efficiency in data exchange is paramount. Serialization formats such as JSON, XML, and Protocol Buffers are widely used. JSON is particularly popular due to its human-readable format and widespread support in various languages.

However, for scenarios requiring efficient binary serialization, Protocol Buffers or similar formats might be preferable.

To illustrate JSON serialization in Nim, consider the following example where data is serialized to JSON and then deserialized:

```nim
import json, strutils

proc serializeToJson(data: JsonNode): string
 return data.toPretty()

proc deserializeFromJson(jsonStr: string): JsonNode
 return parseJson(jsonStr)

let data % {
 "id": 123,
 "name": "Example",
 "tags": @["nim", "programming"]
}
let jsonStr  serializeToJson(data)
echo "Serialized JSON: ", jsonStr

let parsedData  deserializeFromJson(jsonStr)
echo "Deserialized Data: ", parsedData
```

In this code snippet, `serializeToJson` converts a `JsonNode` object into a pretty-printed JSON string, and `deserializeFromJson` parses a JSON string back into a `JsonNode` object. This approach ensures that data can be easily exchanged between systems or stored for later use.

Furthermore, handling file I/O operations for logging or persistent storage is another crucial aspect of networked applications. Nim's `os` module provides functions for file operations, allowing you to read from and write to files efficiently. Properly managing these operations ensures that logs and data are stored reliably, supporting the application's overall functionality and performance.

By integrating these concepts—load balancing, microservices, asynchronous programming, and serialization—developers can build robust and efficient networked applications that meet modern performance and scalability requirements. Understanding and implementing these techniques effectively allows for creating systems capable of handling complex networking scenarios and ensuring seamless communication across diverse platforms.

CHAPTER 12:

When working with external libraries in Nim, understanding how to leverage these resources effectively is crucial for maximizing productivity and efficiency in your projects. Beyond simply finding and installing libraries, the integration process often requires a nuanced understanding of how to utilize these tools in harmony with your existing code. This section will delve into the practical aspects of integrating and using external libraries, with a focus on advanced techniques and considerations for optimal usage.

In addition to basic installation and import procedures, it is important to handle library dependencies and versioning carefully. When you install a library using Nimble, it often brings along other dependencies that your library needs to function correctly. This can sometimes lead to version conflicts if different libraries require incompatible versions of the same dependency. Nimble manages these dependencies by creating a lock file that records the exact versions of dependencies used. However, it's important to regularly update and test your dependencies to ensure compatibility and to benefit from improvements or security patches.

When integrating external C libraries, there are specific considerations to keep in mind. Nim provides the ability to call C functions directly through its Foreign Function Interface (FFI). To ensure seamless integration, you should be familiar with the C library's API and the data types it uses. Often, you need to convert data types between Nim and C, which requires careful handling to avoid data corruption or crashes. Nim's `importc` pragma facilitates this process by allowing you to declare C functions and variables directly in your Nim code. This pragma also allows for specifying the name of the shared library file and the exact C function signatures, ensuring that Nim's interfacing with C functions is accurate.

Moreover, when integrating C libraries, you may need to handle memory management explicitly. Unlike Nim, which has garbage collection, C requires manual memory management. This means you must allocate and deallocate memory correctly to prevent memory leaks or segmentation faults. For instance, if the C library allocates memory that needs to be freed later, you must provide corresponding code in Nim to ensure that memory is properly managed.

In addition to direct integration, Nim also supports using external libraries through dynamic loading. This technique allows you to load a library at runtime rather than linking it at compile time. This can be useful for creating modular applications where certain components can be loaded or unloaded based on specific conditions or user requirements. To dynamically load a library, you use the `dlopen` function from Nim's `os` module. Once loaded, you can use `dlsym` to locate and invoke functions within the library. This approach requires managing the library handle and ensuring that the library is correctly unloaded when no longer needed.

Contributing to the Nim community by developing and sharing your own libraries not only enhances the ecosystem but also fosters collaboration and knowledge sharing. When developing a library, it is crucial to provide clear documentation and examples to help users understand how to integrate and use your library effectively. Proper documentation includes a comprehensive description of the library's functionality, API references, and usage examples. Additionally, providing tests for your library can ensure its reliability and ease of use, as well as facilitate contributions and improvements from other developers.

To contribute your library to the Nim ecosystem, you need to follow a structured process. After creating and testing your library, you should prepare a Nimble package file, which contains metadata about the library, including its name, version, dependencies, and author information. This file also includes a description of the library's purpose and usage, which helps users understand its value and functionality.

Once your package file is ready, you can publish your library to the Nimble repository using the `nimble upload` command. This command uploads your library and makes it available for other Nim developers to install and use. It is also a good practice to maintain your library by addressing issues, updating dependencies, and incorporating feedback from users.

In summary, working with external libraries in Nim involves more than just installation and import. Effective usage requires careful management of dependencies, understanding C library integration, and handling dynamic loading when necessary. Additionally, contributing to the Nim community by developing and sharing libraries involves creating clear documentation, preparing a Nimble package, and maintaining the library through regular updates. By mastering these practices, you can enhance your projects and contribute to the growth of the Nim ecosystem.

When working with external libraries in Nim, you might encounter scenarios that require integrating libraries with varying functionalities, such as those designed for different programming paradigms or language ecosystems. One key aspect of effective integration is managing and resolving potential conflicts between libraries, especially when dealing with libraries that offer overlapping functionality or dependencies.

In such cases, understanding the build and runtime environment becomes crucial. For instance, Nim's build system allows you to customize and manage how libraries are linked and compiled. By adjusting the build configuration, you can control which versions of libraries are used, and how they are integrated into your project. This is particularly important when dealing with C libraries, where discrepancies in library versions or compiler settings might lead to subtle bugs or incompatibilities.

Another advanced technique involves dealing with platform-specific dependencies and ensuring compatibility across different operating systems. When a library is designed to interact with system-specific features, such as networking or file I/O, you must handle these dependencies carefully to ensure your application runs correctly on all targeted platforms. Nim provides mechanisms to define platform-specific code using conditional compilation. This allows you to include or exclude code based on the target platform, ensuring that your integration remains clean and maintainable.

Integrating external libraries also involves considerations related to security and performance. External libraries may introduce vulnerabilities or performance bottlenecks that can impact your application. Therefore, it is advisable to review the library's source code and documentation, and to conduct thorough testing to identify potential issues. Security considerations include validating inputs and outputs when interfacing with libraries that perform sensitive operations or handle user data.

When it comes to performance, profiling tools can help you assess the impact of external libraries on your application's performance. Nim provides support for profiling and benchmarking through various tools and libraries. By analyzing the performance characteristics of integrated libraries, you can make informed decisions about optimizations or alternative libraries that might offer better performance characteristics.

Moreover, understanding how to manage and update external libraries is crucial for long-term project maintenance. As libraries evolve, they may introduce new features or deprecate existing ones. Staying updated with the latest versions of libraries can provide benefits such as bug fixes, performance improvements, and new functionalities. However, updating libraries requires careful testing to ensure that new versions do not introduce breaking changes. It is often useful to maintain a changelog or version history for your project to track which versions of libraries are used and to document any issues or changes encountered during updates.

Handling external libraries also involves considerations around licensing and compliance. When using third-party libraries, you must comply with their licensing terms and ensure that your use of these libraries does not violate any legal agreements. This may include adhering to specific attribution requirements or distributing source code alongside your application. Nim's package manager, Nimble, can help manage licenses by providing metadata about each package, including its licensing information. It is a good practice to review and understand the licensing terms of any library you use and to ensure that your project remains compliant.

Additionally, contributing to the Nim ecosystem by developing and sharing your own libraries is an enriching way to engage with the community and foster collaboration. When creating a new library, it is important to follow best practices for software development, including clear documentation, comprehensive testing, and adherence to coding standards. Providing detailed examples and tutorials can help users get started with your library and can increase its adoption within the Nim community.

As your library gains traction, engaging with users and responding to feedback is crucial for its ongoing development. Addressing issues reported by users, incorporating feature requests, and maintaining compatibility with new versions of Nim and its dependencies are all important aspects of sustaining a successful library. By actively participating in the community and supporting your library, you contribute to the growth and vitality of the Nim ecosystem.

In conclusion, effectively working with external libraries in Nim requires a deep understanding of integration techniques, dependency management, and platform-specific considerations. By carefully managing these aspects, you can ensure that your application leverages external libraries effectively and remains robust and maintainable. Furthermore, contributing to the community through library development and engagement not only enhances the ecosystem but also provides valuable opportunities for collaboration and learning.

Performance Optimization

Performance optimization is essential for building efficient systems capable of handling demanding tasks and large-scale applications. In this exploration of performance optimization within Nim, I will delve into several critical areas: profiling techniques, identifying performance bottlenecks, optimizing memory usage, and crafting high-performance algorithms. Each of these aspects plays a vital role in enhancing the efficiency of your Nim applications.

To begin with, understanding and applying profiling techniques is fundamental to performance optimization. Profiling allows us to gain insights into how our code executes and where time is being spent during execution. In Nim, various profiling tools and methods are available to assist in this process. One common approach is to use built-in profiling utilities that provide detailed reports on function call frequencies, execution times, and memory allocations. By analyzing these reports, we can pinpoint which parts of our code are consuming excessive resources or taking longer to execute than expected.

Profiling in Nim can be achieved using tools such as `gprof` or `perf`, which integrate with the Nim compiler to provide performance metrics. These tools work by instrumenting the code during compilation and recording performance data as the program runs. Once profiling data is collected, it can be analyzed to determine hotspots—areas of the code where optimization efforts should be concentrated. For instance, if a specific function is identified as a performance bottleneck, it becomes a target for optimization.

Identifying performance bottlenecks involves examining the profiling data and interpreting it to understand where inefficiencies exist. Common bottlenecks include inefficient algorithms, excessive memory allocations, or frequent I/O operations. Once identified, these bottlenecks can be addressed through various optimization techniques. For example, if a particular algorithm is found to be slow, we might consider alternative algorithms with better time complexity. If excessive memory allocations are detected, we might refactor the code to reduce memory usage or employ more efficient data structures.

Optimizing memory usage is another critical aspect of performance optimization. In Nim, memory management can be handled both automatically and manually. While Nim's garbage collector simplifies memory management by automatically reclaiming unused memory, there are situations where manual memory management can lead to significant performance improvements. For instance, in performance-critical sections of code, avoiding frequent allocations and deallocations can reduce garbage collection overhead and improve overall efficiency.

To optimize memory usage, start by analyzing memory consumption patterns in your application. Tools such as `valgrind` or Nim's built-in memory profiling utilities can help track memory usage and identify areas where excessive allocations occur. By optimizing data structures and minimizing unnecessary memory allocations, you can reduce memory footprint and enhance performance. Additionally, understanding and leveraging Nim's memory management features, such as `alloc` and `dealloc` procedures, can give you finer control over memory usage.

Writing high-performance algorithms is often the most impactful optimization strategy. Algorithms that are well-designed and efficient can drastically reduce execution time and resource consumption. In Nim, you can optimize algorithms by focusing on algorithmic complexity, data locality, and efficient use of hardware resources. For instance, selecting appropriate data structures, such as hash tables or balanced trees, can significantly impact performance for operations involving large datasets.

Another key consideration in writing high-performance algorithms is parallelism. Nim supports concurrency and parallelism, allowing you to leverage multiple CPU cores to execute tasks concurrently. By breaking down computationally intensive tasks into smaller, parallelizable units, you can achieve substantial performance gains. Nim's threading model and asynchronous programming features facilitate this process, enabling you to design algorithms that efficiently utilize available computational resources.

In practice, achieving high performance requires a combination of these strategies. Profiling provides insights into where optimizations are needed, while memory optimization techniques help reduce resource consumption. Writing efficient algorithms and leveraging parallelism further enhance performance. By applying these techniques in a structured and iterative manner, you can systematically improve the performance of your Nim applications.

As you embark on performance optimization efforts, it is important to adopt a mindset of continuous improvement. Optimization is often an iterative process, involving profiling, analysis, and refinement. By continually assessing the performance of your code and applying targeted optimizations, you can build systems that are not only functional but also efficient and responsive to user needs.

As we delve deeper into performance optimization, the focus shifts to practical strategies and techniques that can significantly impact the efficiency of Nim applications. Profiling and optimizing Nim code are iterative processes that require a meticulous approach to identify and address performance issues. Once performance bottlenecks have been identified through profiling, the next step is to apply targeted optimization techniques to improve overall system efficiency.

A critical aspect of performance optimization is understanding and improving algorithmic efficiency. Algorithms with high time complexity can become significant performance bottlenecks, especially in applications that process large volumes of data or perform intensive computations. To enhance performance, it is often necessary to select or design algorithms with better time complexity. For instance, a sorting algorithm with a time complexity of $O(n \log n)$ is generally more efficient than one with $O(n^2)$ complexity, particularly for large datasets. By analyzing the computational complexity of various algorithms and choosing the most appropriate one for a given task, we can achieve substantial performance improvements.

In addition to algorithmic complexity, data locality and access patterns play a crucial role in performance optimization. Algorithms that access memory in a predictable and sequential manner can benefit from better cache utilization, reducing the number of cache misses and improving execution speed. For example, when working with large arrays or matrices, ensuring that data is accessed in contiguous memory locations can lead to more efficient cache usage. This principle can be applied to both single-threaded and multi-threaded applications to optimize performance.

Another important factor in performance optimization is minimizing I/O operations. Disk and network I/O can introduce significant delays in application performance, especially when dealing with large files or frequent data transfers. Optimizing I/O operations involves techniques such as buffering data, using asynchronous I/O, and reducing the frequency of I/O operations. In Nim, the standard library provides various functions for efficient file handling and network communication, but it is essential to use these functions judiciously to avoid performance degradation.

When dealing with network communication, latency and throughput can be critical factors affecting performance. Efficiently managing network resources and minimizing network overhead can improve the responsiveness and efficiency of networked applications. For instance, employing techniques such as connection pooling, optimizing data serialization, and minimizing the size of transmitted messages can help reduce network latency and improve overall performance.

Memory management is another critical area for optimization. In Nim, memory management can be automatic or manual, and understanding how to leverage both approaches effectively can lead to significant performance gains. While Nim's garbage collector simplifies memory management by automatically reclaiming unused memory, manual memory management allows for more precise control over memory allocation and deallocation. For performance-critical sections of code, minimizing garbage collection overhead by reducing the frequency of allocations and deallocations can lead to improved performance.

Furthermore, using efficient data structures is key to optimizing memory usage. Data structures such as hash tables, balanced trees, and linked lists offer various trade-offs in terms of time and space complexity. Selecting the right data structure for a given application can enhance performance by providing faster access times and reducing memory consumption. For example, hash tables offer average-case $O(1)$ time complexity for lookups and insertions, making them suitable for scenarios where quick access to data is essential.

Parallelism and concurrency are also vital aspects of performance optimization. Nim's concurrency model allows for the creation of concurrent tasks and the utilization of multiple CPU cores to perform computations in parallel. By breaking down computationally intensive tasks into smaller, parallelizable units, applications can achieve substantial performance improvements. Effective use of concurrency requires careful consideration of thread synchronization, data sharing, and task scheduling to avoid common pitfalls such as race conditions and deadlocks.

Nim provides several mechanisms for handling concurrency, including threads and asynchronous programming constructs. Threads enable the concurrent execution of multiple tasks, while asynchronous programming allows for non-blocking operations and efficient handling of I/O-bound tasks. By leveraging these mechanisms, developers can design applications that are responsive and capable of handling multiple tasks simultaneously.

In summary, performance optimization in Nim

involves a comprehensive approach that encompasses profiling, algorithmic efficiency, memory management, I/O optimization, and concurrency. By applying these techniques and continuously refining the performance of your code, you can build systems that are not only functional but also efficient and capable of handling demanding workloads. Optimization is an ongoing process that requires careful analysis, testing, and refinement to achieve the best possible performance outcomes.

To continue the discussion on performance optimization, a nuanced understanding of the profiling tools and techniques available in Nim is essential. Profiling is the process of measuring the performance characteristics of a program to identify areas where optimizations can have the most impact. In Nim, several tools and methods are available to assist with this task.

The Nim programming language provides integrated support for profiling through its built-in tools and third-party libraries. One of the primary tools for performance analysis is the profiler, which can be invoked using the `--profile` flag during compilation. This tool generates detailed reports on the execution time of various parts of the code, including function calls and loop iterations. By analyzing these reports, developers can pinpoint which functions or code segments consume the most resources, allowing for targeted optimization efforts.

Another useful profiling tool in Nim is the heap profiler. This tool provides insights into memory allocation patterns, revealing how much memory is allocated and deallocated during program execution. Understanding memory usage patterns can help identify inefficiencies such as excessive memory allocations or leaks. By optimizing these aspects, developers can reduce the overall memory footprint and improve application performance.

Performance profiling in Nim can also be enhanced by leveraging external libraries and tools. For instance, integrating with profiling tools such as Valgrind or Google's gperftools can offer additional insights into code performance. These tools provide advanced features such as call graphs, cache miss analysis, and detailed memory usage statistics, which can further aid in optimizing Nim applications.

Once performance bottlenecks are identified through profiling, the next step is to apply specific optimization strategies. One critical area of optimization involves refining algorithms and data structures. While selecting the most efficient algorithm is important, optimizing its implementation can further enhance performance. Techniques such as loop unrolling, inlining functions, and minimizing redundant computations can contribute to faster execution times. Additionally, employing advanced data structures like balanced trees or tries can provide more efficient data access and manipulation compared to simpler structures.

Memory management and optimization are also crucial for achieving high performance. Efficient memory use can be achieved through techniques such as object pooling, where frequently used objects are reused instead of being repeatedly allocated and deallocated. This approach reduces the overhead associated with memory allocation and garbage collection, leading to improved performance. Another strategy is to minimize memory fragmentation by allocating large blocks of memory and managing them internally, which can help reduce the impact of memory fragmentation on application performance.

In terms of I/O optimization, several strategies can be employed to enhance performance. For example, batching I/O operations can reduce the number of system calls and improve throughput. By grouping multiple read or write operations into a single batch, the overhead associated with each operation is minimized. Additionally, using asynchronous I/O operations can prevent the application from being blocked while waiting for I/O operations to complete, thereby improving responsiveness and overall performance.

Concurrency and parallelism play a significant role in optimizing performance, especially in modern applications that require handling multiple tasks simultaneously. Nim's concurrency model supports the creation of concurrent tasks using threads and asynchronous programming constructs. Effective use of concurrency can lead to substantial performance improvements by allowing tasks to be executed in parallel. However, it is important to manage concurrent tasks carefully to avoid issues such as race conditions, deadlocks, and contention for shared resources.

When working with concurrency, employing synchronization mechanisms such as mutexes and semaphores can help coordinate access to shared resources and ensure data consistency. Additionally, using concurrent data structures designed for multi-threaded environments can enhance performance by reducing the need for complex synchronization and locking mechanisms.

In parallel computing, dividing a task into smaller, independent units of work that can be executed concurrently is a common approach to improving performance. Techniques such as parallel algorithms, task scheduling, and load balancing are essential for efficiently utilizing multiple CPU cores. Nim's support for parallelism allows developers to write code that can take advantage of modern multi-core processors, leading to faster execution and improved performance.

Finally, continuous performance testing and monitoring are essential for maintaining optimal performance over time.

Performance testing involves running benchmarks and stress tests to evaluate the performance characteristics of the application under different conditions. By regularly testing and monitoring performance, developers can identify and address potential issues before they impact users, ensuring that the application remains responsive and efficient.

In summary, performance optimization in Nim involves a multifaceted approach that includes profiling, algorithm optimization, memory management, I/O optimization, concurrency, and parallelism. By leveraging the available profiling tools, applying targeted optimization strategies, and continuously monitoring performance, developers can build high-performance systems that meet the demands of modern applications. The iterative nature of optimization requires a commitment to ongoing analysis and refinement, but the benefits of improved performance are well worth the effort.

CHAPTER 13:

Effective debugging requires a systematic approach to identify and resolve issues in Nim programs. One of the essential strategies in debugging is leveraging the tools and facilities provided by Nim to gain insights into program behavior and performance. Debugging often begins with understanding the nature of the problem, and this can be achieved through careful examination of symptoms, such as unexpected behavior, crashes, or incorrect results.

Nim's integrated development environment (IDE) and command-line tools offer valuable support for debugging. The `--debug` flag, when used during the compilation process, includes debugging symbols in the output binary. These symbols provide the necessary information for tools like GDB to map machine code back to source code, allowing developers to step through the code, inspect variable values, and observe the program's execution flow. This process is crucial for diagnosing complex issues that cannot be easily pinpointed through code inspection alone.

GDB, as a debugger, supports various commands that are fundamental for interactive debugging. For instance, setting breakpoints using the `break` command allows developers to pause execution at specific lines of code or function calls, making it possible to examine the program state at those critical points. By inspecting variable values, stack frames, and memory contents, one can gather detailed information about the program's state and behavior. Additionally, stepping through the code with commands like `next` and `step` helps trace the execution flow and identify where things may be going awry.

Another powerful technique in debugging involves analyzing core dumps. Core dumps are files that capture the memory state of a program at the time of a crash. They provide a snapshot of the program's memory, including the call stack, registers, and data structures, which can be invaluable for diagnosing crashes and segmentation faults. To generate a core dump, it is necessary to configure the system to allow core files and ensure that the program is compiled with debugging symbols. Tools like GDB can then be used to analyze the core dump, enabling developers to pinpoint the exact location and cause of the crash.

In addition to these debugging techniques, Nim provides logging facilities that can significantly aid in troubleshooting. Logging involves recording runtime information about the program's execution, such as variable values, function calls, and error messages. By incorporating logging statements at strategic points in the code, developers can gain insights into the program's behavior without interrupting its execution. Nim's standard library includes support for logging, with features to configure log levels (e.g., DEBUG, INFO, WARNING, ERROR) and output formats. Properly structured logs can provide a chronological view of events leading up to an issue, making it easier to diagnose and fix problems.

Profiling is another crucial aspect of debugging, especially when it comes to performance issues. Profiling involves analyzing the program's execution to identify performance bottlenecks, such as functions or code segments that consume excessive CPU time or memory. Nim's tooling ecosystem includes profiling tools that can measure various performance metrics, such as execution time, function call counts, and memory usage. Profilers generate reports that highlight hotspots in the code, allowing developers to focus their optimization efforts on areas with the most significant impact on performance.

To complement profiling, developers often use techniques such as code instrumentation, which involves inserting additional code to measure performance metrics directly. For example, inserting timers or counters at critical points in the code can help track the time taken by specific operations or functions. While this approach can provide valuable insights, it is essential to ensure that the instrumentation code itself does not introduce significant overhead or distort the measurements.

Incorporating best practices into testing and debugging workflows can enhance the effectiveness of these processes. For instance, maintaining comprehensive and up-to-date documentation of the codebase and its expected behavior helps ensure that tests are designed to cover all relevant scenarios. Additionally, adopting a systematic approach to testing, such as writing test cases for edge cases and corner cases, can uncover issues that might otherwise go unnoticed. Code reviews and pair programming also contribute to identifying potential problems early in the development process, reducing the likelihood of defects reaching production.

In summary, the combination of testing frameworks, debugging tools, logging, and profiling techniques forms a robust approach to ensuring code quality and performance in Nim. By leveraging these tools and adhering to best practices, developers can effectively identify, diagnose, and resolve issues, ultimately leading to more reliable and high-performing applications. The integration of these practices into the development lifecycle is essential for producing software that meets both functional and performance requirements.

Testing frameworks are vital for ensuring that code behaves

as expected and meets specified requirements. Nim provides several testing libraries that facilitate writing and running tests. One prominent testing framework is Nim's built-in `unittest` module. This module allows developers to write unit tests that verify the functionality of individual components in isolation. The `unittest` framework supports various assertions, such as `assertEqual`, `assertNotEqual`, and `assertTrue`, which enable precise checks on code behavior and outcomes.

Unit tests should be designed to cover a wide range of scenarios, including typical use cases, edge cases, and invalid inputs. Writing comprehensive test cases helps uncover potential issues early in the development cycle, preventing defects from propagating into later stages of the software lifecycle. It's crucial to maintain a clear and organized structure for test cases, often separating them into different test files or modules based on functionality. This organization aids in managing and executing tests efficiently, especially as the codebase grows.

In addition to unit testing, integration testing is essential for verifying the interactions between different components of a system. Integration tests ensure that the components work together as expected and that data flows correctly through the system. Nim provides mechanisms to write integration tests, often using the same `unittest` framework but focusing on the interactions between modules or external systems. For example, integration tests might involve setting up mock services or databases to simulate real-world interactions and validate the overall functionality of the application.

Another critical aspect of testing is end-to-end (E2E) testing, which assesses the complete workflow of an application from the user's perspective. E2E tests simulate user interactions with the application and verify that all parts of the system function correctly together. While Nim does not include a built-in E2E testing framework, it is possible to integrate with external tools or frameworks to perform such testing. For example, tools like Selenium can be used to automate browser interactions and validate web application behavior.

Effective debugging is equally crucial for identifying and resolving issues that may not be caught during testing. Nim's debugging capabilities include integrated support for various debugging tools, such as GDB, which provides a comprehensive set of features for interactive debugging. Using GDB with Nim involves compiling the code with debugging symbols, which allow the debugger to map machine instructions back to the source code. This setup enables developers to set breakpoints, step through code, and inspect the state of the program during execution.

Breakpoints are a fundamental feature of interactive debugging. By setting breakpoints, developers can pause execution at specific lines of code or when certain conditions are met. This pause allows for inspection of variables, evaluation of expressions, and analysis of the call stack. Conditional breakpoints are particularly useful for pausing execution only when specific criteria are satisfied, which can help isolate issues that occur under particular circumstances.

Stepping commands in GDB, such as `step` and `next`, enable developers to control the execution flow of the program. The `step` command enters into functions, allowing for detailed examination of code within those functions, while the `next` command executes over functions, providing a higher-level view of the program's progression. These commands help developers trace the execution path and identify where errors or unexpected behaviors occur.

In addition to interactive debugging, using logs and traces can significantly aid in debugging efforts. Logs provide a record of events and state changes during program execution, which can be invaluable for understanding how the program reached a particular state. By strategically placing logging statements in the code, developers can track the flow of execution and identify issues that may not be apparent through testing alone. Nim's standard library offers logging facilities with configurable log levels and output formats, allowing developers to tailor the logging output to their needs.

Profiling is another essential practice in performance debugging. Profiling tools measure various aspects of program performance, such as execution time, function call frequency, and memory usage. Nim supports profiling through tools like `gprof` or `valgrind`, which can generate detailed reports on performance metrics. Analyzing these reports helps identify bottlenecks and inefficiencies in the code, guiding optimization efforts to improve overall performance.

Code instrumentation is a technique used to gather performance data by adding additional code to measure specific metrics. For instance, inserting timing functions around critical sections of code can help measure the time taken by those sections and identify performance issues. However, it is important to use instrumentation judiciously, as excessive instrumentation can introduce overhead and skew the performance measurements.

By combining these testing and debugging strategies, developers can achieve a high level of confidence in the reliability and performance of their Nim programs. Effective testing ensures that code meets functional requirements and behaves correctly under various conditions, while robust debugging techniques help resolve issues and optimize performance. Integrating these practices into the development workflow is essential for delivering high-quality software that meets user expectations and performs efficiently.

CHAPTER 14:

In examining advanced Nim techniques, it is essential to explore not only the mechanics of macros, metaprogramming, and templates but also their practical applications and implications. These advanced features significantly extend Nim's capabilities, allowing for highly customizable and optimized code. By delving deeper into these constructs, we can better understand how they contribute to writing more efficient and maintainable programs.

Macros in Nim are powerful tools that allow developers to perform complex code transformations during compilation. Unlike traditional functions that operate at runtime, macros operate at compile-time, giving them the ability to generate or modify code before it is executed. This compile-time code generation can be particularly useful for scenarios where repetitive code needs to be created or where certain optimizations are required that cannot be easily achieved through standard code practices.

For instance, consider a scenario where you need to implement multiple variations of a logging function, each tailored to different logging levels or output formats. Writing these functions manually would be time-consuming and error-prone. Instead, you can use a macro to define a logging template that can be instantiated with different parameters. This macro can generate the necessary logging functions with the appropriate logic for each variation, ensuring consistency and reducing the risk of errors.

The power of Nim's macros is further amplified by its ability to work with the abstract syntax tree (AST). By manipulating the AST, macros can introduce sophisticated code generation patterns that are otherwise difficult to achieve. For example, you can write a macro that analyzes existing code structures and automatically generates additional code based on specific patterns or annotations. This capability allows for the creation of domain-specific languages (DSLs) and other advanced code constructs that can streamline complex development tasks.

Moving on to metaprogramming, this concept extends the capabilities of Nim beyond simple macros. Metaprogramming involves writing programs that generate or manipulate other programs, providing a high level of abstraction and flexibility. In Nim, metaprogramming is often achieved through a combination of macros and templates. While macros handle more complex transformations, templates offer a simpler mechanism for generating repetitive code.

Templates in Nim are defined using the `template` keyword and allow for the insertion of code snippets into various parts of a program. Unlike macros, templates operate at a more granular level, focusing on specific code patterns rather than broad transformations. This makes them particularly useful for scenarios where you need to generate multiple versions of a function or method based on different type parameters.

For example, suppose you need to implement a series of functions that perform similar operations but on different types, such as integers, floats, and strings. Instead of writing each function manually, you can define a template that accepts a type parameter and generates the required functions automatically. This approach not only saves development time but also ensures that all generated functions adhere to a consistent structure and logic.

Furthermore, metaprogramming in Nim enables the creation of high-level abstractions that can simplify complex programming tasks. By defining custom language constructs through macros and templates, you can design DSLs tailored to specific problem domains. This can make your code more expressive and easier to understand, as well as improve productivity by reducing the amount of boilerplate code.

Another crucial aspect of advanced Nim techniques is performance optimization. By leveraging macros and templates, you can write code that is not only more concise but also more efficient. For instance, code generated by templates can be optimized by the compiler in ways that manually written code might not be. This can lead to significant performance improvements, particularly in performance-critical applications where every millisecond counts.

Additionally, Nim's support for compile-time execution allows for further performance enhancements. Compile-time execution enables certain computations to be performed before the program runs, reducing runtime overhead and improving overall efficiency. This feature is especially valuable for tasks that involve complex calculations or data transformations that can be precomputed, resulting in faster execution times.

To illustrate, consider a scenario where you need to perform a series of mathematical calculations that are constant across different runs of the program. By performing these calculations at compile-time, you can eliminate the need to repeat them at runtime, thereby reducing computational overhead and improving performance.

In conclusion, the advanced features of Nim, including macros, metaprogramming, and templates, provide powerful tools for writing highly efficient and reusable code. By mastering these techniques, developers can leverage Nim's full potential to create more flexible and optimized programs. The ability to generate and manipulate code at compile-time, create custom language constructs, and optimize performance opens up new possibilities for solving complex programming challenges and developing high-quality software.

To fully leverage the advanced features of Nim, it is essential to understand not just their theoretical aspects but also their practical implications and best practices. As we explore these advanced techniques, it becomes evident that their effective use can significantly enhance the power and flexibility of Nim, allowing developers to tackle complex problems with elegance and efficiency.

A critical aspect of using macros effectively is understanding their impact on code readability and maintainability. While macros can drastically reduce boilerplate code and automate repetitive tasks, they can also introduce complexity that may obscure the code's intent. To mitigate this, it is crucial to use macros judiciously and ensure that they are well-documented. Clear documentation and comments within the macro definitions can help other developers (and yourself) understand the purpose and behavior of the generated code. Furthermore, adhering to consistent naming conventions and structuring macros in a modular fashion can enhance readability and ease of maintenance.

In practice, macros are particularly valuable in scenarios that involve generating code based on specific patterns or configurations. For example, consider a scenario where you need to create multiple data processing functions, each tailored to different data types or processing strategies. Instead of writing each function manually, a macro can be designed to generate these functions automatically based on a set of parameters or templates. This not only reduces the amount of repetitive code but also ensures consistency across all generated functions. By leveraging macros in this way, you can focus on defining the core logic and let the macro handle the repetitive aspects of code generation.

Metaprogramming, as an advanced technique, offers even greater flexibility by allowing code to generate or manipulate other code at compile-time. This can be particularly useful for creating high-level abstractions or domain-specific languages (DSLs) that simplify complex programming tasks. By combining macros with metaprogramming techniques, you can design custom language constructs that enhance code expressiveness and reduce boilerplate.

For instance, if you are developing a library for mathematical computations, you might use metaprogramming to create a DSL for defining mathematical expressions. This DSL could allow developers to write mathematical formulas in a more natural and intuitive way, while the metaprogramming constructs handle the translation of these formulas into efficient code. This approach not only improves the ease of use for library consumers but also ensures that the underlying code is optimized for performance.

Templates, on the other hand, provide a simpler mechanism for code generation compared to macros. They are particularly useful for scenarios where you need to generate multiple variations of a function or method based on type parameters. By defining templates that accept type parameters, you can create generic functions or methods that operate on different data types without duplicating code.

Consider a template that generates a function for computing the sum of elements in an array. By using type parameters, you can create a single template that works with arrays of integers, floats, or any other numeric type. This not only reduces code duplication but also allows for greater flexibility and reusability. The generated code will be type-safe and optimized for the specific type used, ensuring both efficiency and correctness.

Performance optimization through advanced techniques also

plays a crucial role in building high-quality software. By leveraging compile-time execution, you can precompute certain values or perform optimizations before the program runs. This can be particularly valuable for tasks that involve complex calculations or data transformations that are known ahead of time.

For example, if you need to perform a series of calculations that involve constant values or configurations, you can use compile-time execution to perform these calculations during the compilation process. This reduces the runtime overhead associated with these calculations and improves overall performance. The Nim compiler's support for compile-time execution allows you to perform complex computations efficiently, leading to faster and more responsive applications.

Additionally, understanding the performance implications of using macros, metaprogramming, and templates is essential for writing efficient code. While these techniques can significantly enhance code flexibility and expressiveness, they can also introduce overhead if not used judiciously. It is important to profile and analyze the performance impact of generated code to ensure that the benefits of these techniques outweigh any potential drawbacks.

In summary, the advanced features of Nim, including macros, metaprogramming, and templates, offer powerful tools for writing efficient and reusable code. By mastering these techniques and understanding their practical applications, you can create highly optimized programs that are both flexible and maintainable. The key to leveraging these advanced features effectively lies in balancing their power with careful consideration of code readability, maintainability, and performance.

CHAPTER 15:

When integrating Nim with other languages, particularly C, the process involves understanding several key aspects of language interoperability, including type conversion, function linkage, and memory management.

Nim's Foreign Function Interface (FFI) simplifies the integration with C, providing a straightforward mechanism to call C functions and utilize C libraries. To effectively call C functions from Nim, it's crucial to correctly map C data types to their Nim equivalents. Nim supports various C data types natively through its `ffi` module. For instance, C's `int` type is typically mapped to `cint`, and `long` to `clong`. This mapping ensures that the types are compatible and that the function calls behave as expected.

Consider a scenario where you need to interface with a C library that provides mathematical functions. If the C library offers a function to compute the factorial of a number, the function might be defined as follows in C:

```c
// mathlib.c
long long factorial(int n) {
  if (n < 1) return 1;
  return n factorial(n - 1);
}
```

To call this function from Nim, you would first declare it in Nim with the appropriate `importc` pragma. It is essential to ensure that the type definitions and function signatures match exactly. Here's how you might declare and use this function in Nim:

```nim
mathlib.nim
import ffi

proc factorial(n: cint): clong {.importc: "factorial", header: "mathlib.h".}

let result factorial(5)
echo result
```

In this example, the `importc` pragma tells Nim to link with the C library and use the C function `factorial`. The types `cint` and `clong` ensure that the data types passed to and received from the C function are compatible.

When dealing with more complex C libraries, particularly those that use structures, arrays, or pointers, it's crucial to accurately represent these C constructs in Nim. For instance, if a C library uses structures to manage data, you need to define equivalent Nim types. Suppose the C library uses a struct to represent a `Person`:

```c
// person.h
typedef struct {
  char name[100];
  int age;
} Person;
```

You would define a corresponding Nim type as follows:

```nim
person.nim
```

```
import ffi
```

```
type
 Person object
  name: array[100, cchar]
  age: cint
` ` `
```

This definition allows Nim to interact with C functions that operate on `Person` structures. If you have functions in C that manipulate these structures, you would declare them similarly:

```nim
` ` `nim
proc setName(p: var Person, name: cstring) {.importc: "setName", header: "person.h".}
proc getAge(p: Person): cint {.importc: "getAge", header: "person.h".}
` ` `
```

Here, `var` indicates that the `Person` object is passed by reference, allowing the function to modify its contents.

In addition to interfacing with C, Nim's ability to integrate with other languages such as C++ or Fortran requires handling additional complexities. For example, C++ functions and classes often involve name mangling, which can obscure function names. To call C++ functions from Nim, you may need to create a C wrapper around the C++ code, exposing the C++ functionality through a C-compatible interface. This wrapper code provides a bridge between Nim and the C++ code.

Another example of integration is with Python using Nim's `nimpy` library. This library enables Nim to interface with Python, allowing the invocation of Python functions and manipulation of Python objects. To use Python functions from Nim, you would first import the `nimpy` library and then use its APIs to interact with Python code:

```nim
import nimpy
```

Initialize Python interpreter
pyInit()

Import Python module
let math pyImport("math")

Call Python function
let result math.sqrt(16.0).toFloat
echo result
```

This code initializes the Python interpreter, imports the Python `math` module, and calls the `sqrt` function to compute the square root of a number.

When working with multiple languages, it's also important to manage memory and resource allocation carefully. Different languages have different memory management practices, and when passing data between Nim and another language, you must ensure that memory is allocated and deallocated appropriately to avoid leaks and ensure stability.

In summary, interfacing with C and other languages in Nim involves accurately mapping data types, managing memory, and correctly declaring external functions. By leveraging Nim's FFI and understanding the specific requirements of each language, you can effectively integrate with existing libraries and systems, enhancing the power and flexibility of your Nim applications.

When interfacing Nim with other languages beyond C, such as C++, Python, or Fortran, additional nuances come into play, requiring careful consideration of language-specific features and interoperability mechanisms. Understanding
```

these intricacies allows for seamless integration and effective utilization of existing libraries and codebases.

For C++ integration, it is crucial to recognize that C++ introduces complexities such as name mangling and class-based constructs. Name mangling in C++ means that function names are altered during compilation to include additional information about function signatures, leading to difficulties in direct linkage. To overcome this, you can create a C-compatible wrapper around your C++ code. This wrapper exposes a C-style interface that Nim can interact with, as C functions do not experience name mangling. Consider a C++ class with member functions:

```cpp
// example.cpp
class MyClass {
public:
  void doSomething() {
    // implementation
  }
};
```

To expose this class to Nim, you would write a C wrapper:

```cpp
// example_wrapper.cpp
extern "C" {
  MyClass createMyClass() { return new MyClass(); }
  void destroyMyClass(MyClass obj) { delete obj; }
  void doSomething(MyClass obj) { obj->doSomething(); }
}
```

In Nim, you would then declare these functions using `importc`:

```nim
example.nim
import ffi

type
  MyClass object

proc createMyClass(): ptr MyClass {.importc: "createMyClass",
header: "example_wrapper.h".}
proc destroyMyClass(obj: ptr MyClass) {.importc:
"destroyMyClass", header: "example_wrapper.h".}
proc doSomething(obj: ptr MyClass) {.importc: "doSomething",
header: "example_wrapper.h".}
```

This approach allows you to use the C++ class methods from Nim, while the C wrapper handles memory management and method invocation.

When interfacing with Python, Nim's `nimpy` library facilitates interaction with Python code. The library provides mechanisms for importing Python modules, calling Python functions, and managing Python objects. To call a Python function from Nim, you would first ensure that Python is properly initialized in your Nim program. Here's how you can interact with a Python function using `nimpy`:

```nim
import nimpy
```

Initialize the Python interpreter
pyInit()

Import a Python module
let math pyImport("math")

Call a Python function
let result math.sqrt(25.0).toFloat
echo result

```
` ` `
```

In this code, `pyInit` initializes the Python interpreter, `pyImport` imports the specified Python module, and `math.sqrt` calls the Python function `sqrt`. The result is converted to a Nim `float` for further use.

For Fortran integration, interfacing with Nim involves using Fortran's C interoperability features. Fortran provides the `ISO_C_BINDING` module, which allows Fortran code to be compatible with C. To interface with Fortran, you typically write a Fortran subroutine or function that is compatible with C, then call it from Nim using `importc`. Here is an example of a Fortran function and its Nim interface:

Fortran code:

```fortran
` ` `fortran
! example.f90
subroutine        addNumbers(a,        b,        result)        bind(c,
name"addNumbers")
 use iso_c_binding, only: c_int
 integer(c_int), value :: a, b
 integer(c_int), intent(out) :: result
 result  a + b
end subroutine addNumbers
` ` `
```

Nim interface:

```nim
` ` `nim
import ffi

proc  addNumbers(a:  cint,  b:  cint):  cint  {.importc:
"addNumbers", header: "example.h".}

let sum  addNumbers(5, 10)
echo sum
` ` `
```

In this example, the Fortran subroutine `addNumbers` is declared with `bind(c)` to make it callable from C, and Nim calls it using `importc`.

Handling data interchange between Nim and other languages involves not only calling functions but also ensuring that data is correctly converted between types used by different languages. This might include converting strings, arrays, or complex structures. Each language has its own conventions for data representation, and proper conversion is essential for correct behavior.

Memory management is another critical aspect when interfacing with other languages. Each language may have different approaches to memory allocation and deallocation, which necessitates careful coordination. For instance, if a C function allocates memory, Nim must ensure that it appropriately deallocates this memory to avoid leaks.

In conclusion, interfacing Nim with C and other languages involves a detailed understanding of type mapping, function linkage, and memory management. By leveraging Nim's Foreign Function Interface and understanding the specific requirements of each language, you can effectively integrate with existing libraries and systems, thereby enhancing the functionality and flexibility of your Nim applications. This seamless integration empowers developers to utilize a wide array of existing resources and write high-performance, cross-language applications.

CHAPTER 16:

When delving deeper into building and using Nim libraries, it's crucial to focus on the intricacies of library integration and maintenance. As previously discussed, designing, implementing, documenting, and packaging are fundamental steps. However, the real-world application of libraries often involves a range of additional considerations, from dependency management and versioning to integration testing and continuous integration.

To integrate your Nim library effectively into various projects, you must ensure it is both accessible and reliable. This means your library should be able to interact seamlessly with other codebases, whether they are written in Nim or interfaced with external languages. One key aspect of this is managing the library's compatibility with different versions of Nim or other libraries it depends on. It is essential to test your library with various versions of Nim and dependencies to ensure it works correctly across different environments. This process often involves creating a suite of unit tests and integration tests that validate the functionality of your library in diverse scenarios.

Furthermore, when working with external dependencies, it's vital to consider how changes in those dependencies might affect your library. Libraries often rely on third-party packages, and updates to these packages can introduce breaking changes. Thus, regular testing against the latest versions of dependencies and implementing version constraints in your `.nimble` file can help mitigate compatibility issues. The use of continuous integration (CI) tools can automate this testing process, running your library's tests in a controlled environment whenever changes are made. This ensures that any issues are identified and addressed promptly.

Another aspect to consider is how your library will be consumed by others. Providing clear usage examples and tutorials can significantly enhance the user experience. Demonstrating common use cases through sample code helps users understand how to integrate and utilize your library effectively. For instance, if your library provides data manipulation functions, you might include examples that show how to use these functions in different contexts, such as handling JSON data or processing user input. Detailed examples and practical applications make it easier for users to get started and integrate your library into their projects.

In addition to providing usage examples, it is essential to offer comprehensive support for users. This involves creating detailed documentation that explains the library's functionality, including parameter descriptions, return values, and potential error messages. A well-documented library not only aids users in understanding how to use it but also facilitates troubleshooting and debugging. Including a README file with your library that outlines installation instructions, basic usage, and contribution guidelines is also highly beneficial. This file serves as a central reference point for users and contributors alike.

When it comes to maintaining your library, keeping it up-to-date and responsive to user feedback is crucial. Regular updates to address bugs, add features, or improve performance ensure that your library remains relevant and useful. Listening to user feedback and incorporating it into future releases can also help enhance the library's functionality and usability. Engaging with the community through forums, issue trackers, and social media can provide valuable insights into how your library is being used and what improvements are needed.

Versioning is another critical aspect of library maintenance. Semantic versioning provides a standardized way to communicate changes and updates. By following semantic versioning principles, you can indicate whether changes are backward-compatible, introduce new features, or include breaking changes. For example, incrementing the major version number signals breaking changes that require users to update their code, while minor version updates introduce new features in a backward-compatible manner. Patch versions, on the other hand, are used for bug fixes that do not affect the library's API.

Effective versioning also involves managing the transition between different versions of your library. Providing migration guides or release notes that detail what has changed between versions can help users adapt their code to new releases. These notes should highlight any breaking changes, deprecated features, and new functionalities, offering guidance on how to adjust their code accordingly.

Additionally, when working with Nim libraries that interface with other languages, such as C or C++, it's important to handle cross-language interactions carefully. Ensuring that your library's interfaces are compatible with those of the external languages and managing data interchange properly is crucial. For example, when interfacing with C libraries, you must handle memory management and data types correctly to avoid issues such as memory leaks or data corruption. Using Nim's `import` statement to bring in C functions and handling data conversions between Nim and C types is essential for seamless integration.

In summary, building and using Nim libraries encompasses a wide range of activities beyond the initial creation and documentation. Effective integration involves thorough testing, careful management of dependencies and versioning, clear documentation, and responsive maintenance. By addressing these aspects, you can ensure that your library remains robust, user-friendly, and adaptable to evolving requirements.

Once the foundational aspects of library creation and usage have been established, delving into the intricacies of library distribution and version management is imperative. Effective library distribution involves several considerations, from ensuring compatibility across various environments to managing dependencies and handling updates efficiently.

To begin with, packaging your Nim library for distribution involves creating a `.nimble` file, which is essential for defining the library's metadata and dependencies. This file not only specifies the name, version, and description of the library but also outlines its dependencies on other packages. The `.nimble` file enables Nim's package manager to handle the installation and management of these dependencies. Therefore, it's crucial to meticulously list all external dependencies and their versions, ensuring that users can replicate your library's development environment accurately.

Moreover, you should consider the compatibility of your library across different operating systems and Nim versions. Testing your library in various environments can help identify and resolve compatibility issues. Nim's cross-compilation capabilities facilitate this process by allowing you to compile your library for different platforms. This ensures that users on diverse systems can integrate your library without encountering platform-specific issues.

Documentation plays a critical role in the usability and adoption of your library. Beyond the basic usage examples and API descriptions, detailed documentation should include explanations of the library's design decisions, usage patterns, and any limitations or caveats. For instance, if your library interacts with external systems or APIs, documenting these interactions and providing troubleshooting advice can greatly enhance user experience. A comprehensive README file, clear examples, and well-organized documentation contribute to the library's accessibility and ease of integration.

In addition to documentation, creating and maintaining a robust testing framework for your library is vital. Testing ensures that your library functions as intended and remains reliable through various updates. Implementing unit tests to validate individual components and integration tests to check the library's performance in larger systems helps identify issues early. Tools such as Nim's built-in `test` module facilitate writing and running tests. Integrating continuous integration (CI) systems can automate the testing process, running tests on each commit or pull request to detect issues promptly.

Managing dependencies and their versions is another crucial aspect of maintaining a Nim library. Libraries often rely on other packages, and keeping track of these dependencies can be challenging, especially when updates or changes occur. Employing semantic versioning, as previously discussed, provides a clear method for indicating changes and updates in your library. For dependencies, specifying version constraints in the `.nimble` file ensures that users install compatible versions, preventing conflicts that could arise from incompatible updates.

Handling breaking changes and updates requires careful planning. When introducing changes that affect the library's API or behavior, it's important to communicate these changes effectively to users. Providing migration guides or release notes can help users transition to new versions smoothly. These guides should outline what has changed, why the changes were made, and how to adapt existing code to accommodate the new version. By offering detailed explanations and examples, you facilitate a smoother update process for users.

The process of distributing and integrating your library with other systems or languages involves addressing cross-language interoperability. For libraries that interface with languages like C, it is essential to ensure that the interlanguage calls are correctly handled. This involves managing data conversions, memory allocation, and error handling. For instance, when interfacing with C functions, you need to ensure that data types are correctly mapped between Nim and C and that memory allocated in one language is appropriately managed and freed. Additionally, handling errors and exceptions in a way that is compatible with both Nim and the external language prevents potential crashes and data corruption.

Incorporating external tools and frameworks into your library can also enhance its functionality. For example, integrating with build systems or package managers can streamline the build and installation process. Tools like `Nimble` and `Nim's package manager` can assist in managing dependencies and automating tasks related to library distribution and integration. Leveraging these tools can simplify the process of ensuring that your library is correctly built, tested, and deployed across various environments.

Lastly, engaging with the Nim community and gathering feedback can provide valuable insights into the practical use of your library. Community interactions through forums, issue trackers, and social media can reveal common issues, feature requests, and areas for improvement. Actively participating in these discussions and addressing user feedback can help refine your library and ensure that it meets the needs of its users.

In conclusion, the process of building and using Nim libraries extends beyond initial development to include comprehensive documentation, effective distribution, and ongoing maintenance. By focusing on these aspects, you ensure that your library remains robust, user-friendly, and adaptable to various environments and requirements. Engaging with the community, managing dependencies carefully, and leveraging external tools and frameworks contribute to creating a high-quality library that is both valuable and reliable for its users.

CHAPTER 17:

Nim's type system is both versatile and robust, offering a wide range of advanced features to enhance type safety and flexibility in programming. Having explored the fundamentals of type inference and generics, it's important to delve deeper into how these features can be applied in more sophisticated ways, including the use of type operators and advanced type manipulations. These aspects of Nim's type system are pivotal for writing code that is not only flexible and reusable but also precise and reliable.

Expanding on type inference, Nim's ability to automatically deduce types helps streamline coding by reducing redundancy. However, type inference becomes more powerful when combined with explicit type constraints and annotations. While Nim's compiler is adept at inferring types in most scenarios, there are instances where you might want to guide the compiler or enforce specific type behaviors explicitly. This can be achieved by using type annotations to clarify the expected types in ambiguous situations or when dealing with complex expressions.

For example, when working with function overloads or complex type transformations, specifying types explicitly can aid the compiler in resolving ambiguities and ensuring correctness. Consider a scenario where you have a function that performs operations on different numeric types. Explicitly annotating the types involved in these operations helps the compiler understand the intended behavior, particularly when type inference might not suffice. This approach provides additional safety and clarity, ensuring that the operations are performed correctly for each specific type.

Generics, a key feature in Nim, allow for the creation of flexible and reusable code that can handle various types without sacrificing type safety. Beyond basic usage, generics can be employed in more advanced scenarios such as type-safe containers and algorithms. For instance, when implementing a generic data structure like a binary tree, you can define type parameters that specify the type of elements stored in the tree. This allows you to create a single implementation that works with different types, ensuring type safety and code reusability.

Another powerful application of generics is in the creation of type-safe algorithms. By defining algorithms as generic functions or procedures, you can ensure that they operate correctly for any type that meets the specified constraints. For example, you might create a generic sorting function that works with any type that supports comparison operations. This not only reduces code duplication but also enhances the robustness of your code by enforcing type constraints at compile time.

Type operators further extend the capabilities of Nim's type system by enabling advanced type manipulations and transformations. These operators allow you to define custom operations for types, such as combining or transforming them based on specific rules. For instance, you can create a type operator that computes the union of two types, resulting in a new type that encompasses the properties of both. This feature is particularly useful for defining complex type relationships and constraints in a concise and expressive manner.

One practical example of type operators in action is defining custom type-level operations for arithmetic or logical operations. By implementing type operators, you can create types that represent mathematical structures or logical conditions, enhancing the expressiveness and flexibility of your type system. For example, you might define a type operator that represents vectors and supports operations like addition and scaling. This allows you to work with vectors in a type-safe manner while leveraging the benefits of type-level computations.

In addition to type operators, Nim supports type constraints and refinements, which provide more granular control over type safety and correctness. Type constraints enable you to specify conditions that types must satisfy, ensuring that only types meeting these conditions are accepted by functions or data structures. For instance, you can define a type constraint that requires a type to implement a specific interface or support certain operations. This ensures that your code interacts correctly with the types it operates on, reducing the risk of type-related errors.

Type refinements, on the other hand, allow for more precise type checking based on runtime conditions or specific properties. By refining types based on certain criteria, you can narrow down the type of a value, enabling more accurate type operations and validations. For example, you might use type refinements to differentiate between different states of an object, ensuring that your code handles each state appropriately.

Combining these advanced type features allows you to leverage the full power of Nim's type system, creating code that is both flexible and type-safe. By understanding and applying type inference, generics, type operators, and type constraints, you can write code that adapts to a wide range of scenarios while maintaining rigorous type safety. This approach not only improves the robustness and maintainability of your code but also enhances its readability and expressiveness.

In summary, Nim's type system offers a rich set of features that empower developers to create highly flexible and type-safe code. By effectively using type inference, generics, type operators, and advanced type constraints, you can harness the full potential of Nim's type system to handle diverse programming challenges with precision and confidence. These advanced type features contribute to Nim's strength as a language, enabling developers to write code that is both robust and adaptable.

In advancing our exploration of Nim's type system, the focus shifts towards utilizing advanced techniques to harness the language's full potential. This involves diving deeper into the intricacies of type inference, generics, and type operators, and understanding their interplay to create sophisticated, type-safe applications.

Type inference in Nim is a cornerstone of its type system, enabling developers to write cleaner and more concise code. While the compiler's ability to deduce types automatically simplifies code writing, its effectiveness is augmented when combined with explicit type annotations. Explicit annotations become crucial in complex scenarios, such as when dealing with higher-order functions or intricate type interactions. For instance, when designing a function that operates on a variety of input types, specifying the types explicitly can guide the compiler, reducing ambiguity and ensuring correctness. This practice also serves as a form of documentation, clarifying the expected input and output types, which can be invaluable during maintenance or code review.

In scenarios where type inference alone might not suffice, leveraging type annotations and constraints can enhance type safety. This is particularly relevant in generic programming, where the generalization of functions and data structures can introduce type ambiguities. By specifying type constraints, you can restrict the types that are permissible, ensuring that only those meeting certain criteria are used. For example, a generic function designed to sort elements might include constraints to ensure that the elements are comparable. This constraint prevents runtime errors by enforcing type safety at compile time, making the code more robust and reliable.

Generics extend Nim's type system by enabling the creation of reusable components that work with various types. While basic generics involve parameterizing types, advanced usage includes defining constraints and creating complex generic structures. A practical example of advanced generics is the design of a generic data structure like a priority queue, where the elements are ordered based on a custom comparator. By parameterizing both the element type and the comparator type, you can create a highly flexible and reusable data structure that adheres to specific ordering rules.

Beyond simple parameterization, advanced generics in Nim also support the creation of type-safe collections and algorithms. For instance, consider implementing a generic stack that supports type constraints to ensure that only types implementing a specific interface can be pushed onto the stack. This ensures that the stack operations are type-safe and that the stack maintains its integrity regardless of the type of elements it holds.

Type operators in Nim provide a mechanism for defining custom operations on types, allowing for sophisticated type manipulations and transformations. This feature is particularly useful for creating domain-specific languages or implementing custom type-level computations. For example, type operators can be employed to define operations like type-level arithmetic or logical operations, enabling more expressive and flexible type definitions.

One application of type operators is in defining custom type combinators that enhance the expressiveness of type definitions. For instance, you can create a type operator that computes the intersection of two types, resulting in a new type that includes only the common properties of both. This can be useful in scenarios where you need to derive types based on specific criteria or combine types in novel ways.

Another powerful use of type operators is in implementing type-level constraints and validations. By defining type operators that enforce certain conditions, you can create types that adhere to specific rules, ensuring that your code operates within well-defined constraints. For example, you might define a type operator that ensures that a type meets certain invariants, such as non-negativity or boundedness. This approach can be particularly useful in numerical computations or other scenarios where adherence to specific constraints is critical.

In addition to type operators, Nim supports advanced type manipulations through type refinements and dependent types. Type refinements allow you to refine types based on runtime conditions or specific properties, enabling more precise type checking and validation. For instance, you can use type refinements to differentiate between different states of an object, ensuring that your code handles each state appropriately and safely.

Dependent types, although not as extensively supported as some other type features, offer a powerful way to express complex relationships between types and values. By using dependent types, you can encode additional constraints and properties within your types, making it possible to capture and enforce intricate relationships directly in the type system. This can be particularly useful in scenarios where traditional type systems fall short, such as in formal verification or advanced mathematical computations.

In conclusion, leveraging Nim's type system effectively

requires a deep understanding of its advanced features and their interplay. By mastering type inference, generics, type operators, and type constraints, you can create highly flexible, type-safe code that handles a variety of scenarios with precision. These advanced techniques enhance the expressiveness and robustness of your code, enabling you to build sophisticated applications that adhere to stringent type requirements. The ability to manipulate and extend types in Nim not only enhances code reliability but also fosters innovative solutions to complex programming challenges.

CHAPTER 18:

Building on the principles of algorithmic efficiency, it's imperative to explore how to optimize algorithms beyond the basic design. Delving deeper into techniques for enhancing performance, we confront the challenges of balancing time complexity with space efficiency, particularly in the context of algorithmic design.

In practice, the efficiency of an algorithm is not solely determined by its theoretical time complexity but also by its implementation details and the specific use case. This realization underscores the importance of not only selecting the right algorithm but also adapting and refining it to fit the constraints and requirements of the system. For instance, while quicksort generally performs well on average, in-memory optimizations, such as choosing an appropriate pivot or switching to a different sorting algorithm for small partitions, can further enhance its performance.

The practical aspects of sorting algorithms involve considerations of cache performance and memory locality. Modern processors are optimized for sequential memory access, so algorithms that exhibit good spatial locality can perform significantly better. Quicksort's in-place partitioning leverages this locality effectively. Conversely, algorithms like mergesort, which require additional space for merging, may be less efficient in scenarios where memory bandwidth is a limiting factor.

When we turn to searching algorithms, the distinction between theoretical and practical performance becomes more pronounced. While binary search offers logarithmic time complexity, its efficiency is contingent upon the data being sorted. In real-world applications, maintaining sorted data structures, such as balanced binary search trees or heaps, can be beneficial. These data structures support efficient updates and queries, albeit with trade-offs in complexity and overhead.

Hashing techniques, which underpin hash tables, represent another area where practical implementation can vastly influence performance. An effective hash function minimizes collisions and ensures that the hash table's performance approaches constant time complexity. Implementing dynamic resizing strategies, such as expanding the hash table when the load factor exceeds a threshold, can prevent performance degradation due to high collision rates. Furthermore, choosing appropriate collision resolution strategies, such as open addressing or separate chaining, based on the expected load and usage patterns, can significantly impact overall performance.

Graph algorithms are another domain where implementation details play a critical role. Algorithms for finding shortest paths, such as Dijkstra's and A search, are well-known for their theoretical efficiency, but their real-world performance can vary based on factors like graph density and data structure choices. For instance, using a priority queue implemented with a binary heap in Dijkstra's algorithm optimizes the time complexity of extracting the minimum element. However, in cases where the graph is sparse, alternative data structures, such as Fibonacci heaps, can further reduce the algorithm's complexity.

In graph-based problems, the choice of representation— adjacency matrix versus adjacency list—can also influence algorithmic efficiency. Adjacency lists are often preferred for sparse graphs due to their space efficiency, whereas adjacency matrices offer faster edge lookup times but require more memory. The trade-offs between these representations must be carefully evaluated based on the specific characteristics of the graph and the operations to be performed.

Memory efficiency is not confined to data structures and representations; it also encompasses algorithmic techniques for reducing unnecessary space usage. For example, in dynamic programming algorithms, employing techniques like memoization to store intermediate results can significantly reduce redundant computations and enhance performance. However, this must be balanced with the memory overhead of storing these results. In scenarios where memory constraints are tight, iterative solutions or algorithms with lower space complexity may be preferable.

Analyzing and optimizing algorithmic performance necessitates a comprehensive approach that combines theoretical insights with practical considerations. Profiling tools and techniques are essential for identifying performance bottlenecks and understanding the actual behavior of algorithms in practice. Performance profiling can reveal inefficiencies such as excessive memory access or redundant computations that are not evident from theoretical analysis alone.

For optimization, iterative refinement is key. By profiling the algorithm in real-world scenarios, developers can pinpoint specific areas for improvement, such as optimizing critical code paths or reducing memory overhead. Additionally, leveraging empirical testing, such as benchmarking against representative datasets, provides valuable feedback for fine-tuning performance.

Ultimately, the goal of writing efficient algorithms is to design solutions that not only meet theoretical expectations but also excel in practical applications. This involves a continuous process of evaluating and refining algorithms, considering both their theoretical properties and practical implications. By embracing a holistic approach that integrates algorithmic theory with practical implementation strategies, one can achieve superior performance and efficiency in complex systems.

In the exploration of efficient algorithms, attention must be given to various specialized techniques and strategies that can further enhance performance in specific scenarios. Beyond the basic implementations of algorithms, optimization often involves tailoring solutions to the nuances of the problem domain, including considerations of hardware characteristics and application-specific requirements.

For instance, when dealing with large datasets, external sorting algorithms become relevant. These algorithms are designed to handle data that does not fit into main memory and instead rely on external storage. Merge sort, particularly in its external sorting variant, is a common choice. This approach involves dividing the data into manageable chunks, sorting each chunk in memory, and then merging the sorted chunks. This technique effectively minimizes disk I/O operations, which are often a bottleneck in such scenarios. Implementations of external merge sort must be optimized to balance the number of chunks and the size of each, considering factors such as the available memory and the speed of the storage medium.

When addressing searching algorithms, one must also consider the trade-offs between preprocessing time and query time. In many cases, data structures such as suffix trees or tries are used to accelerate search operations, especially in text processing and pattern matching tasks. Suffix trees, for instance, are particularly effective for string matching problems because they allow for efficient substring searches. However, building and storing suffix trees require significant memory, and thus, a trade-off must be evaluated between preprocessing time and the efficiency gained during query operations.

Advanced data structures, like balanced trees and hash tables, provide another layer of optimization. Balanced trees, such as AVL trees and Red-Black trees, maintain sorted data and allow for efficient insertions, deletions, and lookups. These structures ensure that operations remain logarithmic in complexity, even as the dataset grows. Hash tables, on the other hand, provide average-case constant time complexity for insertion, deletion, and search operations. The performance of hash tables is highly dependent on the quality of the hash function and the handling of collisions. Techniques such as double hashing or cuckoo hashing can be employed to improve performance in scenarios where high collision rates are anticipated.

In the context of dynamic programming, optimization techniques such as space reduction are particularly valuable. Many dynamic programming algorithms can be optimized to use less memory by leveraging iterative approaches instead of recursive ones. For instance, in the classic problem of computing the nth Fibonacci number, the space complexity can be reduced from $O(n)$ to $O(1)$ by storing only the last two computed values instead of the entire sequence. This approach illustrates how algorithmic techniques can be tailored to reduce both time and space complexity, resulting in more efficient solutions.

Optimization of algorithms also extends to parallel and distributed computing. In scenarios where problems are too large or too complex for a single processor, parallel algorithms can be employed. These algorithms divide the problem into smaller subproblems that can be processed simultaneously, significantly reducing overall computation time. Techniques such as divide-and-conquer, where the problem is recursively divided into smaller instances, are particularly well-suited for parallel processing. Implementations must consider factors such as synchronization and data sharing to avoid overhead that could negate the benefits of parallelism.

Distributed algorithms address scenarios where computing resources are spread across multiple machines. These algorithms must manage issues related to communication overhead, data consistency, and fault tolerance. For example, in distributed sorting, techniques like parallel merge sort can be used to efficiently sort large datasets by distributing the sorting work across multiple nodes. The challenge lies in coordinating the nodes and managing the data flow to ensure correctness and efficiency.

The optimization process often involves empirical testing and benchmarking. Profiling tools and performance analyzers are essential for identifying bottlenecks and understanding the real-world behavior of algorithms. By running tests with representative datasets and measuring key performance metrics, one can gain insights into how an algorithm performs in practice. This empirical data is invaluable for guiding further refinements and ensuring that theoretical improvements translate into practical benefits.

Ultimately, the pursuit of efficient algorithms is a dynamic and iterative process that combines theoretical knowledge with practical experimentation. It requires a deep understanding of both algorithmic principles and the specific requirements of the application. By employing advanced techniques, optimizing implementations, and continuously evaluating performance, one can develop solutions that are not only theoretically sound but also highly effective in real-world scenarios. The integration of these principles ensures that algorithms can handle complex problems efficiently, making a significant impact on system performance and resource utilization.

CHAPTER 19:

To build command-line tools effectively, it is important to consider both the architecture of the application and its interaction with the user. In addition to parsing arguments, handling user input, and formatting output, there are several other factors that contribute to the success of a command-line tool.

When designing a command-line tool, it is vital to handle configurations and settings. For many tools, users need to specify various parameters, and incorporating configuration files can greatly enhance flexibility. Nim supports file operations through its standard library, allowing you to read from and write to configuration files seamlessly. By using the `os` module's file handling functions, such as `open`, `readFile`, and `writeFile`, you can implement functionality that loads settings from a file or saves user preferences. This approach not only simplifies user interaction but also ensures that default settings can be overridden, providing a tailored experience.

Another critical aspect of command-line tools is error handling and logging. Robust error handling ensures that your tool can gracefully manage unexpected conditions and provide meaningful feedback to the user. In Nim, you can utilize exception handling with `try` and `except` blocks to capture and respond to errors. This mechanism allows you to deal with issues such as file not found, permission denied, or invalid input formats. Incorporating logging is also beneficial for debugging and monitoring purposes. The `logging` module in Nim can be employed to record detailed information about the tool's execution, which can help identify and resolve issues that may arise during operation.

Furthermore, testing command-line tools involves more than just validating functional correctness; it requires ensuring that the tool performs well under various conditions. Automated tests can be designed to simulate different command-line inputs and validate the outputs, ensuring that the tool behaves as expected. Nim's testing framework, which includes the `unittest` module, supports writing and running tests to verify the correctness of your code. By creating a suite of tests that cover a range of scenarios, including edge cases and error conditions, you can improve the reliability of your tool and catch potential bugs early in the development process.

In addition to functionality and performance, command-line tools should be designed with usability in mind. Clear and concise error messages, helpful usage instructions, and consistent behavior all contribute to a positive user experience. The tool's help message, typically accessible via a `--help` or `-h` flag, should provide users with a comprehensive overview of its features and usage. This includes a description of available commands, options, and their respective arguments. Ensuring that error messages are informative and guide users towards corrective actions is crucial for usability. For example, if a user provides an invalid file path, the error message should specify that the file could not be found and suggest checking the path or file name.

Consider also the design of your command-line tool's output. Effective output formatting can make the difference between a tool that is easily usable and one that is frustrating. For instance, when displaying lists of items or results, using table formats or aligning columns can make the information more readable. Nim provides various functions for formatting output, such as those found in the `strutils` module. Using these functions to create neatly formatted tables or reports can enhance the clarity of your tool's output and improve the overall user experience.

Moreover, when building command-line tools, you should also be aware of platform-specific considerations. Different operating systems may have variations in command-line behavior or support. For example, path separators differ between Unix-like systems and Windows, and command-line arguments may be handled differently. Nim's cross-platform capabilities help mitigate these issues, but it is important to test your tool on multiple platforms to ensure consistent behavior. Nim's standard library and community packages offer cross-platform solutions that can help manage these differences, providing a smoother experience across various environments.

Finally, consider the extensibility of your tool. As your tool evolves, you might need to add new features or integrate it with other systems. Designing your tool with extensibility in mind allows for easier updates and modifications. This might involve structuring your code to support plugins, modular components, or configuration-driven behavior. Nim's flexible language constructs and modular approach can facilitate such extensions, allowing you to build a tool that can grow and adapt to new requirements over time.

In conclusion, creating a well-designed command-line tool involves a careful consideration of functionality, user interaction, and robustness. By focusing on effective argument parsing, handling user input securely, formatting output clearly, and incorporating best practices for error handling and testing, you can develop command-line tools that are both powerful and user-friendly. Leveraging Nim's features and adhering to these principles will help you create tools that not only perform efficiently but also provide a positive experience for users.

Developing command-line tools with Nim offers a rich set of features for creating efficient and robust applications. However, to build a truly effective CLI tool, one must consider several additional aspects beyond just parsing arguments and formatting outputs. The focus should be on crafting an intuitive user experience, managing dependencies, and ensuring the tool can be integrated seamlessly into various workflows.

When it comes to user interaction, one of the most critical aspects is providing meaningful feedback and guidance. A well-designed command-line interface should not only execute tasks but also communicate effectively with users. This includes implementing clear and concise error messages that help users understand what went wrong and how to fix it. For instance, if a user provides an invalid option or missing argument, your tool should offer a detailed message explaining the issue and how to resolve it. This approach improves usability and helps prevent user frustration.

Another crucial element of CLI tool design is incorporating logging and diagnostic capabilities. Logging allows you to track the behavior of your tool, providing insights into its performance and aiding in troubleshooting. Nim's standard library includes the `logging` module, which you can use to record various levels of information, from debug messages to critical errors. Configuring logging appropriately can help you monitor the tool's operation, diagnose problems, and make improvements based on real-world usage.

Dependency management is another important consideration when developing command-line tools. Tools often rely on external libraries or modules, and managing these dependencies effectively is essential for maintaining compatibility and functionality. Nim provides a package management system known as Nimble, which simplifies the process of handling dependencies. By defining dependencies in a Nimble package file (`.nimble`), you can ensure that all required libraries are installed and maintained consistently. Additionally, using Nimble for version control allows you to specify which versions of dependencies your tool supports, reducing the risk of conflicts and ensuring a stable development environment.

Furthermore, command-line tools should be designed with extensibility in mind. As requirements evolve, you may need to add new features or adjust existing ones. Designing your tool to support plugins or modular components can facilitate this process. For example, you might structure your tool to allow for dynamically loaded plugins that extend its functionality. Nim's flexible module system and dynamic linking capabilities support such designs, making it possible to enhance your tool without extensive modifications to the core codebase.

Testing is a critical aspect of developing command-line tools. Automated tests help verify that your tool performs as expected across various scenarios and environments. In Nim, the `unittest` module provides a framework for writing and executing tests. By creating a comprehensive test suite that covers different command-line inputs and edge cases, you can ensure that your tool handles various conditions robustly. Testing should include not only functional correctness but also performance considerations. For instance, you might test how your tool performs with large inputs or under heavy load to ensure it meets performance expectations.

Additionally, considering cross-platform compatibility is essential when developing command-line tools that will be used in diverse environments. Nim's cross-compilation capabilities allow you to build tools for different operating systems from a single codebase. However, it is important to test your tool on all target platforms to ensure consistent behavior. Platform-specific issues, such as differences in file system paths or command-line argument handling, should be addressed to ensure that the tool functions correctly across various systems.

User experience can also be enhanced through thoughtful design of command-line options and arguments. Providing sensible defaults, allowing for flexible argument formats, and supporting commonly used conventions can make your tool more intuitive and easier to use. For instance, consider implementing argument parsing libraries like `docopt` or `clap` if they align with your tool's requirements. These libraries offer advanced features for managing command-line arguments and generating help messages, which can further improve the usability of your tool.

Finally, documenting your command-line tool thoroughly is essential for helping users understand how to use it effectively. Documentation should include detailed instructions on installation, usage, and examples of common tasks. Providing clear and comprehensive documentation not only supports users in getting the most out of your tool but also contributes to its overall success and adoption. Consider creating a dedicated section in your documentation for troubleshooting common issues and providing additional resources for users who need further assistance.

In summary, developing command-line tools with Nim involves careful consideration of user interaction, logging, dependency management, extensibility, testing, cross-platform compatibility, and documentation. By focusing on these aspects, you can create tools that are not only functional and efficient but also user-friendly and adaptable. Leveraging Nim's features and best practices will help you build command-line applications that meet the needs of your users and perform reliably in various environments.

CHAPTER 20:

The development of graphical user interfaces (GUIs) in Nim extends its capabilities well beyond traditional systems programming. Delving deeper into GUI creation involves understanding how to leverage different libraries and frameworks that facilitate the design and implementation of user-friendly and interactive applications. This discussion will continue by examining how to integrate these libraries into more complex applications, focusing on layout management, event handling, and practical examples that demonstrate these concepts in action.

Layout management is a crucial aspect of GUI development, as it determines how widgets are arranged within a window. Effective layout management ensures that the interface is both visually appealing and functional, adapting to different screen sizes and resolutions. Nim provides several methods for managing layouts depending on the library used. For example, in `NimQt`, layout managers such as `QVBoxLayout` and `QHBoxLayout` are employed to organize widgets vertically or horizontally. These managers automatically adjust the size and position of child widgets, making it easier to create responsive designs.

Consider an example where you want to create a form with labeled input fields and buttons. Using `QVBoxLayout`, you can stack widgets vertically, aligning labels and corresponding text fields. The following code snippet illustrates how to set up a vertical layout in `NimQt`:

```nim
```

```nim
import nimqt/[QApplication, QMainWindow, QVBoxLayout,
QLabel, QLineEdit, QPushButton]

proc main()
 let app  QApplication()
 let window  QMainWindow()
 window.setWindowTitle("Simple Form")
 window.setGeometry(100, 100, 300, 200)

 let centralWidget  QWidget()
 let layout  QVBoxLayout()

 let nameLabel  QLabel("Name:")
 let nameInput  QLineEdit()
 layout.addWidget(nameLabel)
 layout.addWidget(nameInput)

 let submitButton  QPushButton("Submit")
 layout.addWidget(submitButton)

 centralWidget.setLayout(layout)
 window.setCentralWidget(centralWidget)

 window.show()
 app.exec()
```

In this example, the `QVBoxLayout` is used to place a label, a text field, and a button in a vertical stack. The layout manager automatically handles the positioning and spacing, which simplifies the process of creating a clean and organized interface.

Event handling is another critical component of GUI

development, as it allows the application to respond to user interactions such as button clicks, text input, and window resizing. Each library has its own mechanisms for managing events. In `NimQt`, signals and slots are used to connect user actions to specific functions. When a user clicks a button, a signal is emitted, which can be connected to a slot—a function that performs an action in response.

Expanding on the previous example, let's add functionality to the submit button to display a message box when clicked. This involves connecting the button's `clicked` signal to a custom slot function that shows a dialog box:

```nim
import nimqt/[QApplication, QMainWindow, QVBoxLayout, QLabel, QLineEdit, QPushButton, QMessageBox]

proc showMessage()
 let msgBox QMessageBox()
 msgBox.setText("Form submitted!")
 msgBox.exec()

proc main()
 let app QApplication()
 let window QMainWindow()
 window.setWindowTitle("Simple Form")
 window.setGeometry(100, 100, 300, 200)


 let centralWidget QWidget()
 let layout QVBoxLayout()


 let nameLabel QLabel("Name:")
 let nameInput QLineEdit()
 layout.addWidget(nameLabel)
 layout.addWidget(nameInput)
```

```
let submitButton QPushButton("Submit")
submitButton.clicked.connect(showMessage)
layout.addWidget(submitButton)

centralWidget.setLayout(layout)
window.setCentralWidget(centralWidget)

window.show()
app.exec()
` ` `
```

Here, the `showMessage` procedure is defined to create and display a message box. The `submitButton.clicked.connect(showMessage)` line establishes the connection between the button click event and the `showMessage` slot.

Handling more complex interactions may involve dealing with user input validation, dynamic updates to the interface, and managing application state. For example, if you need to validate user input before submitting a form, you can extend the slot function to check the input values and provide feedback to the user. This can involve displaying error messages or updating the interface based on the input provided.

Nim's support for GUI development also extends to other libraries beyond `NimQt`. When using `NimGtk`, for instance, you will interact with GTK widgets and layout managers, which have their own conventions and methods. `NimGtk` provides a similar approach to layout management and event handling, though the specific classes and methods will differ from those in `NimQt`.

In summary, creating GUIs with Nim involves selecting the appropriate library for your needs, understanding layout management, and handling user events. By leveraging libraries such as `NimQt`, `NimGtk`, or `Nimui`, developers can build a wide range of applications, from simple forms to more complex interfaces, while maintaining the efficiency and performance that Nim is known for. Through practical examples and detailed explanations, you can develop a solid foundation in GUI programming with Nim, enabling the creation of functional and user-friendly applications.

In the realm of GUI development with Nim, the choice of library significantly impacts the approach and features available for creating graphical applications. As I delve deeper into practical aspects, it's essential to explore how these libraries handle more complex features, such as custom widgets, advanced user interactions, and application aesthetics. Each library provides distinct tools and methodologies for addressing these needs, and understanding their capabilities can greatly enhance the functionality and appeal of your applications.

One of the fundamental aspects of creating sophisticated GUIs is the ability to design and use custom widgets. Custom widgets are essential when standard controls do not meet specific needs or when you want to introduce unique visual elements into your application. For example, in `NimQt`, custom widgets can be developed by subclassing existing widget classes and overriding their methods to provide new functionality or appearance.

Let us consider a scenario where you need a custom slider that displays its value dynamically. This can be achieved by creating a subclass of `QSlider` and implementing a method to update the slider's appearance based on its value. Here is an illustrative example:

```nim
import nimqt/[QApplication, QMainWindow, QSlider, QLabel,
QVBoxLayout, QWidget]
```

```nim
type
  CustomSlider  object of QSlider
    valueLabel: QLabel

proc initSlider(slider: var CustomSlider)
  slider.init()
  slider.setOrientation(Qt.Horizontal)
  slider.setRange(0, 100)
  slider.valueLabel  QLabel("Value: 0")
  slider.valueChanged.connect(slider.updateValue)

proc updateValue(slider: var CustomSlider)
  slider.valueLabel.setText(fmt("Value: %d", slider.value()))

proc main()
  let app  QApplication()
  let window  QMainWindow()
  window.setWindowTitle("Custom Slider Example")
  window.setGeometry(100, 100, 400, 200)


  let centralWidget  QWidget()
  let layout  QVBoxLayout()


  var mySlider: CustomSlider
  initSlider(mySlider)
  layout.addWidget(mySlider)
  layout.addWidget(mySlider.valueLabel)


  centralWidget.setLayout(layout)
  window.setCentralWidget(centralWidget)


  window.show()
  app.exec()
```

In this example, `CustomSlider` is a new widget type derived from `QSlider`. It includes an additional `QLabel` to display the current value of the slider. The `initSlider` procedure sets up the slider, and the `updateValue` procedure updates the label whenever the slider's value changes. This custom widget now provides enhanced functionality that was not available in the standard `QSlider`.

Advanced user interactions, such as drag-and-drop functionality or complex gesture handling, also play a significant role in modern GUI applications. Libraries like `NimQt` and `NimGtk` offer mechanisms to manage these interactions. For instance, in `NimQt`, you can enable drag-and-drop support by overriding the relevant methods in your widgets to handle drag events. Here is an example of how to implement a basic drag-and-drop feature in a `QWidget`:

```nim
import nimqt/[QApplication, QMainWindow, QLabel, QVBoxLayout, QWidget, QDragEnterEvent, QDropEvent, QMimeData]

type
  DraggableLabel object of QLabel
    proc dragEnterEvent(event: QDragEnterEvent)
    if event.mimeData().hasText():
      event.acceptProposedAction()


    proc dropEvent(event: QDropEvent)
    let droppedText event.mimeData().text()
    self.setText(droppedText)

proc main()
  let app QApplication()
  let window QMainWindow()
  window.setWindowTitle("Drag and Drop Example")
```

```
window.setGeometry(100, 100, 400, 200)

let centralWidget  QWidget()
let layout  QVBoxLayout()

let sourceLabel  QLabel("Drag this text to the other label")

sourceLabel.setTextInteractionFlags(Qt.TextSelectableByMou
se)

var targetLabel: DraggableLabel
targetLabel.setText("Drop here")
targetLabel.setAcceptDrops(true)

layout.addWidget(sourceLabel)
layout.addWidget(targetLabel)

centralWidget.setLayout(layout)
window.setCentralWidget(centralWidget)

window.show()
app.exec()
```
` ` `

In this code, `DraggableLabel` is a custom widget that overrides `dragEnterEvent` and `dropEvent` to handle drag-and-drop operations. The widget accepts text dropped onto it and updates its content accordingly. This example illustrates how to extend standard widget behavior to support more interactive features.

Aesthetic considerations, including themes and styles, are also crucial in creating appealing GUI applications. Most GUI libraries provide support for styling widgets through CSS-like syntax or built-in theme capabilities. For example, `NimQt` allows for extensive customization of widget appearance using stylesheets, which can define colors, borders, and font styles. Customizing the look and feel of your application enhances user experience and ensures that the application aligns with its intended visual design.

When working with `NimQt`, you can apply stylesheets to widgets as follows:

```nim
import nimqt/[QApplication, QMainWindow, QPushButton,
QWidget, QVBoxLayout]

proc main()
 let app QApplication()
 let window QMainWindow()
 window.setWindowTitle("Styled Button Example")
 window.setGeometry(100, 100, 300, 150)

 let centralWidget QWidget()
 let layout QVBoxLayout()

 let styledButton QPushButton("Styled Button")
     styledButton.setStyleSheet("background-color:    4CAF50;
color: white; font-size: 16px; padding: 10px; border-radius:
5px;")

 layout.addWidget(styledButton)

 centralWidget.setLayout(layout)
 window.setCentralWidget(centralWidget)
```

```
window.show()
app.exec()
```

In this example, a stylesheet is applied to a `QPushButton` to alter its background color, text color, font size, padding, and border radius. This approach allows for significant flexibility in designing the visual appearance of your application.

In conclusion, building GUIs with Nim involves a thorough understanding of the libraries available, as well as the ability to implement custom widgets, handle advanced user interactions, and apply aesthetic customizations. By leveraging Nim's robust support for GUI development, you can create sophisticated and user-friendly applications that extend beyond the boundaries of traditional systems programming.

CHAPTER 21:

Expanding on the techniques of advanced error handling and recovery, I delve deeper into the mechanics and strategies that ensure robust and reliable application behavior under various failure conditions. Error handling is not just about catching exceptions but also involves designing systems that can recover from failures gracefully and maintain operational integrity.

One crucial aspect of error management is the concept of error contexts, which refers to the information and state that should accompany an error to aid in diagnostics and recovery. This involves not only capturing the error itself but also collecting contextual data such as the state of variables, execution paths, and any external conditions that may have contributed to the error. Nim's ability to handle custom exception types facilitates this by allowing developers to create exceptions that carry rich, contextual information. For instance, a network operation might fail due to a timeout, and the custom exception could include details about the attempted URL, the timeout duration, and any partial results that were retrieved before the failure.

Consider the following example of enhancing the `FileError` exception to include additional contextual data:

```nim
type
  FileError object of Exception
    fileName: string
    errorCode: int
```

```
  operation: string
  details: string

proc initFileError(fileName: string, errorCode: int, operation:
string, details: string): FileError
  result.fileName fileName
  result.errorCode errorCode
  result.operation operation
  result.details details

proc getDetailedErrorMessage(e: FileError): string
  return "Error during operation '" & e.operation & "' on file '" &
e.fileName &
    "': " & e.details
` ` `
```

In this extended example, the `FileError` type now includes
`operation` and `details` fields that provide additional
context about the error. This allows for more informative
logging and debugging, as the details can be used to
understand precisely what went wrong during a specific
operation.

Effective error recovery involves not just catching and logging
errors but also implementing mechanisms to handle or
mitigate the impact of these errors. For instance, in a multi-
tiered application, you might have a strategy where lower-level
components attempt to recover from errors autonomously
while higher-level components are responsible for overall
error handling and user notification. This layered approach
allows for more granular control over error handling and
recovery, ensuring that lower-level errors do not necessarily
lead to application-wide failures.

In scenarios where errors may require corrective actions
or retries, it's essential to consider the impact on system
performance and user experience. Implementing exponential
backoff strategies for retries can be more efficient than

fixed delays, particularly in network communication scenarios where transient issues might resolve over time. Here's an example of how to implement an exponential backoff strategy in Nim:

```nim
import times, random

proc exponentialBackoff(attempts: int, baseDelay: TimeSpan)
  var currentAttempt 0
  while currentAttempt < attempts:
   try:
     Perform operation that might fail
     echo "Operation succeeded"
     return
   except Exception as e:
      let delay  baseDelay  (2 ^ currentAttempt) + random(0 ..
100.milliseconds)
     echo "Attempt ", currentAttempt, " failed: ", e.msg
     echo "Retrying in ", delay.seconds, " seconds"
     sleep(delay)
     currentAttempt.inc()
  echo "Operation failed after ", attempts, " attempts"
```

In this code, `exponentialBackoff` increases the delay between retries exponentially based on the number of attempts. This approach reduces the load on the system and network by spacing out retries in a controlled manner, which can be particularly useful when dealing with temporary network issues or service unavailability.

Another key aspect of advanced error handling is resource management. Ensuring that resources such as file handles, network connections, or memory are properly released in the event of an error is crucial for preventing resource leaks and maintaining application stability. Nim's `defer` statement, which ensures that a block of code is executed at the end of the current scope regardless of whether an error occurs, can be particularly useful for this purpose. For example:

```nim
proc openFile(fileName: string)
 var file: File
 try:
  file.open(fileName, fmRead)
  defer: file.close()  Ensures the file is closed when done
   Process file contents
 except Exception as e:
  echo "Error opening file: ", e.msg
```

In this example, the `defer` statement guarantees that the file will be closed after it is opened, whether or not an error occurs during file processing. This ensures that resources are managed properly and prevents potential resource leaks.

Finally, integrating error handling with logging and monitoring systems can provide real-time insights into application health and facilitate proactive issue resolution. Logging frameworks can be configured to capture detailed error information, including stack traces and contextual data, which can be invaluable for diagnosing and fixing issues. Monitoring tools can track application performance and error rates, allowing developers to identify and address potential problems before they impact users.

In summary, advanced error handling and recovery in Nim involve creating custom exceptions with detailed contextual information, implementing error propagation and recovery strategies, managing resources effectively, and integrating with logging and monitoring systems. By applying these techniques, you can develop robust applications that handle errors gracefully and maintain stability even in complex and dynamic environments.

When it comes to advanced error handling and recovery, the importance of proper design cannot be overstated. It is essential to approach error management with a comprehensive strategy that not only addresses how errors are caught and logged but also how they influence the flow of the application and interact with various components.

A critical aspect of advanced error handling is the propagation of errors through the application. Nim's approach to exception propagation allows for fine-grained control over how errors are managed at different levels of the application. Propagation involves not just forwarding an error from one function to another but also making informed decisions about whether to handle it immediately, transform it into a different type of error, or allow it to bubble up to higher levels where it might be handled more appropriately.

Consider a scenario where a function that processes user input might encounter various types of errors, such as invalid data formats or system failures. To handle such scenarios, we can use custom exception types to encapsulate different error conditions, thus allowing the error handler to determine the appropriate course of action based on the error's nature. Here's an example of how different exceptions can be defined and used:

```nim
type
  InputError object of Exception
    reason: string

  SystemError object of Exception
    code: int
    description: string

proc handleInput(input: string)
```

```nim
if input.len < 5:
  raise newException(InputError, "Input too short")
  Process input
 echo "Processing input: ", input

proc processFile(fileName: string)
 try:
  let file  open(fileName, fmRead)
  defer: file.close()
  Read and process file
 except InputError as e:
  echo "Input error: ", e.reason
 except SystemError as e:
  echo "System error (code ", e.code, "): ", e.description
 except Exception as e:
  echo "Unexpected error: ", e.msg
```

In this example, `InputError` and `SystemError` are custom exceptions that provide specific information about different types of errors. The `processFile` function demonstrates how multiple `except` blocks can be used to handle different exceptions differently, ensuring that each type of error is managed appropriately according to its context.

Another sophisticated technique involves using error handling within asynchronous operations. When dealing with asynchronous tasks or concurrency, managing errors becomes more complex due to the non-deterministic nature of task execution. Nim provides support for asynchronous programming through its `async` and `await` constructs. Here's how you might handle errors in an asynchronous context:

```nim
import asyncdispatch

proc asyncTask() {.async.}
```

```
  try:
    Simulate an asynchronous operation that may fail
    await sleepAsync(1000.milliseconds)
    if random(0 .. 1)  0:
          raise  newException(SystemError, "Random  failure
occurred")
    echo "Async task completed successfully"
  except SystemError as e:
    echo "Handled async system error: ", e.description
  except Exception as e:
    echo "Handled async exception: ", e.msg

proc runAsyncTasks() {.async.}
  await asyncTask()
  echo "All async tasks finished"

asyncMain(runAsyncTasks)
` ` `
```

In this snippet, `asyncTask` is an asynchronous procedure that may raise an exception. The error handling within the `asyncTask` procedure ensures that any exceptions are caught and managed without crashing the application. The use of `asyncMain` allows for the execution of asynchronous tasks within the event loop, providing a robust framework for handling errors in concurrent scenarios.

Resource cleanup and recovery are integral to robust error handling. When dealing with resources like file handles or network connections, it is vital to ensure they are released properly even if an error occurs. Nim's `defer` statement helps manage this by guaranteeing that specific code is executed when the scope is exited, regardless of whether an error occurs. For example:

```nim
proc processData(fileName: string)
  var file: File
```

```
try:
  file.open(fileName, fmRead)
  defer: file.close()
  Process the file contents
 except Exception as e:
  echo "Error processing file: ", e.msg
` ` `
```

In this case, `file.close()` is guaranteed to be called, preventing resource leaks even if an error occurs during file processing.

Furthermore, implementing comprehensive logging is essential for understanding and diagnosing errors in a production environment. Logs should capture detailed error information, including timestamps, error types, stack traces, and contextual data. Effective logging can provide insights into the conditions that led to an error, helping to diagnose issues and prevent future occurrences. Nim provides various logging libraries and techniques to facilitate detailed and structured logging.

Finally, integrating error handling strategies with testing and validation processes can help ensure that error handling mechanisms work as intended. Unit tests should cover various error scenarios to verify that exceptions are handled correctly and that the application behaves as expected under failure conditions. By combining effective error handling, resource management, logging, and testing, developers can build resilient applications capable of gracefully managing and recovering from errors.

CHAPTER 22:

Effective memory management goes beyond just detecting leaks; it involves understanding the root causes of memory inefficiencies and applying strategies to mitigate them. After identifying memory leaks using tools and techniques discussed previously, the next step is to implement methods to correct these issues and improve overall memory usage.

To address memory leaks effectively, one must first understand how memory is allocated and deallocated within a Nim application. Nim employs automatic memory management through its garbage collector, but relying solely on this can lead to potential inefficiencies if not used properly. While the garbage collector simplifies memory management, it is crucial to use it wisely and complement it with manual memory management practices when needed.

A fundamental technique for managing memory is to use Nim's built-in mechanisms for resource cleanup. Nim provides several constructs to help with resource management, such as `defer`, `finally`, and `except`. The `defer` statement is particularly useful for ensuring that resources are released even if an error occurs during execution. For example, when working with file handles or network connections, it is essential to close these resources after use. The `defer` statement ensures that the cleanup code is executed when the procedure exits, regardless of how it exits:

```nim
proc processFile(fileName: string)
 var file  open(fileName, fmRead)
```

```
defer: file.close()  Ensure the file is closed when the procedure
exits
  Process the file
` ` `
```

In this snippet, the `defer` statement guarantees that the file is closed properly, preventing resource leaks even if an exception occurs while processing the file.

Another important technique for managing memory is to be mindful of object lifetimes and ownership. When working with dynamic memory allocation, it is crucial to manage the lifetime of objects explicitly. Nim provides several ways to handle object ownership and lifetime, including using `new` and `dispose` for manual memory management. For instance, when you allocate memory for an object, you must ensure that it is properly deallocated when no longer needed:

```
` ` `nim
proc createObject(): ref MyObject
  result  new MyObject()
  Use the object
  ...
  Explicitly dispose of the object when done
  dispose(result)
` ` `
```

In this example, the `dispose` procedure is used to deallocate the memory allocated for `MyObject`. This approach helps avoid memory leaks by ensuring that memory is freed when it is no longer needed.

Additionally, understanding and managing memory fragmentation is crucial for optimizing memory usage. Memory fragmentation occurs when memory is allocated and deallocated in such a way that it leads to inefficient use of memory space. Fragmentation can be particularly problematic in long-running applications where memory is continually allocated and freed. To mitigate fragmentation, consider using memory pools or custom memory allocators that group allocations together, reducing fragmentation and improving overall memory efficiency.

Memory pools are a technique where a block of memory is pre-allocated and divided into smaller chunks. These chunks are then used to satisfy allocation requests. This approach can significantly reduce fragmentation and improve performance for applications with frequent memory allocations. In Nim, you can implement memory pools by managing your own memory blocks and allocating memory from these blocks:

```nim
type
 MemoryPool object
  pool: seq[byte]
  currentIndex: int

proc initMemoryPool(size: int): MemoryPool
 result.pool newSeq[byte](size)
 result.currentIndex 0

proc allocateFromPool(pool: var MemoryPool, size: int): ptr byte
 if pool.currentIndex + size > pool.pool.len:
    raise newException(ValueError, "Not enough memory in pool")
 result cast[ptr byte](pool.pool[pool.currentIndex])
 pool.currentIndex + size

proc freePool(pool: var MemoryPool)
 pool.currentIndex 0
```

In this implementation, the `MemoryPool` object manages a block of memory and provides methods for allocating and freeing memory. By allocating memory from the pre-allocated pool, you reduce the risk of fragmentation and improve allocation efficiency.

When dealing with complex systems, it is also helpful to employ runtime analysis tools to monitor memory usage in real-time. Tools such as Valgrind, while not specific to Nim, can be invaluable for detecting memory-related issues during development. Valgrind provides detailed information about memory allocation, deallocation, and usage patterns, helping you identify and address problems such as memory leaks, invalid memory accesses, and buffer overflows.

To use Valgrind with Nim applications, compile your code with debugging information and run it through Valgrind:

```bash
nim c --debug myapp.nim
valgrind --leak-checkfull ./myapp
```

The Valgrind output will provide detailed reports on memory usage, highlighting areas where leaks or inefficiencies occur. By analyzing these reports, you can take corrective actions to improve memory management in your application.

In summary, effective memory management in Nim involves a combination of using built-in tools and techniques, manual memory management practices, and runtime analysis. By leveraging Nim's memory profiling tools, applying best practices for resource cleanup, managing object lifetimes, and utilizing memory pools, you can address memory-related issues and ensure that your applications are both performant and reliable. Regularly profiling and analyzing your application's memory usage will help maintain optimal performance and prevent memory-related problems from impacting your software.

To effectively manage memory in Nim applications,

understanding and addressing memory fragmentation is crucial. Fragmentation occurs when memory is allocated and freed in such a way that leads to inefficient use of memory, either through unused gaps between allocations or excessive overhead. This can degrade performance and increase the risk of memory-related issues over time. One effective strategy to combat fragmentation is to use memory pools. Memory pools involve pre-allocating a large block of memory and then dividing it into smaller chunks for allocation as needed. This approach minimizes fragmentation by ensuring that memory is allocated from a contiguous block, reducing the number of gaps that can form between allocations.

In Nim, you can implement memory pools using arrays or sequences to manage the pool of memory. For example, you might define a memory pool as a sequence of bytes and keep track of the current allocation index. By allocating memory from this pool, you can avoid frequent allocations and deallocations from the heap, which can contribute to fragmentation. Implementing a memory pool might look like this:

```nim
type
  MemoryPool object
    pool: seq[byte]
    currentIndex: int

proc initMemoryPool(size: int): MemoryPool
  result.pool newSeq[byte](size)
  result.currentIndex 0

proc allocateFromPool(pool: var MemoryPool, size: int): ptr byte
  if pool.currentIndex + size > pool.pool.len:
    raise newException(ValueError, "Not enough memory in pool")
```

```
result  cast[ptr byte](pool.pool[pool.currentIndex])
pool.currentIndex + size

proc freePool(pool: var MemoryPool)
  pool.currentIndex 0
```

In this implementation, `initMemoryPool` initializes a memory pool of a specified size, and `allocateFromPool` allocates memory from this pool. By managing memory allocations in this way, you reduce the likelihood of fragmentation and improve allocation efficiency.

Another important aspect of memory management is understanding and applying strategies for memory leak detection and recovery. Memory leaks occur when memory that is no longer needed is not released, leading to an increase in memory consumption over time. Detecting and fixing memory leaks is essential for maintaining application performance and preventing resource exhaustion.

Nim offers several tools and techniques for detecting memory leaks. The `memtrace` module is particularly useful for this purpose. By enabling memory tracing in your Nim application, you can generate detailed reports on memory allocations and deallocations, helping to identify areas where memory is not being properly freed. To use `memtrace`, you must compile your application with the `--memtrace` option:

```bash
nim c --memtrace myapp.nim
```

After running your application, you can analyze the generated memory trace files to identify leaks. The trace files provide detailed information about memory allocations, allowing you to pinpoint where memory is being allocated without corresponding deallocations.

In addition to using `memtrace`, you can employ runtime analysis tools such as Valgrind to detect memory leaks and other memory-related issues. Valgrind is a powerful tool for analyzing memory usage and can be used to profile your Nim application in detail. To use Valgrind with your Nim application, compile your code with debugging information and run it through Valgrind:

```bash
nim c --debug myapp.nim
valgrind --leak-checkfull ./myapp
```

Valgrind's output will include detailed reports on memory leaks, invalid memory accesses, and other issues. By analyzing these reports, you can identify and address memory leaks in your application.

Memory management also involves considering the implications of using third-party libraries and dependencies. When integrating external libraries into your Nim application, it is essential to ensure that these libraries manage memory correctly and do not introduce memory leaks or inefficiencies. Review the documentation for any third-party libraries you use and, if possible, examine their source code to understand their memory management practices.

In addition to these practices, adopting good coding habits can further enhance memory management in your applications. Regularly reviewing and refactoring your code to identify and address potential memory issues, conducting code reviews with a focus on memory management, and writing unit tests to cover edge cases can all contribute to more robust memory handling.

As you continue to develop and optimize your Nim applications, remember that memory profiling and leak detection are ongoing processes. Regularly profiling your application's memory usage, using tools to detect and address memory leaks, and applying best practices for memory management will help ensure that your applications remain performant and reliable.

In summary, effective memory management in Nim involves a combination of techniques for detecting and addressing memory leaks, managing fragmentation, and using tools for runtime analysis. By implementing memory pools, using memory tracing and runtime analysis tools, and adopting good coding practices, you can improve memory efficiency and prevent issues that could impact your application's performance. Regularly profiling and reviewing your application's memory usage will help maintain optimal performance and ensure that your applications remain robust and reliable over time.

CHAPTER 23:

When delving deeper into concurrency patterns and practices, it is essential to explore not only the basic mechanisms for managing concurrent tasks but also advanced patterns that can help address more complex scenarios. These patterns and practices ensure that your application can handle concurrency effectively while minimizing potential issues related to performance and correctness.

One such advanced pattern is the producer-consumer model, which is particularly useful when dealing with tasks that involve producing and consuming data at different rates. This pattern relies on a shared buffer or queue to decouple the production and consumption processes. The producer generates data and places it into the queue, while the consumer retrieves and processes this data. This model can be implemented in Nim using threads and synchronization primitives like mutexes and condition variables. Here's a conceptual example:

```nim
import threads, locks, os, queues

const bufferSize 10
var buffer Queue[int]()
let mutex Mutex()
let notEmpty Condition()
let notFull Condition()

proc producer()
  for i in 1..100:
```

```nim
    mutex.lock()
    while buffer.len  bufferSize:
     notFull.wait(mutex)
    buffer.enqueue(i)
    notEmpty.signal()
    mutex.unlock()
    sleep(500)

proc consumer()
  for _ in 1..100:
    mutex.lock()
    while buffer.isEmpty:
     notEmpty.wait(mutex)
    let item  buffer.dequeue()
    notFull.signal()
    mutex.unlock()
    echo "Consumed: ", item
    sleep(1000)

let p  createThread(producer)
let c  createThread(consumer)

p.join()
c.join()
` ` `
```

In this example, the `producer` thread generates integers and places them into a queue. The `consumer` thread retrieves these integers from the queue. Mutexes and condition variables synchronize access to the buffer and handle situations where the buffer is either full or empty.

Another important pattern in concurrent programming is the fork-join model. This pattern involves splitting a task into smaller subtasks that can be executed concurrently and then combining the results of these subtasks. The fork-join model is particularly useful in divide-and-conquer algorithms and parallel processing. In Nim, this can be implemented by creating multiple threads to handle the subtasks and then aggregating the results. For instance, consider a parallel implementation of a merge sort algorithm:

```nim
import threads, os, sequtils

proc mergeSort(arr: seq[int]): seq[int]
  if arr.len < 1:
    return arr
  let mid  arr.len div 2
  var left, right: seq[int]
  var sortedLeft, sortedRight: seq[int]


  createThread(proc()                                    sortedLeft
mergeSort(arr[0..mid-1])).join()
                  createThread(proc()                    sortedRight
mergeSort(arr[mid..^1])).join()


  return merge(sortedLeft, sortedRight)

proc merge(left, right: seq[int]): seq[int]
  var result: seq[int]
  var i, j  0
  while i < left.len and j < right.len:
    if left[i] < right[j]:
      result.add(left[i])
      i.inc()
    else:
      result.add(right[j])
      j.inc()
  result.addAll(left[i..^1])
  result.addAll(right[j..^1])
  return result

let unsorted  @[38, 27, 43, 3, 9, 82, 10]
```

```nim
let sorted  mergeSort(unsorted)
echo "Sorted array: ", sorted
```

In this example, the `mergeSort` function splits the array into two halves, processes each half in parallel using threads, and then merges the sorted halves. This approach effectively demonstrates the fork-join pattern, where the sorting task is divided, executed concurrently, and then results are combined.

Another aspect of concurrent programming in Nim involves the use of asynchronous tasks and futures, which are particularly suited for I/O-bound operations. The `asyncawait` module in Nim provides facilities for writing asynchronous code using `async` and `await` constructs, which allow for non-blocking operations and improved responsiveness in applications.

Here's a basic example of using `asyncawait` to perform asynchronous HTTP requests:

```nim
import httpclient, asyncawait, logging

proc fetchURL(url: string): Async[HttpResponse] {.async.}
 let client  newAsyncHttpClient()
 return await client.get(url)

proc processURL(url: string) {.async.}
 let response  await fetchURL(url)
 echo "Response from ", url, ": ", response.body

asyncMain:
 let urls  ["http://example.com", "http://example.org", "http://example.net"]
 for url in urls:
  spawn processURL(url)
 Wait for all asynchronous tasks to complete
```

```
await for url in urls:
  processURL(url)
```

In this example, `fetchURL` performs an asynchronous HTTP GET request, and `processURL` waits for the response and processes it. The `asyncMain` procedure spawns asynchronous tasks for each URL and then waits for all tasks to complete. This approach allows multiple I/O-bound tasks to run concurrently without blocking the main thread.

By leveraging these advanced concurrency patterns and practices, you can effectively manage complex concurrent tasks and build efficient, responsive applications in Nim. Understanding and applying these patterns will enable you to handle a wide range of concurrency scenarios, ensuring that your applications can perform optimally while avoiding common pitfalls associated with concurrent programming.

In further exploring concurrency patterns and practices, it becomes crucial to address the subtleties of synchronization and the efficient handling of shared resources. Concurrency introduces challenges related to ensuring data consistency and preventing race conditions. To manage these issues, various synchronization techniques are employed, including locks, semaphores, and atomic operations.

Locks are a fundamental synchronization mechanism, ensuring that only one thread can access a particular piece of data at a time. In Nim, the `Mutex` type from the `locks` module is used to implement mutual exclusion. While locks are effective in preventing race conditions, they also introduce the risk of deadlocks—situations where two or more threads are waiting indefinitely for each other to release resources. To mitigate this risk, it's essential to follow best practices such as acquiring locks in a consistent order and avoiding nested locks when possible.

For example, consider a scenario where multiple threads are updating a shared counter. The following Nim code demonstrates how to use a `Mutex` to synchronize access to the counter:

```nim
import threads, locks, os

var counter: int 0
let mutex Mutex()

proc increment()
  mutex.lock()
  counter.inc()
  mutex.unlock()

proc decrement()
  mutex.lock()
  counter.dec()
  mutex.unlock()

let thread1 createThread(increment)
let thread2 createThread(decrement)

thread1.join()
thread2.join()

echo "Final counter value: ", counter
```

In this example, the `increment` and `decrement` procedures modify the shared `counter` variable. The `Mutex` ensures that these modifications are performed atomically, preventing race conditions.

Semaphores offer another synchronization mechanism, which is useful for managing access to a fixed number of resources. A semaphore maintains a count that is decremented when a resource is acquired and incremented when it is released. This approach can be implemented in Nim using the `Semaphore` type. Semaphores are particularly useful in scenarios where a limited number of resources need to be shared among threads, such as controlling access to a pool of database connections.

Consider a situation where a thread pool is used to process tasks concurrently. A semaphore can be employed to limit the number of threads accessing a shared resource, like a database connection pool:

```nim
import threads, locks, os

const maxConnections 5
var semaphore Semaphore(maxConnections)

proc processTask(taskId: int)
  semaphore.acquire()
  echo "Task ", taskId, " is processing..."
  sleep(1000)  Simulate task processing
  echo "Task ", taskId, " finished."
  semaphore.release()

for i in 1..10:
  createThread(processTask, i)
```

In this code, the semaphore ensures that no more than `maxConnections` tasks can be processed concurrently, effectively managing access to the limited resource.

Atomic operations provide a lower-level synchronization mechanism for performing operations on shared data without the need for locks. They are particularly useful for counters and flags where the overhead of locks would be too high. Nim supports atomic operations through the `atomic` module, which provides types like `AtomicInt` for thread-safe integer operations.

An example of using atomic operations in Nim is the following implementation of a thread-safe counter:

```nim
import threads, atomic, os

var counter: AtomicInt AtomicInt(0)

proc increment()
  atomicAdd(counter, 1)

proc decrement()
  atomicAdd(counter, -1)

let thread1 createThread(increment)
let thread2 createThread(decrement)

thread1.join()
thread2.join()

echo "Final counter value: ", counter.get()
```

In this example, the `atomicAdd` procedure is used to modify the `AtomicInt` counter in a thread-safe manner without locking.

While synchronization mechanisms are vital for managing concurrent access, it is also important to consider performance implications and avoid common pitfalls. One such pitfall is the "thundering herd" problem, where multiple threads are awakened simultaneously when a shared resource becomes available. This situation can lead to inefficiencies and excessive context switching. To address this, it is often beneficial to use techniques such as condition variables or redesigning the locking strategy to minimize contention.

Another common issue is the "lost wakeup" problem, where a thread may miss a signal indicating that a resource is available. This issue can be mitigated by employing reliable signaling mechanisms and ensuring that threads do not proceed without proper synchronization.

In addition to these synchronization techniques, it is essential to profile and analyze the performance of concurrent applications. Profiling tools help identify bottlenecks and inefficiencies, such as excessive locking or contention. Nim provides integration with various profiling tools that can be used to measure the performance of concurrent code and optimize it accordingly.

In summary, managing concurrency in Nim involves understanding and applying various synchronization techniques, including locks, semaphores, and atomic operations. By carefully selecting and implementing these techniques, you can build robust and efficient concurrent applications that handle shared resources effectively while avoiding common pitfalls. Profiling and performance analysis further enhance the reliability and efficiency of your concurrent systems, ensuring they perform optimally in real-world scenarios.

CHAPTER 24:

When managing network security, ensuring the integrity of data during transmission is just as critical as protecting data at rest. This necessitates a thorough understanding of encryption techniques and their proper implementation in networked environments. In practice, choosing the right encryption method depends on the specific requirements and constraints of the application. For instance, while symmetric encryption offers high performance due to its straightforward key management, asymmetric encryption provides enhanced security through its public-private key pair system, albeit with a performance trade-off.

Implementing secure communication channels using TLS (Transport Layer Security) is a common approach in network programming. TLS ensures that data transmitted over the network is encrypted, thereby preventing eavesdroppers from reading or tampering with the data. Nim's support for TLS is typically facilitated through bindings to libraries such as OpenSSL or via dedicated packages. When setting up a TLS connection, it's essential to configure it correctly to avoid common pitfalls. This includes ensuring that the server's certificate is valid, the certificate chain is properly established, and that secure ciphers are used.

For practical implementation, consider using the `httpbeast` library in Nim, which can be configured to support HTTPS. Here's an example of setting up an HTTPS server:

```nim
import httpbeast, openssl
```

```
proc setupHTTPS()
 let server newAsyncHttpServer()
 server.addHandler(proc (req: Request) {.async.}
  req.respond(Http200, "Secure connection established!"))


  Configure OpenSSL for HTTPS
 let ctx newSslContext()
 ctx.useCertificateFile("server.crt")
 ctx.usePrivateKeyFile("server.key")
 server.sslContext ctx


 echo "HTTPS server is running on port 443"
 await server.serve(Port(443))

asyncMain(setupHTTPS())
` ` `
```

In this code, we initialize an HTTP server and configure it to use SSL/TLS for secure communication. The `useCertificateFile` and `usePrivateKeyFile` methods load the SSL certificate and private key required for encryption. By doing so, we ensure that all data exchanged with the server is encrypted.

Beyond encryption, authentication plays a crucial role in establishing trust between entities in a network. In networked applications, various authentication mechanisms can be employed to verify the identities of users or systems. One common approach is to use token-based authentication, where users authenticate once and receive a token that can be used for subsequent requests. This token is then validated on each request to ensure that the user or system has the appropriate permissions.

JWT (JSON Web Tokens) is a popular choice for implementing token-based authentication. It allows for the secure exchange of claims between parties and can be used to verify the authenticity of requests. The use of JWTs in Nim can be facilitated through libraries such as `jwt` or `jose`, which provide functionality for encoding and decoding JWTs. Here is an example of generating and validating a JWT:

```nim
import jwt, json

let secretKey "mysecretkey"

proc generateToken(userId: int): string
  var claims  %{"user_id": userId}
  return JWT.encode(claims, secretKey, JWTAlgorithm.HS256)

proc validateToken(token: string): JsonNode
  try:
    return JWT.decode(token, secretKey, JWTAlgorithm.HS256)
  except JWTError as e:
    echo "Invalid token: ", e.msg
    return %

let token  generateToken(12345)
let claims  validateToken(token)

echo "Generated token: ", token
echo "Claims: ", claims
```

In this snippet, we define functions to generate and validate JWTs, which can be used to authenticate users and secure access to resources.

While encryption and authentication are fundamental, addressing vulnerabilities is equally important for maintaining a secure network application. Vulnerabilities often arise from flaws in the code, misconfigurations, or unpatched software. A proactive approach to security involves regular code reviews, vulnerability assessments, and applying patches to address known issues.

For instance, input validation is a crucial aspect of preventing attacks such as SQL injection, cross-site scripting (XSS), and buffer overflows. Ensuring that inputs are sanitized and validated before processing can mitigate many common security issues. This involves checking that inputs conform to expected formats and rejecting or escaping any inputs that do not meet these criteria.

Additionally, employing secure coding practices and utilizing static analysis tools can help identify potential security vulnerabilities early in the development process. Nim provides various tools for static code analysis that can help developers catch security issues before they become problems.

Regular updates to libraries and dependencies are essential to maintaining security. Many vulnerabilities are discovered post-release, and updates often include fixes for these issues. By keeping all components up-to-date, you minimize the risk of exploitation from known vulnerabilities.

Finally, implementing monitoring and logging mechanisms can aid in detecting and responding to security incidents. Proper logging allows you to track activities and identify unusual patterns that may indicate an attack or breach. Combining logging with intrusion detection systems (IDS) can provide real-time alerts and enhance the overall security posture of your application.

In summary, securing networked applications in Nim involves a multifaceted approach that includes implementing robust encryption, employing effective authentication methods, addressing vulnerabilities through best practices, and maintaining vigilance through regular updates and monitoring. By adhering to these principles, you can build secure network applications that protect data integrity and maintain user trust.

In the realm of network security, beyond encryption and authentication, securing data integrity and ensuring secure communication practices are paramount. One effective way to maintain data integrity is through the use of cryptographic hash functions. These functions generate a unique hash value from input data, which can be used to verify that the data has not been altered. When a data packet is transmitted, its hash value can be included along with the data. The receiver can then recalculate the hash of the received data and compare it to the received hash value to ensure that the data has not been tampered with.

Nim provides various libraries for implementing cryptographic hash functions. The `crypto` module, for example, supports algorithms like SHA-256, which can be used for creating hashes. Here's how you might use it to hash a piece of data:

```nim
import crypto, strutils

let data  "Sensitive data to be hashed"
let hash  sha256(data)
echo "SHA-256 Hash: ", hash.toHex()
```

In this example, the `sha256` function generates a hash for the given data. This hash can then be sent along with the data to the recipient, who can use it to verify the integrity of the data upon receipt.

Moreover, securing data in transit also involves implementing secure transport layers. Network communications often rely on protocols such as HTTPS for secure data transmission. Nim's `httpbeast` library, when configured with TLS, can help establish a secure HTTPS connection. However, it's crucial to ensure that the TLS configuration adheres to best practices, including using strong cipher suites and enforcing certificate validation. This mitigates risks associated with weaker encryption standards and potential man-in-the-middle attacks.

A common practice is to set up a secure connection using the TLS configuration and regularly update the security settings to adhere to the latest standards. For instance, you might disable outdated protocols like SSLv2 and SSLv3 and ensure that only TLS versions with strong encryption algorithms are supported.

In addition to encryption and data integrity, network security also involves the management of network services and the protection of network endpoints. Ensuring that services are properly configured and restricted to only those necessary can reduce the attack surface. For instance, if a server only needs to serve HTTP traffic, it should be configured to reject or ignore non-HTTP requests. This can be achieved through proper firewall settings and by employing network policies that restrict access to only authorized entities.

Network segmentation is another important strategy for protecting networked applications. By segmenting networks, you can isolate critical systems and sensitive data from less secure areas of the network. This limits the potential impact of a security breach to a specific segment and prevents unauthorized access to critical resources. Implementing Virtual LANs (VLANs) or using network security groups can effectively segment traffic and control access between different network zones.

Furthermore, monitoring and auditing play a critical role in network security. Continuous monitoring allows for the detection of anomalies or potential security incidents in real-time. Tools and techniques such as intrusion detection systems (IDS) and intrusion prevention systems (IPS) can be used to identify and respond to suspicious activities. Logs and audit trails are also valuable for analyzing past incidents and understanding attack patterns.

In Nim, integrating logging into your network applications is straightforward and can be accomplished using libraries like `logging`. By configuring appropriate log levels and destinations, you can ensure that relevant events are recorded and stored for later review. Here's an example of setting up basic logging:

```nim
import logging

let log newFileLogger("application.log", level LogLevel.Info)
log.info("Application started")
```

This configuration creates a file logger that records informational messages to a log file. Regularly reviewing these logs helps in identifying potential security threats and assessing the effectiveness of implemented security measures.

Another aspect of network security involves handling and mitigating denial-of-service (DoS) attacks. These attacks aim to overwhelm a network service or application, rendering it unavailable to legitimate users. Techniques such as rate limiting, implementing web application firewalls (WAFs), and using load balancers can help mitigate the impact of DoS attacks. By controlling the rate of incoming requests and distributing traffic across multiple servers, you can reduce the risk of service disruptions caused by excessive traffic.

Finally, adherence to security best practices and regular updates are critical in maintaining the security of networked applications. This includes patching vulnerabilities as they are discovered, reviewing and updating security policies, and conducting periodic security assessments. By staying informed about emerging threats and adapting security practices accordingly, you can better protect your applications and data from evolving risks.

In summary, effective network security encompasses a range of practices beyond basic encryption and authentication. It involves ensuring data integrity, securely configuring transport layers, managing network services, segmenting networks, implementing robust monitoring and logging, and mitigating threats such as DoS attacks. By employing these strategies and continuously evaluating and updating security measures, you can create a resilient and secure networked application environment.

Performance Tuning for Nim Applications

Performance tuning is an essential part of developing high-performance applications. In the context of Nim, optimizing performance involves understanding the interplay between various aspects of the application, including memory usage, CPU cycles, and I/O operations. The process begins with identifying performance bottlenecks and inefficiencies through profiling and continues with applying specific techniques to enhance the runtime efficiency of your applications.

To begin with, performance tuning starts with profiling, which is the systematic analysis of a program's runtime behavior. Profiling tools help in pinpointing parts of the application that consume excessive amounts of resources or cause slowdowns. In Nim, you have access to various profiling tools and libraries that can help in assessing the performance characteristics of your applications.

One common profiling tool is the `perf` utility, which provides detailed insights into CPU usage, function execution times, and other performance metrics. Although `perf` is not specific to Nim, it is widely used in conjunction with Nim applications to gain a deeper understanding of performance issues. For example, running `perf` with your compiled Nim application can reveal which functions are taking the most time to execute, allowing you to focus your optimization efforts where they will have the most impact.

Another valuable tool for performance profiling in Nim is the `heaptrack` utility. This tool specializes in memory profiling by tracking memory allocations and deallocations. `heaptrack` can help identify memory leaks, excessive memory consumption, and inefficient memory usage patterns. By analyzing the output from `heaptrack`, you can make informed decisions about memory management and address issues such as unintentional memory growth or fragmentation.

In addition to these tools, Nim offers built-in support for performance profiling through its standard library. The `profiling` module, for instance, allows you to measure the time taken by different sections of your code. By strategically placing profiling markers in your code, you can obtain timing information that highlights which areas are most in need of optimization. Here's a basic example of using the `profiling` module:

```nim
import profiling

var start Time.now()
Code block to be profiled
let elapsedTime Time.now() - start
echo "Time taken: ", elapsedTime, " seconds"
```

Once you have identified performance bottlenecks through profiling, the next step is to implement optimization strategies. Optimization techniques can vary widely depending on the specific issues identified. For instance, if your profiling results indicate that a particular function is a hotspot, you might consider optimizing its algorithm or reducing the complexity of its operations.

One common optimization technique is to reduce the time complexity of algorithms. For example, if you are using an O(n^2) algorithm for sorting or searching, switching to a more efficient O(n log n) algorithm can yield significant performance improvements. Nim provides various algorithms and data structures that are optimized for different use cases. Leveraging these built-in features can help you avoid reinventing the wheel and ensure that your code is as efficient as possible.

Another important aspect of performance tuning is memory management. Efficient memory usage can drastically improve application performance. In Nim, you can manage memory allocation and deallocation manually to gain finer control over memory usage. For example, using stack-based memory allocation instead of heap-based allocation can reduce overhead and improve performance. However, it is crucial to balance manual memory management with the risk of introducing memory leaks or fragmentation.

To complement manual memory management, Nim also offers garbage collection, which can automatically handle memory deallocation. Fine-tuning garbage collection settings can help optimize performance by adjusting the frequency and behavior of garbage collection cycles. For instance, you might configure the garbage collector to run more or less frequently based on the specific needs of your application.

I/O operations are another critical area for performance tuning. Applications that perform frequent disk or network I/O can experience significant slowdowns if these operations are not optimized. Techniques such as asynchronous I/O and buffering can help mitigate the performance impact of I/O operations. For instance, using asynchronous file operations allows your application to continue processing while waiting for I/O operations to complete, thus reducing idle time and improving overall throughput.

In addition to optimizing individual components, it is also essential to consider the overall architecture and design of your application. Efficient use of concurrency and parallelism can help fully utilize available hardware resources and improve performance. Nim provides robust support for concurrency through its threading and asynchronous programming features. By designing your application to take advantage of concurrent execution, you can achieve better performance and responsiveness.

Finally, performance tuning is an iterative process. It involves continuously measuring, analyzing, and refining your application to achieve optimal performance. Regularly revisiting your profiling results and optimization strategies ensures that you can adapt to changing requirements and address new performance challenges as they arise.

In summary, performance tuning for Nim applications involves a systematic approach to profiling, optimizing, and refining your code. By utilizing profiling tools to identify bottlenecks, implementing targeted optimization techniques, and managing memory and I/O operations efficiently, you can enhance the runtime efficiency of your applications. Through iterative testing and refinement, you ensure that your application performs optimally under various conditions, providing a smooth and responsive experience for users.

When it comes to performance tuning, understanding and managing the interaction between different components of your application is crucial. One of the advanced techniques involves fine-tuning the performance of specific algorithms and data structures used in your Nim applications. The choice of algorithms can significantly impact performance, especially in terms of computational complexity and memory usage.

For example, consider a scenario where your application processes large datasets and performs frequent search operations. Choosing an appropriate data structure such as a hash table or balanced binary search tree can drastically improve performance. Nim's standard library provides various data structures optimized for different tasks. By selecting the right data structure and algorithm, you can enhance your application's efficiency and reduce execution time.

Moreover, optimizing critical sections of your code often requires a deep understanding of both the algorithmic complexity and the underlying hardware architecture. Profiling tools can help you identify hotspots in your application, but optimizing these hotspots requires a more nuanced approach. Techniques such as loop unrolling, inlining functions, and minimizing cache misses can contribute to better performance. Loop unrolling involves expanding loops to reduce the overhead of loop control, while inlining functions reduces the function call overhead by embedding the function's code directly. Minimizing cache misses, on the other hand, requires optimizing data access patterns to align with the CPU cache's architecture.

In addition to optimizing algorithms and data structures, another critical aspect of performance tuning involves reducing contention in concurrent applications. Contention occurs when multiple threads or processes compete for the same resources, leading to performance degradation. Techniques such as lock-free data structures and fine-grained locking can help mitigate contention. Lock-free data structures, such as concurrent queues and stacks, allow multiple threads to operate concurrently without the need for traditional locks. Fine-grained locking involves using multiple locks to reduce contention by allowing threads to access different parts of the data simultaneously.

Memory management plays a significant role in performance tuning, and Nim provides several tools and strategies to manage memory efficiently. For instance, Nim's garbage collector helps manage memory automatically, but fine-tuning garbage collection parameters can further optimize performance. By configuring the garbage collector to adjust the frequency and timing of garbage collection cycles, you can balance memory usage and application performance. Additionally, using memory pools and object recycling techniques can reduce the overhead associated with frequent memory allocations and deallocations.

Another strategy to enhance performance involves optimizing I/O operations. Applications that perform extensive I/O operations, such as file reading and writing or network communication, can benefit from various techniques to improve throughput and reduce latency. Asynchronous I/O operations allow your application to perform other tasks while waiting for I/O operations to complete, reducing idle time and improving overall performance. Buffered I/O is another technique that involves reading or writing data in chunks, which can reduce the number of I/O operations and improve performance.

Performance tuning also requires attention to how your application interacts with external systems and services. For example, when dealing with database interactions, optimizing queries and reducing the number of database round-trips can significantly impact performance. Indexing frequently queried fields and using query optimization techniques can reduce the time spent on database operations and improve the responsiveness of your application.

Additionally, adopting a holistic approach to performance tuning involves considering the overall system architecture. Ensuring that your application is designed to efficiently use available hardware resources, such as CPU cores and memory, is crucial. Techniques such as load balancing and horizontal scaling can help distribute the workload across multiple servers or instances, improving overall performance and reliability.

Real-world examples illustrate the practical application of these techniques. For instance, in a web server application that handles a high volume of concurrent requests, profiling and optimizing the request handling code can lead to significant improvements in response time. By identifying and optimizing bottlenecks in the request processing pipeline, you can enhance the server's throughput and reduce latency.

Similarly, in a data processing application that performs complex calculations on large datasets, optimizing the algorithms and data structures used for processing can lead to faster execution and reduced resource consumption. By profiling the application and applying targeted optimizations, you can achieve better performance and scalability.

Performance tuning is not a one-time task but an ongoing process. As your application evolves and its requirements change, continuous monitoring and optimization are necessary to maintain and improve performance. Regularly revisiting profiling results, reassessing optimization strategies, and adapting to new technologies and techniques will ensure that your application remains efficient and responsive over time.

In summary, advanced performance tuning for Nim applications involves a comprehensive approach to optimizing algorithms, managing memory, reducing contention, and improving I/O operations. By leveraging profiling tools, understanding the intricacies of algorithmic performance, and applying targeted optimization techniques, you can enhance the efficiency and responsiveness of your applications. Through continuous monitoring and refinement, you ensure that your applications deliver optimal performance and meet the evolving demands of users and systems.

When delving into advanced performance tuning for Nim applications, one must consider not just the immediate gains but the broader implications on the system's architecture and overall efficiency. Beyond algorithmic optimizations and data structure choices, an integral aspect of performance tuning is managing and optimizing the runtime environment itself.

In Nim, as in many modern programming languages, the runtime environment includes the garbage collector, the memory allocator, and the threading model. Each of these components can significantly impact application performance. Fine-tuning these aspects requires a deep understanding of how they interact with your application's workload.

The garbage collector, for instance, plays a pivotal role in memory management by automatically reclaiming unused memory. However, its operation can introduce pauses, which might be detrimental in performance-sensitive applications. To mitigate this, one approach is to employ a more aggressive strategy for garbage collection tuning. This could involve adjusting parameters such as the frequency of collection cycles, the size of the memory regions used for allocation, or even opting for a different garbage collection algorithm if Nim provides alternatives. For example, using a generational garbage collection strategy can help in reducing the frequency of full garbage collections by focusing more on short-lived objects.

Moreover, understanding and optimizing the memory allocator's behavior can also yield significant performance improvements. Nim's standard library uses a general-purpose memory allocator, but for performance-critical applications, you might want to implement or integrate a custom allocator that better suits your specific usage patterns. This custom allocator can be optimized for particular allocation sizes or access patterns, thus reducing fragmentation and improving allocation speed.

In terms of threading, efficient management of threads is crucial for applications that perform concurrent tasks. Nim provides abstractions for threading, but fine-tuning the performance requires managing thread pools and understanding thread contention. Thread pools help limit the number of concurrent threads, thereby reducing the overhead associated with creating and destroying threads frequently. Efficiently managing the thread pool size to match the number of available CPU cores and the nature of the workload can improve overall throughput.

When dealing with concurrency, another key consideration is minimizing contention. Contention occurs when multiple threads attempt to access shared resources simultaneously, leading to performance degradation. Employing techniques such as lock-free data structures or applying fine-grained locking can help alleviate contention. Lock-free data structures, such as concurrent queues or hash maps, allow threads to operate without traditional locks, thus reducing the overhead of acquiring and releasing locks. Fine-grained locking involves using multiple locks to limit contention to smaller sections of data, enabling more threads to operate concurrently.

Additionally, profiling tools are indispensable for identifying performance bottlenecks and understanding the impact of optimizations. In Nim, various profiling tools can be employed to analyze different aspects of application performance, such as CPU usage, memory allocation, and thread activity. Profilers can provide insights into which parts of the code consume the most resources, which in turn guides targeted optimization efforts.

For instance, if a profiler indicates that a particular function is a hotspot in terms of CPU usage, it might be beneficial to examine the function's implementation for opportunities to optimize. This could involve algorithmic improvements, reducing the function's complexity, or even parallelizing its execution if appropriate.

In addition to profiling, performance metrics offer valuable insights into how well your optimizations are working. Metrics such as execution time, throughput, and latency can be used to gauge the impact of changes. By monitoring these metrics before and after applying optimizations, you can quantify the improvements and ensure that the changes lead to the desired outcomes.

Consider a scenario where an application experiences high latency due to frequent disk I/O operations. Profiling may reveal that disk access is a significant bottleneck. In such cases, optimizing I/O operations can involve strategies like asynchronous I/O, where operations are performed in a non-blocking manner, or implementing a caching mechanism to reduce the number of disk reads and writes.

Finally, it's crucial to recognize that performance tuning is not a one-time task but an ongoing process. As your application evolves, new performance bottlenecks may emerge, and previously optimized areas may need revisiting. Regular performance reviews and iterative optimizations are essential to maintaining and improving application performance over time.

By adopting a systematic approach to performance tuning —focusing on algorithmic efficiency, memory management, threading, and profiling—you can significantly enhance the performance of your Nim applications. Understanding and applying these advanced techniques will enable you to build applications that are not only functional but also highly efficient, scalable, and responsive to user demands.

CHAPTER 25:

Integrating Nim with web technologies involves understanding various components and how they interact to build and manage web applications effectively. Beyond the basics of HTTP servers and frameworks, there are additional considerations and tools that play a crucial role in the integration process. One of the essential aspects of working with web technologies is handling data, which often involves interacting with databases.

Nim provides several libraries for database interaction, such as `db_postgres` for PostgreSQL, `db_mysql` for MySQL, and `db_sqlite` for SQLite. These libraries facilitate connecting to and querying databases, allowing your web application to store and retrieve data efficiently. When integrating Nim with databases, it's important to understand how to manage database connections, execute queries, and handle results.

For instance, using `db_postgres`, you can establish a connection to a PostgreSQL database by specifying the connection parameters such as host, port, user, password, and database name. Once connected, you can execute SQL queries and process the results. The library provides methods for performing CRUD (Create, Read, Update, Delete) operations, which are fundamental for web applications that require persistent data storage. For more advanced use cases, you might need to handle transactions, prepared statements, and database migrations.

Handling authentication and authorization is another critical aspect when building web applications. Nim's libraries and frameworks offer various ways to implement these security measures. For instance, when using `Jester`, you can integrate authentication mechanisms such as sessions, cookies, and OAuth. Implementing secure authentication involves ensuring that user credentials are handled safely, using techniques like password hashing and secure token management.

Sessions and cookies are commonly used to manage user sessions in web applications. In `Jester`, you can create and manage sessions to track user activity and maintain state between requests. This includes storing session data on the server and sending session identifiers to the client via cookies. Ensuring the security of sessions involves using secure cookies and implementing proper session expiration and invalidation policies.

OAuth is another authentication mechanism that allows users to log in using their credentials from third-party services, such as Google or Facebook. Integrating OAuth involves setting up an OAuth provider and handling the authorization flow, which includes redirecting users to the provider's authentication page and handling the response. Nim's libraries and frameworks can help manage the OAuth flow and handle tokens securely.

Another important aspect of web development with Nim is error handling and logging. Proper error handling ensures that your web application can gracefully manage unexpected issues and provide meaningful feedback to users. Nim's `logging` module provides a robust framework for logging application events, errors, and other important information. By configuring loggers and setting appropriate logging levels, you can capture and analyze runtime information, which is crucial for debugging and maintaining your application.

Error handling in web applications often involves catching

exceptions and providing user-friendly error messages. In Nim, you can use try-catch blocks to handle exceptions that may occur during request processing. By catching exceptions and logging them, you can ensure that your application remains stable and provides informative error messages to users.

Performance considerations are also crucial when integrating Nim with web technologies. Efficient handling of HTTP requests, database interactions, and resource management are key to building high-performance web applications. Profiling and optimizing your code can help identify bottlenecks and improve overall performance.

Nim's profiling tools can assist in analyzing the performance of your web applications. Tools such as `profile` and `timeit` help measure execution time and resource usage, allowing you to pinpoint areas that may require optimization. By analyzing profiling data, you can make informed decisions about optimizing algorithms, improving database queries, and managing resources more effectively.

Finally, testing is an essential part of the development process when integrating Nim with web technologies. Ensuring that your application behaves as expected and handles various scenarios correctly requires thorough testing. Nim provides testing frameworks such as `unittest` that facilitate writing and running tests for your web application. Writing unit tests, integration tests, and end-to-end tests helps ensure that your application functions correctly and meets its requirements.

In conclusion, integrating Nim with web technologies involves a comprehensive understanding of HTTP servers, web frameworks, database interaction, authentication, error handling, performance optimization, and testing. By leveraging Nim's libraries and tools, you can build robust and efficient web applications that harness the power of Nim while addressing the complexities of web development.

When working with Nim for web development, it's crucial to understand how to effectively integrate it with various web technologies to build robust and scalable applications. Building on the previous discussions of HTTP servers, frameworks, and authentication, I now turn to the more nuanced aspects of client-side scripting, web services, and the overall architecture of web applications using Nim.

Client-side scripting is an essential part of modern web applications, allowing developers to create dynamic and interactive user interfaces. Although Nim itself is primarily a server-side language, it can be effectively used in conjunction with client-side technologies through WebAssembly. Nim's ability to compile to WebAssembly opens up possibilities for running Nim code directly in the browser, which can enhance client-side performance and interactivity.

To leverage Nim in the browser, you would typically use the `nim-web` library, which provides tools for compiling Nim code to WebAssembly. This approach involves writing Nim code that can be executed in the browser, interacting with JavaScript and the Document Object Model (DOM) to manipulate page content. The `nim-web` library facilitates this integration by allowing Nim to call JavaScript functions and handle browser events, bridging the gap between server-side logic and client-side behavior.

Incorporating WebAssembly into your web applications allows for performance improvements in scenarios where computationally intensive tasks are required. For instance, if your web application needs to perform complex calculations or process large datasets on the client side, leveraging Nim's performance advantages can lead to a more responsive and efficient user experience. It's important to manage the interactions between WebAssembly and JavaScript carefully, ensuring that data passed between the two is correctly handled and that performance overheads are minimized.

Interaction with web services is another critical area in web development, involving both consuming third-party APIs and exposing your own services. Nim provides several libraries for making HTTP requests and handling responses, such as `httpbeast` for HTTP server functionality and `httpclient` for client-side requests. When working with web services, you often need to handle JSON or XML data formats, which Nim supports through libraries like `json` and `xmltree`.

For example, when consuming a RESTful API, you might use `httpclient` to send GET or POST requests and receive JSON responses. Parsing these responses involves using the `json` library to convert the JSON data into Nim data structures. This process includes handling various data types and managing potential errors that might occur during data parsing or network communication. Proper error handling ensures that your application can gracefully manage issues such as network failures or invalid responses.

When exposing your own web services, you will often set up an HTTP server using Nim's `httpbeast` or `jester` frameworks. These frameworks enable you to define routes, handle incoming requests, and generate responses. For example, you might create a RESTful API endpoint that responds to GET requests by returning JSON data. Implementing such endpoints involves defining the appropriate route handlers and ensuring that your service adheres to best practices for API design, including proper status codes and data formatting.

Securing web services is paramount to ensure that data exchanged between clients and servers is protected. This involves implementing encryption protocols such as HTTPS to secure data in transit and applying authentication and authorization mechanisms to restrict access to sensitive endpoints. Nim's `httpbeast` and `jester` frameworks support HTTPS by configuring the server to use SSL/TLS certificates. Additionally, implementing token-based authentication, such as JWT (JSON Web Tokens), helps manage user sessions and protect endpoints from unauthorized access.

The overall architecture of a web application built with Nim involves considering both server-side and client-side components and ensuring that they work together seamlessly. This includes designing a well-structured application with clear separation of concerns, such as handling business logic, data access, and presentation. Good architectural practices ensure that your application is maintainable, scalable, and easy to extend with new features.

In a typical Nim web application, the server-side component handles business logic, data processing, and interaction with databases and external services. The client-side component, which may include WebAssembly or JavaScript, manages user interactions and updates the UI dynamically. Effective communication between these components is essential for creating a cohesive and functional web application. This involves defining clear interfaces and protocols for data exchange and ensuring that both sides adhere to these definitions.

Testing and debugging are also critical aspects of developing web applications. Ensuring that both server-side and client-side components function correctly and interact as expected requires comprehensive testing strategies. This includes writing unit tests for individual components, integration tests for interactions between components, and end-to-end tests for the entire application workflow. Nim's testing frameworks, such as `unittest`, facilitate the creation and execution of tests, helping you identify and fix issues early in the development process.

In conclusion, integrating Nim with web technologies involves a multifaceted approach that encompasses server-side logic, client-side scripting, web services, and application architecture. By leveraging Nim's capabilities and libraries, you can build efficient and scalable web applications that harness the strengths of both server-side and client-side processing. Ensuring that your application adheres to best practices in security, performance, and testing will help create a robust and reliable web solution.

Portability and Cross-Platform Development

Ensuring that Nim applications are portable across various platforms and operating systems is crucial for broadening their usability and market reach. In the realm of systems programming, where applications often need to run on different environments, the ability to write cross-platform code can significantly impact development efficiency and application performance. This discussion delves into strategies and techniques for achieving portability in Nim applications, focusing on writing code that is adaptable across diverse systems and handling platform-specific issues effectively.

To begin with, understanding Nim's design philosophy regarding portability is fundamental. Nim is inherently designed to be a cross-platform language, with its compiler supporting a variety of target platforms, including Windows, macOS, and Linux. However, achieving true portability involves more than just compiling code on different systems; it requires careful consideration of how code interacts with underlying operating systems and hardware.

One of the primary strategies for writing portable code in Nim is to minimize dependencies on platform-specific features. This means avoiding or abstracting away direct calls to operating system APIs or system libraries that may not be available or behave differently on other platforms. Instead, it is advisable to use cross-platform libraries and abstractions that provide a consistent interface across various operating systems.

Nim's standard library includes several modules designed with portability in mind. For example, modules like `os` and `strutils` provide cross-platform functionality for file operations, string manipulation, and other common tasks. By relying on these standard library modules, you ensure that your code adheres to a consistent interface that works uniformly across different platforms.

When dealing with external libraries or third-party dependencies, it is crucial to select those that support cross-platform development. Nim's package manager, Nimble, facilitates this by providing access to a range of libraries that are designed to be portable. It is beneficial to evaluate the portability of these libraries before incorporating them into your project, ensuring they meet your cross-platform requirements.

Another key aspect of cross-platform development is handling differences in file paths and directory structures. Different operating systems have distinct conventions for file paths, such as the use of forward slashes (`/`) versus backslashes (`\`). Nim provides mechanisms to abstract these differences through its `os` module, which includes functions for handling paths in a platform-independent manner. By using these functions, you can write code that constructs and manipulates file paths in a way that is compatible with various operating systems.

For applications that require network functionality, such as HTTP clients or servers, Nim's network libraries also support cross-platform development. Networking code can often be more challenging due to differences in network stack implementations and protocols across platforms. Nim's network libraries abstract these differences and provide a unified interface for network operations, making it easier to write portable networking code.

When developing cross-platform applications, it is also essential to address platform-specific issues that may arise. One common challenge is managing platform-specific configuration settings or build parameters. Nim's build system, which utilizes `.nimble` files, allows you to specify different configurations for various platforms. By defining platform-specific build options and conditional compilation flags, you can tailor your code to handle platform-specific quirks while maintaining a unified codebase.

Debugging and testing cross-platform code is another critical aspect of ensuring portability. It is important to test your application on all target platforms to identify and address any platform-specific issues that may not be apparent during development. Automated testing frameworks and continuous integration systems can help streamline this process by running tests across different platforms and environments.

Additionally, documentation plays a crucial role in cross-platform development. Providing clear and comprehensive documentation for your application's installation, configuration, and usage on different platforms helps users navigate any platform-specific considerations. This documentation should include instructions for building and running the application on various operating systems, as well as any known issues or limitations.

For advanced cross-platform development, Nim supports the use of conditional compilation to include or exclude code based on the target platform. This feature allows you to write platform-specific code sections that are only compiled when targeting a particular platform, helping to manage platform-specific differences while keeping the main codebase clean and maintainable.

In summary, achieving portability in Nim applications involves leveraging Nim's built-in support for cross-platform development, using portable libraries and abstractions, and addressing platform-specific issues through conditional compilation and configuration management. By adopting these strategies and thoroughly testing your applications across different platforms, you can ensure that your Nim code runs effectively and reliably on a wide range of operating systems, enhancing its usability and reach.

In delving deeper into strategies for cross-platform development with Nim, it is crucial to explore various techniques and best practices to ensure that applications maintain their functionality and performance across different environments. This section addresses additional aspects of cross-platform development, focusing on managing platform-specific features, optimizing code for different systems, and leveraging Nim's capabilities to enhance portability.

When working with platform-specific features, it is often necessary to include conditional code that caters to different operating systems or environments. Nim provides a way to handle this through its preprocessor directives, which allow developers to conditionally compile code based on the target platform. For instance, using the `when defined` construct enables you to include or exclude code blocks depending on the compilation target. This method ensures that platform-specific code is only compiled when necessary, reducing the risk of introducing errors or inconsistencies across platforms.

Another essential aspect of cross-platform development is managing system-specific dependencies and libraries. Different platforms may have varying requirements for external libraries or system services. To handle these dependencies gracefully, you can use Nim's package management system, Nimble, to manage and specify library dependencies in a way that is adaptable to different platforms. Nimble allows you to define platform-specific dependencies and configuration options within your `.nimble` file, making it easier to ensure that the correct libraries are used for each target environment.

Furthermore, understanding and addressing differences in system resources and performance characteristics is vital for optimizing cross-platform applications. Different operating systems and hardware configurations can exhibit varying performance characteristics, such as differences in memory management, CPU architecture, and I/O operations. To address these variations, it is important to profile your application on each target platform and identify performance bottlenecks or inefficiencies. Nim's profiling tools can assist in analyzing application performance and guiding optimizations specific to each platform, ensuring that the application runs efficiently across diverse environments.

Handling file and directory operations is another critical area where platform differences come into play. File paths, permissions, and directory structures can vary significantly between operating systems. Nim's standard library provides abstractions for file and directory operations that help mitigate these differences. By using functions from modules like `os` and `strutils`, you can manage file paths and perform operations in a way that is consistent with the underlying platform. For instance, functions for manipulating paths and handling file I/O are designed to accommodate platform-specific conventions, allowing your code to work seamlessly across different systems.

In cases where direct interaction with system APIs is required, such as for accessing hardware features or system-specific functionality, it is essential to encapsulate these interactions within platform-specific modules or abstractions. By isolating system-specific code in dedicated modules, you can reduce the complexity of your main codebase and make it easier to maintain and extend. This approach also facilitates testing and debugging, as you can focus on platform-specific issues within their respective modules without affecting the rest of the application.

Networking code often presents additional challenges for cross-platform development due to variations in network stack implementations and protocols across different operating systems. Nim's network libraries offer abstractions that help manage these differences by providing a consistent interface for network operations. Utilizing these libraries allows you to write networking code that functions correctly regardless of the underlying platform. However, it is still important to test network-related functionality on all target platforms to ensure compatibility and performance.

Another consideration in cross-platform development is handling user interface (UI) elements and interactions. When developing graphical applications or user interfaces, it is necessary to account for differences in UI frameworks and conventions across platforms. Nim supports various UI libraries and frameworks, some of which are specifically designed to be cross-platform. By choosing libraries that offer consistent UI components and behavior across different systems, you can create applications with a unified look and feel while addressing platform-specific nuances.

In addition to managing platform-specific code and dependencies, thorough testing and quality assurance are crucial for ensuring portability. Automated testing frameworks can help in validating the functionality of your application across different platforms by running a suite of tests on each target environment. Continuous integration systems further enhance this process by automating the build and testing of your application on multiple platforms, ensuring that any issues are identified and addressed promptly.

Finally, documentation plays a significant role in cross-platform development. Providing detailed documentation on how to build, configure, and run your application on different platforms helps users and developers understand and navigate any platform-specific requirements or issues. Clear instructions on platform-specific setup, as well as information on known limitations or considerations, contribute to a smoother user experience and reduce the likelihood of encountering unexpected problems.

By employing these strategies and practices, you can effectively manage the complexities of cross-platform development and ensure that your Nim applications perform reliably and efficiently across a variety of operating systems and environments.

When extending the discussion on ensuring portability in Nim applications, it is essential to delve into the practical aspects of cross-platform development, focusing on various approaches for managing and optimizing platform-specific features and interactions.

One critical aspect of cross-platform development is handling system-specific APIs and libraries. Nim's ability to interface with external libraries through its Foreign Function Interface (FFI) is a powerful feature that facilitates interaction with native code written in C, C++, or other languages. To achieve portability, it is important to encapsulate FFI calls within conditional code blocks that target specific platforms. By abstracting these calls into platform-specific modules, you can isolate platform-dependent logic from the rest of your application, making it easier to maintain and test. For instance, you might have a module that contains FFI declarations and implementation for Windows-specific APIs and another for Unix-like systems, allowing your main application logic to remain platform-agnostic.

Furthermore, error handling and debugging across different platforms can present unique challenges. Each operating system may have different error codes and debugging tools, so it is vital to include platform-specific error handling routines that can translate or adapt error messages and diagnostic information accordingly. Implementing robust logging mechanisms that provide detailed context and can be tailored for different platforms will aid in diagnosing issues effectively. Leveraging Nim's built-in support for various logging libraries and integrating them with platform-specific error handling practices will enhance your ability to troubleshoot and resolve issues in a cross-platform environment.

Another important consideration is ensuring compatibility with different file systems and storage mechanisms. File operations such as reading from and writing to files, managing directories, and handling file permissions can vary between operating systems. Nim's standard library offers abstractions that simplify file and directory manipulations, but it is important to test these operations thoroughly on each target platform. For example, file path delimiters differ between Windows and Unix-based systems, so using Nim's cross-platform path manipulation functions will help ensure consistency across environments.

In the context of networking, managing platform-specific networking stack variations is crucial. While Nim provides abstractions for networking tasks, such as HTTP requests and socket operations, these abstractions may behave differently depending on the platform. To address this, testing network-related functionality on all target platforms is essential. Additionally, considering variations in network protocol implementations and handling platform-specific nuances in network configuration and behavior will contribute to a more robust and portable application.

Developing graphical user interfaces (GUIs) introduces its own set of challenges for cross-platform compatibility. Different operating systems have distinct UI frameworks and conventions, which can affect the appearance and behavior of your application's interface. Nim supports various GUI libraries, some of which are designed to be cross-platform, providing a consistent UI experience across different systems. It is important to choose libraries that are well-maintained and actively supported, ensuring that they handle platform-specific quirks effectively. Additionally, testing the application's UI on different platforms to verify consistent behavior and appearance is a crucial step in the development process.

To further enhance portability, consider adopting a modular approach in your application's architecture. By organizing your code into modular components that can be individually tested and adapted for different platforms, you can streamline the development process and simplify the management of platform-specific functionality. This approach not only aids in maintaining a clean and organized codebase but also facilitates easier updates and enhancements in response to changes in platform requirements.

Cross-platform development also involves addressing differences in runtime environments and system resources. Variations in available memory, CPU performance, and hardware capabilities can impact your application's performance. Profiling and optimizing your application for different platforms can help identify performance bottlenecks and ensure that your application runs efficiently across a range of systems. Nim's profiling tools and performance analysis capabilities are valuable assets in this process, enabling you to gather performance metrics and make informed optimizations.

Documentation is another vital aspect of cross-platform development. Providing comprehensive documentation that details how to build, configure, and run your application on various platforms will greatly benefit users and developers. Including platform-specific setup instructions, known limitations, and troubleshooting tips will help users navigate any challenges they may encounter and contribute to a smoother experience.

Finally, maintaining a robust testing strategy is crucial for ensuring portability. Automated testing frameworks that can execute tests across different platforms will help ensure that your application behaves consistently and correctly in various environments. Continuous integration and deployment systems that support cross-platform testing will further enhance your ability to detect and address issues early in the development cycle.

By employing these practices and techniques, you can effectively manage the complexities of cross-platform development with Nim, ensuring that your applications remain portable, reliable, and performant across a diverse range of operating systems and environments.

Building and Managing Projects

In navigating the landscape of Nim development, structuring and managing projects efficiently is crucial for maintaining productivity and ensuring code quality. This discussion delves into the methodologies and tools available within the Nim ecosystem to facilitate effective project management, focusing on structuring projects, managing build processes, and leveraging package management tools.

When starting with Nim, the organization of a project significantly impacts its maintainability and scalability. A well-structured project typically includes a clear directory layout, separating concerns and modularizing functionality. For instance, placing source code in a dedicated `src` directory helps isolate application logic from configuration files, documentation, and other auxiliary materials. Within the `src` directory, it is often beneficial to further organize code into subdirectories based on functionality or domain, which aligns with principles of modular design and encapsulation. This organization not only aids in managing complex codebases but also facilitates easier navigation and understanding of the project structure.

To ensure a smooth development workflow, Nim's build system plays a pivotal role. The `nim` command-line tool provides a robust mechanism for compiling and managing Nim code. The `nim c` command compiles source files into executable binaries, while `nim build` offers additional functionality for managing build configurations and dependencies. It is prudent to utilize the `nim.cfg` file to define build settings and compiler options, allowing for customized build processes that cater to the specific needs of the project. This configuration file can specify compiler flags, linker options, and paths to include directories, among other settings, thereby streamlining the build process and ensuring consistency across different environments.

Effective project management also involves handling dependencies and external libraries. Nim's package manager, Nimble, is instrumental in managing these dependencies. By defining dependencies in the `nimble` file, you can specify external packages required by your project, including their versions and sources. This file also allows you to configure project metadata, such as the project name, description, and author, which facilitates better project documentation and sharing. Using `nimble` to install and update packages ensures that your project remains aligned with the latest versions of external libraries, minimizing compatibility issues and leveraging the latest improvements.

Managing build processes efficiently often involves addressing platform-specific requirements and configurations. Nim's cross-platform capabilities necessitate handling different build configurations for various operating systems. This can be managed through conditional compilation and platform-specific code blocks within your source files. For example, using `when defined(Windows)` or `when defined(Linux)` allows for platform-specific code paths, ensuring that your application behaves correctly regardless of the underlying operating system. This approach minimizes the need for extensive modifications when porting your application across different platforms, thus enhancing its portability and ease of maintenance.

In addition to structuring and managing code, version control is a fundamental aspect of project management. Utilizing version control systems such as Git allows for tracking changes, collaborating with team members, and managing different versions of your project. Incorporating a `.gitignore` file to exclude unnecessary files from version control, such as build artifacts and temporary files, helps maintain a clean repository. Regular commits and clear commit messages facilitate better collaboration and documentation of changes, while branching strategies enable parallel development and experimentation without disrupting the main codebase.

Testing is another critical component of project management, ensuring that your code performs as expected and meets quality standards. Nim supports various testing frameworks, including its built-in `unittest` module, which allows for writing and executing unit tests to validate individual components of your application. Integrating testing into your build process, through tools like Nim's `test` command or continuous integration systems, helps identify issues early and maintains code quality throughout the development cycle. Establishing a comprehensive testing strategy that includes unit tests, integration tests, and end-to-end tests ensures that your application remains robust and reliable.

Documentation is an integral part of managing projects, providing essential information about the project's structure, usage, and development process. Including documentation files such as README.md and CONTRIBUTING.md helps communicate the purpose and usage of your project to other developers and users. Documenting build instructions, configuration settings, and any platform-specific considerations ensures that others can easily set up and contribute to your project. Additionally, generating API documentation using tools like Nim's `doc` command provides detailed information about your code's functionality and usage, further aiding in project maintenance and collaboration.

Effective project management also involves monitoring and optimizing performance throughout the development lifecycle. Nim provides profiling and benchmarking tools that help identify performance bottlenecks and optimize resource usage. Regularly profiling your application and addressing performance issues ensures that it operates efficiently and meets performance requirements.

In summary, managing Nim projects effectively requires a combination of good practices in structuring code, managing builds, handling dependencies, and maintaining documentation. By leveraging Nim's tools and adhering to these principles, you can ensure that your projects remain organized, maintainable, and efficient, ultimately contributing to successful and productive development efforts.

When delving deeper into managing Nim projects, it's important to address the intricacies of dependency management and version control, which are crucial for maintaining a stable and scalable development environment. Nimble, the package manager for Nim, plays a significant role in this process. It simplifies the task of managing external libraries and dependencies, which can otherwise become a complex challenge as projects grow.

The `nimble` file, central to Nimble's functionality, allows you to declare dependencies and configure project settings in a straightforward manner. By specifying dependencies in this file, you can easily integrate third-party libraries into your project. Nimble ensures that these dependencies are installed and updated consistently across different development environments. It's essential to manage these dependencies carefully to avoid conflicts and ensure compatibility. For instance, you might specify exact versions of libraries to ensure that your project remains compatible with the dependencies it relies upon. This approach helps in avoiding the issues that can arise from updates or changes in external libraries that might introduce breaking changes or unexpected behavior.

To effectively manage build processes in Nim, understanding the build configuration options is crucial. The `nim.cfg` file provides a flexible way to customize the build process by specifying compiler flags, include paths, and other configuration settings. This file can be tailored to suit different build environments, such as development, testing, and production. By setting up separate configurations for these environments, you can optimize the build process for specific needs, such as enabling debugging information for development or optimizing for performance in production.

Furthermore, addressing platform-specific issues is a key aspect of building cross-platform applications. Nim's support for conditional compilation allows you to write code that adapts to different operating systems or hardware architectures. By using constructs such as `when defined(Windows)` or `when defined(Linux)`, you can include or exclude code based on the target platform. This technique is invaluable when dealing with platform-specific features or APIs, ensuring that your application remains functional across diverse environments.

Handling platform-specific configurations also extends to managing different toolchains and build environments. For example, when targeting different operating systems, you might need to configure different compiler options or link against different libraries. Nim's ability to interface with native system libraries and tools is a powerful feature, but it requires careful management to ensure compatibility and performance. Setting up automated build processes using continuous integration tools can help streamline this process, allowing you to test your application across multiple platforms and configurations with minimal manual intervention.

Version control systems, such as Git, are indispensable for managing changes and collaborating on projects. Incorporating Git into your development workflow enables you to track changes, manage branches, and handle merge conflicts effectively. It is essential to establish a consistent branching strategy, such as Git Flow or trunk-based development, to streamline collaboration and manage feature development. Additionally, using meaningful commit messages and regularly committing changes helps maintain a clear project history, making it easier to track progress and identify issues.

A well-maintained `.gitignore` file is crucial for managing which files and directories are excluded from version control. This file typically includes entries for build artifacts, temporary files, and other non-essential files that should not be tracked by Git. By keeping the repository clean and focused on source code and essential resources, you ensure that version control remains effective and manageable.

Testing and quality assurance are integral to effective project management. Integrating testing frameworks into your development process ensures that your code remains robust and reliable. Nim's built-in testing capabilities, along with third-party testing libraries, provide various options for writing and executing tests. Automated testing, combined with continuous integration practices, helps catch issues early and ensures that new changes do not introduce regressions.

Documentation is another critical aspect of project management. Clear and comprehensive documentation helps onboard new developers, facilitates collaboration, and provides valuable information about the project's structure and usage. Documenting your project's setup, configuration, and usage instructions, as well as providing API documentation for your code, enhances its accessibility and usability. Tools like Nim's `doc` command can generate detailed API documentation, which is especially useful for larger projects with extensive public interfaces.

As projects evolve, performance tuning and optimization become increasingly important. Profiling tools and benchmarks can help identify performance bottlenecks and areas for improvement. Regularly profiling your application and analyzing performance metrics enable you to address issues proactively and ensure that your application remains efficient and responsive.

In summary, managing Nim projects effectively involves a multifaceted approach, encompassing project structuring, dependency management, build process optimization, and version control. By leveraging Nimble for dependency management, configuring build processes with `nim.cfg`, and addressing platform-specific considerations, you can streamline development and ensure cross-platform compatibility. Integrating version control, testing practices, and thorough documentation further enhances project management, facilitating collaboration and maintaining code quality. These practices collectively contribute to the successful development and maintenance of Nim applications, supporting long-term project sustainability and efficiency.

Effective project management in the Nim ecosystem extends beyond the initial setup and into ongoing maintenance and optimization. As projects grow, the need for systematic organization and efficient management becomes even more critical. To manage complex Nim projects efficiently, adopting best practices in project structure, build processes, and tool usage is essential.

Organizing a Nim project involves more than just laying out files and directories. It requires creating a clear and logical structure that facilitates development, testing, and deployment. For instance, a well-organized project might separate source code from test cases and documentation, ensuring that each component is easy to locate and manage. Typically, the source code resides in a `src` directory, with individual modules and packages neatly organized within. Tests are often placed in a `tests` directory, following a similar structure to the source code to mirror the organization of functionality. Documentation files, such as README files and API documentation, should be in a `docs` directory, providing a centralized location for project-related information.

Utilizing Nim's package manager, Nimble, is vital for managing dependencies and facilitating development. Nimble supports creating and managing project-specific dependencies through a `nimble` file, which specifies the packages required for the project. By defining dependencies explicitly in this file, you ensure that all necessary libraries are available and up-to-date across different development environments. Additionally, Nimble provides commands for updating dependencies, installing packages, and managing version constraints. Using these commands effectively helps maintain a consistent and reliable development environment, reducing the risk of compatibility issues.

Build processes are another crucial aspect of project management. Nim's build system relies on the `nim` compiler and `nim.cfg` configuration file. The `nim.cfg` file allows you to specify compiler options, include paths, and other settings tailored to different build scenarios. For example, you might configure separate settings for development, testing, and production builds, adjusting optimizations and debugging options as needed. Ensuring that the build process is well-configured and efficient can significantly impact the performance and stability of the final application.

As projects become more complex, automation becomes increasingly important. Automating build and deployment processes through scripts or continuous integration (CI) systems streamlines development and ensures consistency. Setting up CI pipelines can automate tasks such as building, testing, and deploying applications, allowing for rapid feedback on changes and ensuring that issues are detected early. CI tools can also handle cross-platform builds, running tests on different operating systems to ensure compatibility and stability.

Managing platform-specific issues requires a nuanced approach. While Nim's conditional compilation features allow for platform-specific code inclusion or exclusion, handling different environments often involves additional configuration. For instance, you might need to specify different compiler flags or link against different libraries depending on the target platform. Automated build scripts and configuration management tools can help manage these variations, ensuring that your application builds and functions correctly across all supported platforms.

Version control is indispensable for managing code changes and facilitating collaboration. Using a version control system like Git helps track changes, manage branches, and coordinate work among team members. Establishing a clear branching strategy, such as feature branching or Git Flow, supports organized development and enables effective management of new features, bug fixes, and releases. Regularly committing changes with descriptive messages and conducting code reviews further ensures code quality and coherence.

In addition to version control, managing project artifacts and dependencies effectively is crucial for maintaining project integrity. This involves handling build outputs, temporary files, and other artifacts that should not be included in version control. A `.gitignore` file helps specify which files and directories to exclude, keeping the repository clean and focused on essential source code and configuration files.

Testing and quality assurance are integral components of effective project management. Incorporating automated testing into the development workflow helps ensure that code changes do not introduce new issues. Nim's testing framework supports writing unit tests and integration tests, providing mechanisms to verify the correctness and functionality of the code. Integrating these tests into the build process, using continuous integration tools, helps catch issues early and ensures that the application remains reliable and robust.

Documentation is also a key aspect of project management, particularly for larger projects or those involving multiple contributors. Providing clear and comprehensive documentation helps onboard new developers, facilitates collaboration, and ensures that the project's goals and usage are well-understood. Documentation should include setup instructions, API references, and usage examples, contributing to the overall accessibility and maintainability of the project.

Maintaining and optimizing a Nim project requires ongoing attention to detail, organization, and best practices. By structuring projects effectively, utilizing Nimble for dependency management, configuring build processes thoughtfully, and leveraging automation and version control, you can manage complex Nim projects efficiently. Additionally, addressing platform-specific issues, incorporating testing and quality assurance, and maintaining thorough documentation contribute to the overall success and sustainability of the project. This comprehensive approach to project management ensures that Nim applications remain well-organized, reliable, and adaptable throughout their lifecycle.

Testing and Debugging Techniques

Testing and debugging form the backbone of producing reliable and high-quality software. In the context of Nim, these processes are essential for ensuring that applications function correctly and efficiently. To achieve this, it is imperative to understand and apply various testing methodologies and debugging techniques specific to the Nim ecosystem.

When beginning with testing, it is crucial to recognize the different levels of testing that contribute to overall software quality. Unit testing is a fundamental practice that involves testing individual components or functions in isolation. In Nim, unit testing is facilitated by the built-in `unittest` module, which provides a straightforward framework for writing and executing tests. Each test is typically defined within a `test` block, allowing developers to assert expected outcomes and validate that their code behaves as intended.

Writing effective unit tests involves defining test cases that cover a range of scenarios, including typical use cases, edge cases, and error conditions. For example, when testing a function that performs calculations, you would include tests for both normal and boundary values to ensure accuracy across all potential inputs. Additionally, using descriptive names for test cases and providing clear assertions helps in understanding the purpose of each test and identifying issues when they arise.

Integration testing, on the other hand, focuses on verifying that different components of the application work together as expected. This type of testing often involves combining multiple units or modules to test their interactions and ensure they function cohesively. In Nim, integration tests can be written using the same `unittest` module, but they typically involve setting up more complex scenarios and verifying the overall system's behavior. Integration tests are particularly important for identifying issues that may not be evident during unit testing, such as problems with data flow or interactions between modules.

Beyond writing tests, utilizing debugging techniques is crucial for diagnosing and resolving issues in Nim applications. Nim offers several debugging tools that can aid in identifying and fixing problems. One of the primary tools is the `gdb` debugger, which is commonly used for debugging applications written in C and C++ but can also be applied to Nim programs. Integrating `gdb` with Nim involves compiling the code with debugging symbols enabled, typically using the `-d:nodebug` flag, and then running the program through `gdb` to set breakpoints, inspect variables, and step through the code.

Another valuable tool in the Nim ecosystem is `Nim's own debugging facilities`, which provide a more Nim-centric approach to debugging. These facilities include features such as `echo` statements for printing variable values and `assert` statements for verifying conditions during runtime.

While these methods are less formal than using dedicated debuggers, they can be incredibly effective for quickly diagnosing issues and understanding the program's state.

In addition to traditional debugging methods, leveraging logging can provide significant insights into the application's behavior. Implementing logging allows you to capture detailed information about the program's execution, including variable values, function calls, and error messages. Nim supports various logging libraries that facilitate this process, enabling you to configure different log levels, such as `info`, `warn`, and `error`, to capture relevant information. Properly managing log output and reviewing logs systematically can help identify patterns, track down issues, and understand the application's behavior in different scenarios.

Moreover, Nim's type system and compile-time checks can serve as valuable debugging aids. By utilizing Nim's strong typing and compile-time assertions, you can catch certain types of errors early in the development process. For example, type mismatches and invalid operations are often detected at compile time, reducing the likelihood of runtime errors and improving overall code reliability. Embracing these features and designing your code with strong typing in mind can lead to fewer bugs and more maintainable software.

As applications grow in complexity, maintaining test coverage becomes increasingly important. Comprehensive test coverage ensures that all critical parts of the application are tested and that potential issues are identified early. Tools like `coverage` can help analyze test coverage, providing insights into which parts of the code are exercised by tests and which are not. By regularly reviewing and improving test coverage, you can enhance the reliability of your code and reduce the likelihood of undetected issues.

In summary, effective testing and debugging are vital for

producing robust and reliable Nim applications. By employing a combination of unit testing, integration testing, debugging tools, and logging, you can systematically identify and address issues in your code. Leveraging Nim's debugging facilities and type system further aids in catching errors early and ensuring the correctness of your software. With a comprehensive approach to testing and debugging, you can achieve a high level of confidence in your application's functionality and performance.

To advance the discussion on testing and debugging, it is essential to delve deeper into various methodologies and techniques that play a crucial role in ensuring software reliability. Testing is not only about writing tests but also about adopting a strategic approach to cover different aspects of an application. This approach involves utilizing both manual and automated testing methods to validate the functionality and performance of Nim applications.

Manual testing, though often less favored due to its labor-intensive nature, remains an important component of the testing strategy. It involves the actual execution of the software to uncover defects that automated tests might miss. Manual testing is particularly useful in exploratory testing scenarios where testers use their intuition and experience to discover unexpected issues. This type of testing can complement automated tests by addressing edge cases and ensuring that the application behaves correctly in real-world scenarios.

Automated testing, on the other hand, leverages tools and frameworks to execute predefined tests automatically. In the Nim ecosystem, automated testing is facilitated by tools that integrate with the `unittest` module. Automated tests can be classified into various types, including unit tests, integration tests, and end-to-end tests. Each type serves a specific purpose and contributes to the overall quality assurance process.

Unit tests, as previously discussed, focus on individual components or functions. However, to create effective unit tests, it is crucial to follow best practices such as test isolation and determinism. Test isolation ensures that each test is independent of others, preventing side effects from one test affecting another. This isolation is achieved by mocking dependencies and using test-specific data. Determinism refers to the ability of a test to produce consistent results every time it is run, which is crucial for reliable test outcomes.

Integration tests, while broader in scope, require careful planning to cover interactions between components. These tests often involve setting up a more complex environment, such as databases or external services, to simulate real-world conditions. When writing integration tests in Nim, it is essential to use fixtures and setup/teardown methods to prepare the environment and clean up afterward. This preparation ensures that tests run in a controlled and repeatable manner, providing accurate results.

End-to-end tests encompass the entire application workflow, validating that all components work together as expected from the user's perspective. These tests often involve simulating user interactions with the application and verifying the expected outcomes. In Nim, end-to-end testing can be achieved using external tools and frameworks that interact with the application's user interface or APIs. Integrating these tests into the continuous integration pipeline ensures that they are executed regularly, helping to identify issues early in the development process.

Debugging, as a complementary practice to testing, involves identifying and resolving issues that arise during the execution of the software. Effective debugging requires a systematic approach, starting with the reproduction of the issue. Reproducing the issue involves understanding the conditions under which it occurs and creating a controlled environment to observe its behavior. This process often involves analyzing logs, reviewing error messages, and using debugging tools to pinpoint the root cause.

One of the primary tools for debugging in Nim is the built-in `gdb` debugger. `Gdb` allows developers to set breakpoints, inspect variables, and step through the code to understand its execution flow. When using `gdb`, it is essential to compile the Nim code with debugging symbols enabled to provide detailed information during the debugging session. By setting breakpoints at strategic locations in the code, developers can pause execution and examine the state of the application, making it easier to identify issues and understand their origins.

In addition to `gdb`, Nim provides debugging facilities that are integrated with the language. For instance, using `echo` statements allows developers to print variable values and track the execution flow. While `echo` statements are less formal than using dedicated debuggers, they can be a quick and effective way to gain insights into the application's behavior during development.

Another important aspect of debugging is the use of assertions. Assertions are statements that check whether a condition holds true during runtime. In Nim, assertions can be used to validate assumptions and detect discrepancies early. For example, an assertion might be used to ensure that a function returns the expected result or that a variable falls within a certain range. When assertions fail, they provide immediate feedback and help identify issues that might otherwise go unnoticed.

As software complexity increases, maintaining an effective debugging strategy becomes more critical. Leveraging advanced debugging techniques, such as conditional breakpoints and watchpoints, can provide deeper insights into complex issues. Conditional breakpoints allow developers to pause execution only when specific conditions are met, while watchpoints monitor changes to variables and trigger actions when they occur.

In summary, effective testing and debugging are integral to producing reliable Nim applications. By employing a combination of manual and automated testing, developers can ensure comprehensive coverage and address various aspects of the application. Debugging techniques, including the use of `gdb`, integrated debugging facilities, and assertions, play a crucial role in identifying and resolving issues. Adopting a systematic approach to both testing and debugging contributes to higher software quality and a more robust development process.

To address the advanced aspects of testing and debugging, it is crucial to delve into how these methodologies can be employed effectively within Nim's development environment. A nuanced understanding of testing frameworks and debugging strategies enhances our ability to maintain high software quality, ensuring that the applications we develop are both robust and resilient to faults.

One of the key strategies in advanced testing is the use of property-based testing. Unlike traditional unit tests, which check specific inputs and outputs, property-based tests are designed to validate properties or invariants that should hold true for a wide range of inputs. In Nim, property-based testing can be facilitated using libraries that allow for the generation of random test cases. This technique can uncover edge cases and unexpected issues that might not be apparent through conventional testing methods. By defining properties that should always be true and letting the testing framework generate diverse inputs, we can enhance the thoroughness of our test suite and improve confidence in the correctness of our code.

Another significant practice is test-driven development (TDD). TDD involves writing tests before implementing the actual code. This approach not only ensures that the code fulfills the requirements but also drives the design of the software. In Nim, adopting TDD involves writing initial failing tests that define the expected behavior of the code. Once these tests are in place, developers write the minimal amount of code necessary to pass the tests, followed by refactoring to improve the code's structure while ensuring that the tests continue to pass. This iterative process helps in building a comprehensive test suite that guides development and maintains high code quality.

Integration testing, while broader than unit testing, requires careful management of dependencies and interactions between various components. In Nim, integration tests often involve setting up a realistic environment that mimics production conditions. This setup can include initializing databases, configuring network services, and populating data sources. Effective integration testing also involves handling test data and ensuring that tests do not interfere with each other. For example, using database transactions that are rolled back after each test can prevent test data from persisting across test runs. Additionally, employing techniques such as dependency injection can help in isolating components and managing their interactions more effectively.

Debugging strategies are deeply intertwined with testing practices, as the insights gained from debugging can inform improvements in the testing approach. Beyond traditional debugging tools like `gdb`, which are invaluable for stepping through code and inspecting variables, Nim developers can leverage more advanced techniques to streamline the debugging process. For instance, integrating logging into the application can provide valuable runtime insights that aid in diagnosing issues. Effective logging involves not only recording error messages but also capturing contextual information, such as the state of relevant variables and the sequence of operations leading up to an issue.

Advanced debugging techniques, such as the use of profiling tools, can also provide deeper insights into performance-related issues. Profiling involves measuring various aspects of application performance, such as execution time and memory usage, to identify bottlenecks and optimize resource utilization. In Nim, profiling tools can help identify parts of the code that consume excessive resources, enabling targeted optimizations. By analyzing profiling data, developers can make informed decisions about where to focus their optimization efforts and how to address performance issues effectively.

Another important consideration in debugging is handling asynchronous operations and concurrency. As applications become more complex, they often involve multiple threads or asynchronous tasks that can complicate debugging. Techniques such as logging thread activity and using synchronization primitives to manage concurrent operations are crucial for diagnosing issues in multi-threaded environments. In Nim, leveraging concurrency primitives and ensuring proper synchronization can help avoid common pitfalls such as race conditions and deadlocks.

Finally, continuous integration and continuous deployment (CI/CD) pipelines play a critical role in maintaining software quality. By integrating automated tests into the CI/CD pipeline, we can ensure that tests are run frequently and consistently, catching issues early in the development process. CI/CD tools can automatically execute tests whenever code changes are committed, providing immediate feedback and facilitating rapid identification of issues. This integration fosters a proactive approach to testing and debugging, aligning with best practices for maintaining high-quality software.

In conclusion, effective testing and debugging in Nim involve a combination of traditional methods and advanced practices. By employing property-based testing, embracing test-driven development, and managing integration tests with care, we can enhance the reliability of our applications. Debugging techniques, including advanced tools and strategies for handling concurrency, contribute to identifying and resolving issues efficiently. Integrating these practices into a robust CI/CD pipeline further supports ongoing software quality and resilience. Through a comprehensive approach to testing and debugging, we can ensure that our Nim applications meet high standards of performance and reliability.

Leveraging Nim's Standard Library

Nim's standard library stands as a testament to its design philosophy of providing a comprehensive toolkit for a wide range of programming tasks. It encompasses a rich collection of modules and functions that significantly ease the development process by offering pre-built solutions to common programming problems. This discussion delves into the most useful components of Nim's standard library, focusing on data structures, algorithms, and utility functions. By exploring these features, we can streamline development and enhance code efficiency and readability.

A cornerstone of Nim's standard library is its robust set of data structures. The library provides a variety of collections, including arrays, sequences, sets, and tables, each serving specific needs and use cases. For instance, sequences in Nim are dynamic arrays that automatically adjust their size, making them ideal for situations where the number of elements is not known in advance. Sequences are implemented efficiently and provide operations such as appending, inserting, and deleting elements, which are crucial for many dynamic applications. The sequence module also includes powerful functions for sorting, filtering, and transforming data, thus facilitating complex data manipulation tasks with minimal effort.

In addition to sequences, Nim's standard library includes sets, which are unordered collections of unique elements. Sets are particularly useful when the primary requirement is to maintain a collection of distinct items, such as in scenarios involving membership testing or eliminating duplicates. The set operations provided—such as union, intersection, and difference—enable efficient set-based computations, which are common in various algorithmic problems. The implementation of sets in Nim is optimized for performance, offering constant-time complexity for most operations, making it a reliable choice for handling large datasets.

Dictionaries, or tables, are another crucial data structure provided by the standard library. These collections map keys to values, allowing for fast lookups, insertions, and deletions. The table module supports various types of keys and values, including user-defined types, and offers a range of functionalities for managing mappings. By leveraging the table module, developers can efficiently manage associative data and implement complex algorithms that rely on key-value associations.

Nim's standard library also offers a wide array of algorithms and utilities that can be utilized to address common programming challenges. Among these, the sorting algorithms stand out as particularly valuable. The library includes implementations for various sorting techniques, including quicksort, mergesort, and heapsort. These algorithms are designed to handle different types of data and performance requirements, enabling developers to choose the most suitable sorting method for their specific needs. The ability to sort data efficiently is essential for many applications, from data analysis to optimizing search operations.

Beyond sorting, the standard library provides a comprehensive suite of algorithms for searching and manipulating data. For example, functions for binary search enable fast retrieval of elements in sorted collections, while algorithms for finding minimum and maximum values assist in determining the boundaries of datasets. Additionally, the library includes algorithms for transforming and aggregating data, such as mapping functions and reductions, which simplify the process of processing and analyzing data in bulk.

Utility functions are another important aspect of the standard library, offering essential tools for various programming tasks. Functions for handling strings, such as pattern matching, parsing, and formatting, are included, which facilitate the manipulation of textual data. The string module provides methods for searching, splitting, and replacing substrings, as well as for converting between different string representations. These functions are vital for tasks involving data extraction, transformation, and presentation.

File and directory manipulation is another area where the standard library excels. The file module provides functions for reading, writing, and managing files, while the directory module offers tools for navigating and manipulating directory structures. These modules simplify the process of working with files and directories, handling tasks such as file I/O operations, file path manipulation, and directory traversal.

Furthermore, the standard library includes modules for handling various system-related tasks, such as interacting with the operating system, managing processes, and working with networking protocols. These modules provide high-level abstractions for performing common system operations, allowing developers to focus on application logic rather than dealing with low-level system details.

To effectively leverage Nim's standard library, it is crucial to understand the documentation and the best practices for using these tools. The standard library documentation provides detailed information about the available modules, their functions, and their usage. By familiarizing oneself with this documentation, developers can make informed decisions about which components to use and how to integrate them into their projects.

In conclusion, Nim's standard library is a powerful resource that offers a wide range of data structures, algorithms, and utility functions designed to streamline development and enhance productivity. By utilizing these built-in features, developers can tackle various programming challenges more efficiently and build robust, high-quality applications. Understanding and effectively leveraging the standard library is essential for maximizing the capabilities of Nim and achieving successful software development outcomes.

The standard library in Nim extends its capabilities to encompass a wide array of modules that facilitate the development process by providing pre-built solutions for common programming tasks. One of the standout features of this library is its comprehensive set of data structures. These include sequences, sets, and tables, each of which serves a unique purpose and provides specific functionalities that are essential for various applications.

Sequences, for example, are dynamic arrays that are crucial for scenarios where the size of the array may change during execution. They offer the flexibility to add or remove elements as needed, which is particularly useful for handling collections of data whose size is not predetermined. In Nim, sequences are not only easy to work with but are also equipped with a host of methods for managing and manipulating the data they hold. Operations such as appending, inserting, or deleting elements are efficiently handled, ensuring that developers can focus on implementing functionality rather than managing data storage intricacies.

The library's implementation of sets is another vital component, offering an unordered collection of unique elements. Sets are highly efficient for operations that require checking membership or ensuring the uniqueness of elements within a collection. The set data structure supports fundamental operations such as union, intersection, and difference, which are essential for many algorithmic applications. The constant-time complexity for these operations makes sets an excellent choice for tasks that involve large datasets where performance is a critical consideration.

Tables, or dictionaries, provided by the standard library offer a way to map keys to values, which is indispensable for managing associative data. They enable quick lookups, insertions, and deletions, facilitating efficient management of key-value pairs. The flexibility of tables is demonstrated through their support for various key and value types, including user-defined types. This versatility allows developers to implement complex data structures and algorithms with ease, leveraging the efficiency of hash-based lookups for rapid data retrieval.

Beyond data structures, the standard library includes a robust set of algorithms and utilities that enhance the development process. Sorting algorithms, such as quicksort, mergesort, and heapsort, are available and tailored to handle different performance needs and data types. The ability to choose an appropriate sorting method based on the context allows developers to optimize performance and handle data efficiently. Similarly, searching algorithms, including binary search, facilitate quick data retrieval from sorted collections, further supporting the need for efficient data handling in applications.

The utility functions provided by the standard library are equally important, encompassing a range of functionalities that simplify common programming tasks. String manipulation functions, such as pattern matching, parsing, and formatting, are crucial for handling textual data. The string module offers a suite of methods for working with strings, including searching for substrings, splitting strings, and replacing text. These capabilities are fundamental for tasks such as data extraction, transformation, and presentation, making string handling in Nim both powerful and straightforward.

File and directory operations are another area where the standard library excels. The file module allows for comprehensive management of file operations, including reading from and writing to files. It provides functionalities for handling file paths, opening files in different modes, and performing file I/O operations efficiently. The directory module complements this by offering tools for navigating and manipulating directories, such as creating, deleting, or listing files and directories. These utilities simplify the process of working with file systems, which is essential for applications that involve data storage and retrieval.

The standard library also addresses system-level tasks through its modules, which provide high-level abstractions for interacting with the operating system. This includes managing processes, handling networking protocols, and performing system-level operations. These modules abstract away the complexities of low-level system interactions, allowing developers to focus on higher-level application logic while relying on the library to manage system-specific details.

Leveraging Nim's standard library effectively requires a thorough understanding of its documentation and functionalities. The documentation provides detailed descriptions of the available modules, their functions, and their intended use cases. Familiarity with this documentation is crucial for selecting the right tools for a given task and for integrating them into your projects effectively. By mastering the standard library, developers can streamline their workflow, reduce the need for custom implementations, and build robust, efficient applications with ease.

In summary, Nim's standard library offers a wealth of features designed to support a wide range of programming needs. From versatile data structures and efficient algorithms to powerful utility functions and system-level abstractions, the library provides essential tools that enhance development productivity. By understanding and utilizing these components, developers can leverage the full potential of Nim, streamline their development process, and create high-quality software solutions.

One of the most compelling aspects of Nim's standard library is its support for concurrent programming, which is increasingly essential in modern software development. The library includes powerful modules for managing concurrency, such as `async` and `threads`. These modules provide abstractions that simplify the implementation of parallel and asynchronous operations, allowing developers to write more efficient and responsive applications.

The `async` module, for instance, is central to asynchronous programming in Nim. It introduces concepts like asynchronous procedures and tasks, which facilitate the execution of non-blocking operations. This is particularly useful for I/O-bound tasks, where waiting for external resources like file systems or network responses can otherwise halt the progress of the application. By leveraging the `async` module, developers can structure their code to perform these operations concurrently, improving the responsiveness and performance of their applications.

Nim's threading capabilities, provided through the `threads` module, offer another dimension of concurrency. This module enables the creation and management of multiple threads within a single process, allowing different parts of the application to execute simultaneously. Threading is advantageous for CPU-bound tasks where tasks can be distributed across multiple processor cores. The `threads` module includes functions for creating and synchronizing threads, managing shared resources, and ensuring thread safety. This module helps in building applications that require parallel processing, such as real-time data analysis or complex computational tasks.

In addition to concurrency, Nim's standard library excels in network programming. The `net` module provides a range of functionalities for building networked applications, including TCP and UDP communication. This module simplifies the process of setting up network connections, sending and receiving data, and handling network protocols. The abstraction provided by the `net` module allows developers to focus on higher-level application logic without getting bogged down by the intricacies of raw network programming.

For instance, creating a basic TCP server in Nim involves setting up a listening socket, accepting incoming connections, and handling client requests. The `net` module provides straightforward functions to accomplish these tasks. By utilizing this module, developers can efficiently manage network connections and ensure their applications are capable of handling network traffic effectively.

The standard library also supports various serialization formats through modules like `json`, `xml`, and `yaml`. These modules are essential for applications that need to exchange data with other systems or store data in a structured format. The `json` module, for example, provides functions for encoding and decoding JSON data, a format widely used for data interchange. Similarly, the `xml` module supports parsing and generating XML data, and the `yaml` module facilitates working with YAML, a format favored for configuration files. Each of these modules simplifies the process of handling structured data, ensuring compatibility with different systems and reducing the complexity of data processing tasks.

Another area where Nim's standard library shines is in its support for mathematical and statistical operations. The `math` module includes a comprehensive set of mathematical functions and constants, supporting operations ranging from basic arithmetic to complex mathematical computations. For more advanced statistical and numerical tasks, the `math` module integrates with additional libraries and tools, providing capabilities for performing sophisticated analyses and calculations.

The standard library's approach to file I/O is also noteworthy. It provides a range of functions for reading from and writing to files, managing file paths, and handling file metadata. This functionality is crucial for applications that need to interact with the file system, whether for storing user data, logging application activity, or processing external data files. By using the `os` and `file` modules, developers can perform these operations with ease, ensuring that their applications can manage file-based data efficiently.

Furthermore, Nim's standard library includes modules for working with dates and times, which essential for applications that need to handle temporal data. The `datetime` module provides classes and functions for representing and manipulating dates and times, supporting operations such as date arithmetic and formatting. This module is invaluable for applications that require precise handling of temporal information, such as scheduling systems or event-driven applications.

The comprehensive nature of Nim's standard library means that developers have a rich set of tools at their disposal for tackling a wide variety of programming challenges. From concurrency and networking to data serialization and mathematical computations, the standard library offers built-in solutions that streamline development and enhance productivity. By mastering these tools and understanding how to leverage them effectively, developers can build robust and efficient applications, taking full advantage of the capabilities provided by Nim.

CHAPTER 26:

When delving into the Nim ecosystem, it's essential to understand not only the tools and libraries available but also the processes and best practices for incorporating them into your development workflow. Leveraging the extensive resources within this ecosystem involves more than simply identifying and installing libraries; it requires an understanding of how these components fit together and how they can be used effectively to meet specific project needs.

One of the core aspects of integrating third-party libraries into Nim projects is managing dependencies. This is where `Nimble` truly shines, acting as the central hub for package management. Through `Nimble`, developers can resolve dependencies, handle versioning, and ensure that the libraries used in a project are compatible with each other. For instance, when you include a package in your `nimble` file, `Nimble` automatically fetches the required versions and integrates them into your project. This seamless integration reduces the complexity of managing external libraries and helps maintain project stability.

However, it is crucial to ensure that the libraries you choose align well with the needs of your project. Given the variety of libraries available, from those handling data structures to those supporting web development, assessing each library's functionality, performance, and maintenance status is important. For instance, when selecting a web framework such as `Jester` or `Karax`, evaluating their support for modern web standards, ease of use, and active community involvement can significantly impact your project's success.

In addition to leveraging libraries, integrating frameworks into Nim projects can offer substantial benefits. Frameworks such as `NimX` provide higher-level abstractions and tools for developing applications, especially for graphical user interfaces and cross-platform needs. For example, `NimX` is designed to facilitate the creation of applications that can run on multiple operating systems, including Windows, macOS, and Linux. By utilizing such frameworks, developers can avoid the complexities of handling platform-specific details manually, thus focusing more on application logic and user experience.

In the realm of data processing, the ecosystem offers libraries that simplify handling various data formats. Libraries such as `tables` for tabular data manipulation and `csv` for handling CSV files provide robust solutions for managing and processing data. When dealing with large datasets or requiring complex data transformations, these libraries can significantly streamline development, ensuring that data operations are both efficient and reliable. For instance, the `tables` library offers advanced features for filtering and sorting data, which can be crucial for applications involving substantial amounts of information.

For developers working with databases, understanding the range of available libraries and their capabilities is essential. Libraries like `db_sqlite` and `nim-mysql` provide interfaces for interacting with different database systems, each tailored to specific use cases. `db_sqlite`, for instance, is optimized for lightweight, embedded database applications, while `nim-mysql` supports more robust database operations suited to larger-scale applications. By selecting the appropriate library, developers can ensure that their database interactions are efficient and well-suited to their application requirements.

Another important aspect of working within the Nim ecosystem is ensuring compatibility with external tools and services. Libraries such as `httpclient` and `json` enable seamless communication with web services and APIs, making it easier to integrate external data and functionality into your applications. The `httpclient` library facilitates sending and receiving HTTP requests, while the `json` library handles JSON encoding and decoding, which is particularly useful for interacting with RESTful APIs and other web-based services.

Beyond libraries and frameworks, the Nim ecosystem includes various tools that enhance development productivity. Integrated Development Environments (IDEs) and code editors equipped with Nim support, such as `Visual Studio Code` with the Nim extension, offer features like syntax highlighting, code completion, and debugging capabilities. These tools are instrumental in improving the development workflow, allowing developers to write, test, and debug Nim code more efficiently.

Engagement with the Nim community is also a key factor in successfully navigating the ecosystem. Community forums, mailing lists, and social media platforms provide valuable resources for obtaining support, sharing knowledge, and collaborating on projects. Participating in these communities can offer insights into best practices, emerging tools, and common challenges faced by other developers. Additionally, contributing to open-source projects and sharing your own experiences can help strengthen the ecosystem and support its growth.

In conclusion, effectively navigating and leveraging the Nim ecosystem involves a combination of understanding available tools and libraries, integrating them into your projects thoughtfully, and engaging with the broader community. By mastering these aspects, developers can enhance their projects with powerful resources, streamline their development processes, and contribute to the ongoing evolution of the Nim language and its ecosystem.

The Nim ecosystem is characterized by its dynamic and supportive environment, offering an array of libraries, frameworks, and tools that significantly enhance development efficiency and capability. Exploring these resources involves not only understanding their functions but also mastering the processes for their effective integration into projects.

When working with third-party libraries, one important consideration is understanding the licensing and usage policies associated with each library. Open-source libraries often come with specific licenses that dictate how they can be used, modified, and distributed. For instance, libraries under the MIT license are generally permissive, allowing for broad usage with minimal restrictions. On the other hand, libraries under the GPL license require that any derivative works also be open-source. Being aware of these licensing terms is crucial to ensure compliance and avoid potential legal issues.

Moreover, keeping libraries up-to-date is essential for maintaining project stability and security. The Nim ecosystem, like many others, frequently updates its libraries to address bugs, introduce new features, and improve performance. Using outdated libraries can introduce vulnerabilities and compatibility issues. Tools like `Nimble` facilitate easy updates by checking for new versions and managing dependencies automatically. Regularly updating libraries ensures that you benefit from the latest improvements and security patches.

In addition to libraries, exploring Nim's frameworks can provide substantial benefits for specific types of projects. Frameworks such as `Jester` for web development offer a higher level of abstraction compared to standalone libraries, simplifying the development of web applications by providing built-in features for routing, middleware, and templating. Similarly, `NimX` offers a comprehensive toolkit for building cross-platform graphical applications, streamlining the development process by abstracting away many of the complexities associated with different operating systems and windowing systems.

When integrating external tools, it's important to consider their compatibility with Nim's build system and development workflow. Tools such as `Nimble` are designed to work seamlessly with Nim's compiler and build process, allowing you to manage dependencies and build configurations with ease. For projects that require more complex build setups, tools like `Nim`s `c2nim` can be invaluable. This utility facilitates the integration of C libraries into Nim projects by generating Nim bindings for C code, thereby enabling the use of existing C libraries without needing to rewrite them.

Testing and debugging within the Nim ecosystem also benefit from the array of available tools. The `nimcheck` utility is a powerful tool for performing static analysis on Nim code, helping to identify potential issues before runtime. Coupled with Nim's built-in debugging features, such as the GDB integration, developers can diagnose and resolve issues efficiently. For more complex debugging scenarios, the `Nim Debugger` offers an interactive environment for stepping through code, inspecting variables, and evaluating expressions, providing a comprehensive approach to identifying and fixing bugs.

Community involvement plays a significant role in navigating the Nim ecosystem. Engaging with forums, mailing lists, and social media platforms helps stay informed about new developments, best practices, and emerging trends within the Nim community. Platforms such as the Nim Forum and the Nim Reddit community offer spaces for developers to seek advice, share experiences, and collaborate on projects.

Participation in these communities not only provides access to a wealth of knowledge but also fosters collaboration and innovation within the ecosystem.

Furthermore, contributing to open-source projects within the Nim ecosystem can be a rewarding experience. By participating in the development and maintenance of libraries, frameworks, and tools, you can help improve the quality and functionality of these resources. Contributions can range from fixing bugs and adding new features to enhancing documentation and providing support to other developers. Engaging with open-source projects also allows you to gain insights into best practices, coding standards, and collaborative development workflows.

In summary, effectively exploring and leveraging the Nim ecosystem involves understanding the wide range of available resources, from libraries and frameworks to tools and community support. By mastering the integration of these components into your projects, adhering to licensing and update policies, and actively participating in the community, you can enhance your development process and contribute to the growth and evolution of the Nim language. The Nim ecosystem, with its rich array of tools and supportive community, offers a robust environment for building efficient, reliable, and innovative software.

CHAPTER 27:

Understanding and optimizing the performance of code in Nim necessitates a closer examination of how the language interacts with hardware and how to utilize its features effectively. One critical aspect of high-performance coding is optimizing data access patterns. Efficient data access is essential for minimizing latency and improving throughput, especially in applications that handle large volumes of data or perform frequent read and write operations.

When working with large datasets, it is crucial to consider how data is stored and accessed. Sequential access patterns are generally more efficient than random access patterns because they take advantage of the memory hierarchy. For example, accessing elements in contiguous memory locations can reduce cache misses and improve overall performance. In Nim, this can be achieved by using data structures such as arrays and sequences that store data in contiguous blocks of memory. When designing algorithms, one should aim to process data in a way that aligns with the underlying memory architecture to minimize costly memory access penalties.

Additionally, the choice of data structures can have a significant impact on performance. For instance, using hash tables can provide constant-time average complexity for insertions and lookups, but they also have overhead associated with hashing and handling collisions. On the other hand, balanced trees like AVL or Red-Black trees offer logarithmic time complexity for these operations, but with lower overhead compared to hash tables. The decision on which data structure to use should be guided by the specific requirements of the application, including the type of operations performed and the expected dataset size.

Another important factor in writing high-performance code is understanding the impact of compiler optimizations. Nim's compiler performs various optimizations to generate efficient machine code from high-level constructs. By default, the compiler applies several optimization techniques, but developers can influence the optimization process through compiler flags and pragmas. For instance, the `--opt:size` flag can be used to prioritize smaller code size, while the `--opt:speed` flag focuses on maximizing execution speed. Leveraging these compiler options can help tailor the generated code to meet specific performance goals.

In addition to compiler optimizations, using inline assembly code can provide even finer control over performance. Nim allows embedding assembly instructions directly within the code, which can be beneficial for performance-critical sections where the high-level abstractions may not suffice. This low-level approach enables direct manipulation of processor instructions and registers, potentially leading to significant performance improvements. However, it requires a deep understanding of the target architecture and careful management to ensure that the benefits outweigh the complexity introduced.

Parallelism and concurrency are other crucial elements in high-performance code. Modern processors feature multiple cores, and effectively utilizing these resources can result in substantial performance gains. Nim provides robust support for concurrent and parallel programming through its `async` and `await` constructs, which simplify writing non-blocking code. For CPU-bound tasks, employing parallel processing can significantly speed up computations by distributing workloads across multiple cores. Nim's `threads` module facilitates the creation and management of threads, enabling developers to implement parallel algorithms and perform simultaneous operations.

In addition to parallelism, optimizing communication between threads or processes is essential. Minimizing synchronization overhead and avoiding contention are key to achieving high performance in concurrent systems. Techniques such as lock-free data structures and efficient inter-thread communication can help reduce the overhead associated with managing concurrent execution. Nim's support for low-level synchronization primitives, such as mutexes and condition variables, allows for fine-tuned control over thread interactions.

Profiling tools play a vital role in identifying performance bottlenecks and guiding optimization efforts. Nim provides several profiling tools that can help analyze different aspects of code execution. By profiling an application, one can pinpoint areas where performance improvements are needed and evaluate the impact of various optimizations. Tools such as the `Nim Profiler` offer detailed insights into function call times, memory usage, and other performance metrics, helping developers make informed decisions about where to focus their optimization efforts.

Lastly, efficient error handling is an often-overlooked aspect of performance optimization. Error handling mechanisms that introduce excessive overhead or complexity can detract from overall performance. Nim provides several ways to handle errors, including exception handling and result types. For performance-critical applications, minimizing the use of exceptions in performance-critical paths and using more lightweight error-handling strategies can help maintain optimal performance.

In summary, writing high-performance code in Nim involves

a multifaceted approach that includes optimizing data access patterns, choosing appropriate data structures, leveraging compiler optimizations, using inline assembly, and effectively managing parallelism and concurrency. Profiling tools and efficient error handling also contribute to achieving and maintaining high performance. By applying these techniques thoughtfully and systematically, developers can harness the full potential of Nim to create efficient and responsive systems.

When optimizing code in Nim, memory management plays a crucial role in achieving high performance. Nim's approach to memory management includes a combination of garbage collection, manual memory management, and efficient allocation strategies. Understanding how to effectively manage memory can help reduce overhead and improve the performance of your applications.

Nim's garbage collector provides automatic memory management, which can simplify development by handling memory allocation and deallocation. However, relying solely on garbage collection might introduce unpredictable pauses during execution due to garbage collection cycles. For performance-critical applications, it is often beneficial to complement garbage collection with manual memory management techniques. Nim allows developers to manually manage memory using its `new` and `dispose` operators, which can be useful for optimizing performance in scenarios where garbage collection overhead is a concern.

To further optimize memory usage, it is important to be mindful of how objects are allocated and deallocated. Nim supports various memory allocation strategies, including stack allocation and heap allocation. Stack allocation is generally faster because it involves simple pointer manipulations and does not require dynamic memory management. However, stack allocation is limited by the size of the stack and the lifetime of the data. For larger or long-lived data structures, heap allocation is more appropriate. Efficient use of heap memory requires careful management to avoid fragmentation and excessive allocations.

Another technique to optimize memory usage is to use memory pools or custom allocators. Memory pools allow you to manage memory more efficiently by pre-allocating a large block of memory and then allocating smaller chunks from this pool. This approach can reduce the overhead of frequent memory allocations and deallocations, especially in applications with high allocation rates. Nim provides the `mem` module, which can be utilized to create and manage memory pools.

In addition to memory management, optimizing computational performance involves selecting appropriate algorithms and data structures. Choosing the right algorithm for a given problem can significantly impact performance. For instance, when sorting data, different algorithms such as quicksort, mergesort, or heapsort offer varying performance characteristics. Nim's standard library provides implementations for various algorithms, but understanding their time and space complexities allows you to select the most suitable one for your use case.

Data structures also play a critical role in performance. For example, when implementing search functionalities, hash tables offer constant-time average complexity, while balanced trees provide logarithmic complexity. Selecting the right data structure based on the nature of operations—such as frequent insertions and deletions versus fast lookups—can optimize performance. Nim's standard library includes several efficient data structures, including arrays, sequences, and hash tables, which can be leveraged based on the specific requirements of your application.

In parallel with choosing the right algorithms and data

structures, it is important to consider how you write and structure your code. Efficient code organization can reduce overhead and enhance performance. For example, minimizing function call overhead by inlining small functions or using local variables instead of global ones can improve performance. Nim supports function inlining through the `inline` pragma, which allows you to suggest that certain functions should be inlined by the compiler to reduce function call overhead.

Profiling and benchmarking are essential tools for understanding and improving performance. Profiling tools help identify performance bottlenecks by providing detailed information about where time is spent during execution. Nim includes profiling tools that allow you to analyze various aspects of your application, such as CPU usage, memory allocation, and function call frequencies. By using these tools, you can identify hotspots in your code and focus optimization efforts where they will have the most impact.

Benchmarking, on the other hand, involves measuring the performance of specific code segments or algorithms to compare different approaches or optimizations. Nim's standard library includes facilities for benchmarking, such as the `benchmark` module, which allows you to write and execute performance tests. By creating benchmarks, you can empirically evaluate the performance of different implementations and choose the most efficient solution.

Another consideration for high-performance code is to utilize SIMD (Single Instruction, Multiple Data) instructions when appropriate. SIMD allows for parallel processing of multiple data elements with a single instruction, which can accelerate computations involving large datasets. While Nim does not provide direct support for SIMD instructions, you can use inline assembly or external libraries to leverage SIMD capabilities and enhance performance for specific tasks.

Finally, optimizing I/O operations is another aspect of writing high-performance code. Input and output operations, such as reading from or writing to files or network sockets, can be slow and impact overall performance. Efficiently managing I/O operations involves using buffering techniques, asynchronous I/O, and minimizing the number of I/O operations. Nim's standard library includes facilities for file and network I/O, and using these facilities effectively can help improve performance in applications that rely heavily on I/O.

In summary, writing high-performance code in Nim requires a multifaceted approach, including effective memory management, selecting appropriate algorithms and data structures, optimizing code organization, profiling and benchmarking, and managing I/O operations. By understanding and applying these techniques, you can enhance the efficiency of your Nim applications and achieve optimal performance.

CHAPTER 28:

When dealing with large codebases, the complexity of managing and integrating different parts of the system becomes increasingly evident. Effective strategies for handling these complexities can greatly impact the maintainability and performance of a project. One critical aspect of managing a substantial codebase involves adopting a structured approach to organizing code and resources.

A fundamental technique for achieving this is modular design. Modular design facilitates the division of a large codebase into discrete, manageable modules. Each module should encapsulate a specific functionality or domain of the application, allowing developers to focus on smaller, more manageable segments of the code. This separation of concerns not only enhances code readability but also simplifies maintenance and debugging. In Nim, modules are defined using the `import` statement, which allows different parts of the code to communicate and share functionality without creating unnecessary dependencies.

Effective modular design also requires careful attention to the boundaries and interfaces between modules. Clearly defined interfaces and minimal coupling between modules ensure that changes in one part of the system do not inadvertently affect others. This practice is particularly important in large projects where the risk of introducing unintended side effects is higher. By adhering to the principles of encapsulation and abstraction, developers can build a robust architecture that supports both flexibility and scalability.

Alongside modular design, refactoring is an essential practice for managing large codebases. Over time, code can accumulate technical debt, making it harder to understand and maintain. Refactoring involves restructuring the existing codebase to improve its design, readability, and efficiency without altering its external behavior. This process includes techniques such as extracting methods to simplify complex functions, renaming variables and functions for clarity, and consolidating redundant code. Refactoring should be an ongoing activity, integrated into the regular development cycle to ensure that the code remains clean and manageable.

Another critical component in managing large codebases is handling dependencies effectively. Dependencies refer to external libraries, modules, or components that your code relies on. As the number of dependencies grows, it becomes essential to manage them systematically to avoid conflicts and ensure compatibility. Nim provides tools such as Nimble, its package manager, to facilitate dependency management. Nimble allows developers to specify required libraries and their versions in a configuration file, streamlining the process of installing and updating dependencies. It is crucial to regularly review and update these dependencies to incorporate the latest improvements and security patches.

In addition to managing dependencies, configuring the build process is another important aspect of handling large projects. As the complexity of the project increases, the build process can become more intricate. Nim's build configuration file, `nim.cfg`, plays a crucial role in defining compiler options, include paths, and other build parameters. Properly configuring this file helps ensure that the project builds consistently across different environments. Utilizing build automation tools can further enhance efficiency by automating repetitive tasks such as compilation, testing, and deployment.

The organization of large codebases also benefits from a strong focus on documentation. Comprehensive and up-to-date documentation serves as a valuable resource for understanding and navigating the codebase. This documentation should cover various aspects of the project, including its architecture, module descriptions, API references, and usage examples. Tools like NimDoc can assist in generating and maintaining detailed documentation, which is essential for onboarding new team members and facilitating ongoing maintenance.

In addition to technical practices, effective project management practices are also vital. Establishing coding standards and guidelines ensures consistency across the codebase, reducing the likelihood of errors and improving code quality. Code reviews and pair programming can also be effective techniques for maintaining high standards and fostering collaboration among team members. Regular code reviews provide an opportunity to identify and address potential issues early, while pair programming encourages knowledge sharing and collective problem-solving.

The integration of robust testing strategies is another key factor in managing large codebases. Comprehensive testing helps ensure that changes to the code do not introduce new issues or regressions. Employing unit tests, integration tests, and end-to-end tests can provide coverage for various aspects of the application. Nim's testing framework supports writing and executing tests, and integrating these tests into the build process can help maintain code quality throughout the development lifecycle.

Ultimately, managing large codebases in Nim requires a combination of strategic practices, including modular design, regular refactoring, effective dependency management, and comprehensive documentation. By implementing these strategies and fostering a collaborative development environment, you can maintain a clean, manageable, and high-quality codebase. This approach not only supports the ongoing development and evolution of the project but also enhances its overall robustness and scalability.

As projects expand in scope and complexity, effective management of a large codebase becomes increasingly critical. Among the essential practices for maintaining such a codebase is the strategic use of version control systems. Version control is not merely a tool for tracking changes; it is a fundamental aspect of modern software development that enables collaborative work, manages code changes, and ensures that the project remains in a stable and deployable state. Using a system like Git, I can track modifications, revert to previous states if necessary, and branch out to explore new features without disrupting the main line of development.

In the context of large codebases, managing version control effectively requires a structured approach to branching and merging. Adopting a branching strategy, such as Git Flow or GitHub Flow, can streamline development processes by defining clear guidelines for feature development, testing, and deployment. Git Flow, for example, involves a series of well-defined branches for features, releases, and hotfixes, which helps in organizing development efforts and maintaining a stable main branch. This structured branching strategy not only enhances coordination among team members but also simplifies the integration of new features and fixes.

Maintaining consistency across different parts of a large codebase also involves adhering to coding standards and style guides. Establishing and enforcing coding conventions helps ensure that code is written in a uniform manner, which improves readability and reduces the likelihood of errors. Code linters and formatters can be integrated into the development workflow to automatically enforce these standards, providing real-time feedback and helping maintain code quality throughout the development process.

In addition to coding standards, establishing effective communication and documentation practices is crucial. Large codebases often involve multiple developers and teams, making clear communication essential for ensuring that everyone is on the same page. Regular meetings, detailed documentation, and collaborative tools can facilitate this communication. For instance, maintaining up-to-date documentation that includes detailed descriptions of code modules, architectural decisions, and usage examples can be invaluable for onboarding new team members and ensuring that all contributors understand the system's design and functionality.

Managing build configurations and automation is another critical aspect of handling large codebases. In complex projects, build processes can become intricate, involving various tools and configurations. Automating these processes through continuous integration (CI) systems can streamline development and ensure that the code is consistently tested and built in a controlled environment. CI tools, such as Jenkins, GitHub Actions, or GitLab CI, can be configured to automatically build and test the code upon each commit, providing immediate feedback on potential issues and ensuring that the codebase remains in a deployable state.

Effective build configuration also involves managing build artifacts and deployment pipelines. As the codebase grows, the complexity of deployment processes can increase. Implementing automated deployment pipelines can help manage this complexity by defining clear steps for building, testing, and deploying the application. Tools like Docker can be used to create containerized environments for consistent deployments, while orchestration platforms like Kubernetes can manage and scale these deployments efficiently.

Addressing performance considerations is also a key aspect of managing large codebases. As the size and complexity of the codebase grow, performance issues may arise, affecting the overall efficiency and responsiveness of the application. Conducting performance profiling and optimization can help identify bottlenecks and improve performance. Profiling tools, such as Nim's built-in profiler or external tools like Valgrind, can provide insights into resource usage and performance characteristics, allowing for targeted optimizations.

Maintaining security in a large codebase is another critical consideration. As the codebase expands, the potential attack surface also grows, making it essential to implement security best practices. This includes regular security audits, code reviews focused on security aspects, and integrating security testing into the CI pipeline. Tools for static code analysis and vulnerability scanning can help identify and address security issues before they become critical.

Lastly, managing large codebases often involves dealing with legacy code and technical debt. Over time, parts of the codebase may become outdated or suboptimal, requiring refactoring and modernization. Establishing a strategy for addressing technical debt, such as prioritizing and scheduling refactoring tasks, can help manage this aspect effectively. It is important to balance the need for maintaining existing functionality with the need for continuous improvement and modernization.

In summary, managing a large codebase involves a multifaceted approach that includes effective version control, adherence to coding standards, clear communication, automation of build and deployment processes, performance optimization, and security considerations. By implementing these strategies and practices, I can ensure that the codebase remains manageable, maintainable, and scalable, supporting the long-term success of the project.

CHAPTER 29:

When navigating the process of contributing to open source projects, particularly within the Nim ecosystem, understanding the nuances of effective communication and collaboration is crucial. Successful open source contributions are not solely about writing code but also about interacting constructively with the project's community. This interaction begins with establishing clear, respectful communication channels and extends to understanding the project's culture and norms.

Effective communication with project maintainers and other contributors starts with clarity and precision. When reporting issues or discussing potential improvements, provide as much detail as possible. For instance, if you encounter a bug, include steps to reproduce the issue, screenshots if applicable, and details about your environment. This level of detail can significantly accelerate the process of identifying and resolving problems. Similarly, when proposing enhancements or new features, outline the problem, propose a solution, and explain how it fits into the project's goals.

Engagement in community discussions and forums related to the project can offer valuable insights into the project's current status and future directions. These discussions are often the breeding ground for new ideas and improvements. Participating in these conversations not only helps in understanding the project's needs but also builds rapport with other contributors and maintainers. It is through such interactions that you can gauge the project's priorities and align your contributions with its strategic objectives.

Respecting the project's norms and culture is another important aspect of contributing effectively. Each open source project may have its own conventions for code style, commit messages, and documentation. Familiarizing yourself with these conventions helps in ensuring that your contributions are consistent with the project's standards. This alignment not only facilitates smoother integration of your changes but also demonstrates your commitment to maintaining the project's quality and coherence.

Handling feedback during the review process is a vital component of successful open source contribution. When your pull request undergoes review, be open to constructive criticism and willing to make necessary adjustments. Reviewers may suggest changes or improvements that could enhance the quality and functionality of your contribution. Addressing this feedback promptly and professionally shows respect for the maintainers' time and expertise. If you disagree with a reviewer's suggestion, engage in a reasoned discussion, providing evidence or alternative solutions to justify your perspective.

Moreover, building a reputation within the open source community can lead to more significant opportunities for involvement. Regular contributions, whether through code, documentation, or community support, help establish you as a valuable member of the community. As your reputation grows, you may be invited to take on more prominent roles, such as reviewing other contributors' pull requests or even managing aspects of the project's development. This progression not only enhances your own skills but also amplifies your impact on the project's success.

In addition to direct contributions to code, open source projects often benefit from contributions to documentation, tutorials, and user support. Clear and comprehensive documentation is essential for both new and existing users of the project. By contributing to documentation, you help make the project more accessible and user-friendly, which can significantly increase its adoption and success. Writing tutorials or guides also assists in demonstrating the project's capabilities and encouraging new contributors to get involved.

Finally, recognizing the importance of ongoing involvement in the open source community cannot be overstated. The landscape of open source projects is dynamic, with frequent updates, new contributors, and evolving needs. Staying engaged with the community, continuously improving your understanding of the project, and adapting to changes ensures that your contributions remain relevant and impactful. Embrace the opportunity to learn from others, share your knowledge, and contribute to the collective growth of the project and its community.

In essence, contributing to open source projects involves more than just submitting code; it requires effective communication, adherence to project norms, and active engagement with the community. By approaching contributions with a collaborative mindset, respecting feedback, and continually participating in the project's ecosystem, you can make meaningful and lasting contributions that benefit both yourself and the broader open source community.

When embarking on the journey of contributing to open source projects, it is crucial to understand the etiquette and norms that govern the community. This awareness not only helps in making valuable contributions but also ensures that your interactions are constructive and positive. The process begins with selecting the right project that aligns with your interests and expertise. Choosing a project with active maintainers and a welcoming community increases the likelihood of your contributions being appreciated and integrated. Platforms like GitHub, GitLab, and Bitbucket host numerous open source projects, and exploring these repositories can provide insights into their activity levels, open issues, and ongoing discussions.

Once you have identified a project of interest, the next step involves familiarizing yourself with its contribution guidelines. Most projects have a `CONTRIBUTING.md` file or a dedicated section in their documentation that outlines the process for submitting contributions. This typically includes details on coding standards, commit message conventions, and the procedure for submitting pull requests. Adhering to these guidelines demonstrates respect for the project's established practices and increases the likelihood of your contributions being accepted.

Engaging with the project's community is another vital aspect of contributing effectively. This engagement can take many forms, such as participating in discussions, reporting issues, or providing feedback on existing contributions. Community forums, mailing lists, and chat channels are often used to facilitate communication among contributors. By actively participating in these platforms, you not only stay informed about the project's developments but also build relationships with other contributors and maintainers. Such interactions can lead to collaborative opportunities and provide valuable insights into the project's needs and future directions.

When it comes to submitting code contributions, the process typically involves creating a fork of the project's repository, making changes on your fork, and then submitting a pull request. A well-prepared pull request should include a clear description of the changes, the rationale behind them, and any related issue numbers. Providing a comprehensive description helps reviewers understand the context and purpose of your contribution, making the review process smoother and more efficient.

Before submitting a pull request, ensure that your code is thoroughly tested and adheres to the project's coding standards. Many projects include automated testing frameworks and continuous integration (CI) pipelines that run tests on new contributions. Running these tests locally before submitting your pull request can help catch errors early and prevent unnecessary delays. Additionally, reviewing the project's existing codebase and understanding its structure and conventions will aid in ensuring that your contribution aligns with the project's overall design and style.

Feedback is an integral part of the contribution process. When your pull request is reviewed, you may receive comments or suggestions from maintainers or other contributors. Approach this feedback with an open mind and a willingness to improve. Addressing review comments promptly and effectively demonstrates your commitment to the project's quality and helps build your credibility within the community. If you encounter disagreements or challenges during the review process, engage in constructive discussions, providing evidence or alternative solutions to support your viewpoint.

In addition to code contributions, there are other valuable ways to contribute to open source projects. Improving documentation, creating tutorials, or assisting with user support are all crucial activities that enhance the project's accessibility and usability. Well-maintained documentation helps new users understand the project's functionality and integration, while tutorials and guides provide practical insights and examples. Contributing to these areas not only supports the project's growth but also showcases your versatility and commitment to its success.

Maintaining ongoing involvement with the project is essential for long-term contributions. Open source projects are dynamic, with frequent updates and evolving needs. By staying engaged with the project's community and regularly contributing, you ensure that your involvement remains relevant and impactful. This continuous engagement also provides opportunities for learning and growth, as you stay updated with new developments and best practices in the field.

Ultimately, contributing to open source projects is a mutually beneficial experience. It offers an opportunity to enhance your skills, collaborate with like-minded individuals, and make a meaningful impact on projects that align with your interests. By following best practices, engaging constructively with the community, and maintaining a commitment to quality and improvement, you can make significant contributions that support the project's success and foster a positive and productive open source environment.

CHAPTER 30:

In examining the real-world applications of Nim, it becomes clear that the language's capabilities and characteristics are well-suited for various domains, each presenting unique challenges and requiring specific solutions. A thorough analysis of these applications highlights how Nim's features can be effectively utilized and where its limitations may influence the development process.

Consider the development of a real-time communication application, such as a chat or messaging platform. This type of application demands high performance, low latency, and scalability. Nim's `async` and `net` libraries are particularly useful for handling real-time communication efficiently. These libraries enable asynchronous operations, which are crucial for maintaining responsiveness in applications that handle multiple concurrent connections. By utilizing Nim's coroutine-based concurrency model, developers can manage I/O operations without blocking the main execution thread, thereby enhancing the application's ability to handle high volumes of messages and connections. The real challenge in such projects often revolves around ensuring that the asynchronous code remains easy to read and maintain, as complex concurrency patterns can introduce subtle bugs. Nim's clean syntax and robust error handling help mitigate these issues, allowing for more reliable and maintainable code.

Another compelling case study involves the use of Nim for building a high-performance numerical simulation application. Simulations that require heavy computational tasks, such as scientific modeling or financial forecasting, benefit greatly from Nim's performance characteristics. By leveraging Nim's ability to generate efficient machine code and its support for low-level operations, developers can write code that executes with minimal overhead. For instance, a financial modeling application that calculates complex statistical measures can achieve significant performance improvements through optimized algorithms and efficient memory usage. Nim's support for interfacing with C libraries also allows developers to integrate specialized numerical libraries, further enhancing the simulation's capabilities. The main challenge here is to ensure that the numerical accuracy and precision are maintained while optimizing performance, which requires careful profiling and tuning of the code.

Exploring the use of Nim in the context of embedded systems provides additional insights into its real-world applications. Embedded systems often have stringent constraints regarding memory and processing power, making efficiency a top priority. Nim's ability to generate lightweight executables and its support for low-level hardware access are advantageous in this domain. An example can be found in the development of firmware for microcontrollers, where Nim's efficient handling of resources and its straightforward integration with C-based hardware libraries prove beneficial. However, developers must contend with limited debugging tools and a smaller ecosystem tailored to embedded systems compared to more established languages. Despite these challenges, Nim's design allows for effective management of low-level operations, making it a viable choice for certain embedded applications.

In the realm of web development, Nim's performance advantages are increasingly being recognized. A web application requiring both high speed and efficiency, such as a real-time analytics dashboard or a high-traffic API service, can leverage Nim's capabilities to deliver robust performance. By using Nim's `httpbeast` library, developers can build scalable web servers that handle numerous requests per second with minimal latency. The integration of Nim with modern web frameworks and tools further enhances its utility in web development, although it may involve additional work to bridge gaps in library support and ecosystem maturity. The primary challenge in this area is balancing the performance benefits of Nim with the need for a rich set of web development features, often necessitating the development of custom solutions or the adaptation of existing libraries.

Furthermore, the application of Nim in game development highlights its strengths in scenarios requiring real-time performance and resource management. Game engines built with Nim can benefit from its low-level access to memory and high execution speed, which are critical for rendering and processing game logic. For example, a 2D or 3D game engine can leverage Nim's capabilities to handle complex graphics and physics simulations efficiently. Nim's ability to interact with C libraries also allows for the integration of existing game development tools and assets. The main challenge in game development with Nim lies in the relatively smaller community and fewer specialized libraries compared to more established game development environments. Nonetheless, Nim's performance attributes and versatility make it a strong candidate for developing high-performance game engines.

These diverse applications illustrate Nim's ability to address various real-world challenges through its design and features. The language's performance-oriented nature and its capacity to interface with low-level systems and existing libraries make it suitable for a broad range of applications. However, the practical use of Nim also reveals areas where its ecosystem and toolset may require further development to fully support all aspects of application development. By examining these case studies, we gain a deeper understanding of how Nim can be effectively utilized in different contexts, and how developers can navigate its strengths and limitations to achieve successful outcomes.

When analyzing Nim's role in various real-world scenarios, it's essential to consider not only the language's strengths but also the practical challenges developers encounter. In real-world implementations, Nim's design choices offer a mix of benefits and constraints that shape the development process. Here, we delve into several more nuanced applications to gain a deeper understanding of how Nim performs in diverse contexts.

Consider a project where Nim is employed to develop a robust data processing pipeline for handling large-scale datasets. In this scenario, the efficiency of data manipulation and transformation becomes paramount. Nim's performance capabilities shine through when dealing with intensive data operations. For instance, in processing logs or analytical data, the ability to handle large volumes of information swiftly can be critical. Nim's support for compile-time checks and optimizations allows developers to build highly efficient data processing routines. However, working with large datasets also introduces challenges related to memory management and data serialization. The language's garbage collection and memory handling features must be carefully tuned to avoid performance bottlenecks. Efficient memory usage and data structuring become essential considerations, especially when dealing with high-throughput data streams.

In the realm of desktop applications, Nim has been employed to create lightweight, high-performance tools. A notable example is a desktop application designed for real-time video processing and editing. In this context, Nim's capability to interface with low-level system libraries and leverage its high-performance features proves advantageous. For instance, video processing applications often require real-time frame manipulation and rendering, which demand both speed and efficiency. Nim's ability to generate optimized machine code and its support for interfacing with C libraries for hardware acceleration can be leveraged to achieve the required performance. Despite these advantages, developers must handle complex interactions between Nim's abstractions and the lower-level video processing APIs. Ensuring compatibility and stability across different platforms can also pose challenges, necessitating thorough testing and platform-specific adjustments.

A compelling application of Nim is in the development of networked applications, such as a distributed file storage system. These systems require efficient network communication, fault tolerance, and data consistency across multiple nodes. Nim's concurrency model, which is based on coroutines, facilitates the development of networked applications by allowing asynchronous handling of multiple connections and tasks. This is crucial for maintaining responsiveness and scalability in distributed environments. The language's `async` library provides powerful tools for managing asynchronous operations, but developers must navigate the complexities of distributed systems, such as handling network failures and ensuring data integrity. Effective error handling and robust protocol design become central to maintaining a reliable and performant distributed file storage system.

Another area where Nim has demonstrated its utility is in the development of cross-platform command-line tools. These tools often require efficient parsing of user input, file management, and integration with various system utilities. Nim's ability to produce small, efficient executables that run across different platforms is beneficial for creating lightweight command-line applications. The language's standard library includes powerful modules for file I/O, string manipulation, and command-line argument parsing, which facilitate the development of such tools. However, cross-platform development introduces challenges related to varying system behaviors and library dependencies. Ensuring that a command-line tool behaves consistently across different operating systems requires careful consideration of platform-specific nuances and thorough testing.

In the domain of scientific computing, Nim's performance and ease of integration with existing libraries make it a strong candidate for certain computational tasks. For example, in numerical simulations or data analysis applications, leveraging Nim's capabilities to interface with high-performance scientific libraries can significantly enhance computational efficiency. Nim's ability to call C libraries and its support for efficient memory management allow it to handle complex numerical computations effectively. Nevertheless, scientific computing often demands high precision and extensive mathematical functionality. Developers must ensure that numerical accuracy is preserved while optimizing performance, which may involve implementing custom algorithms or tuning existing libraries.

Each of these case studies illustrates the diverse applications of Nim and highlights the language's adaptability to various domains. While Nim offers substantial performance benefits and a flexible programming model, real-world scenarios often reveal the complexities and trade-offs associated with its use. By understanding these practical challenges and leveraging Nim's strengths, developers can effectively address the needs of different applications, from data processing and video editing to distributed systems and command-line tools. The insights gained from these applications not only showcase Nim's potential but also provide valuable lessons for optimizing and adapting the language to meet specific project requirements.

CHAPTER 31:

When delving deeper into advanced metaprogramming techniques in Nim, it becomes evident that understanding and leveraging these concepts can significantly enhance the flexibility and functionality of your code. Building upon the foundation of code generation, reflection, and custom macros, we will explore more intricate aspects of these techniques, focusing on practical applications and real-world examples that highlight their power and utility.

Starting with code generation, it is essential to recognize that Nim's templating system provides not only a way to insert repetitive code but also to generate complex data structures and algorithms dynamically. For instance, you can use templates to create a suite of data types that share common functionality but vary in specific details. This approach is particularly useful in scenarios where you need to handle multiple types of data in a uniform manner, such as implementing a set of similar classes or interfaces for different data entities.

Consider the case of implementing a generic serialization framework. By utilizing templates, you can create a generalized mechanism that automatically generates serialization and deserialization code for various data types. The template could take type parameters and generate the necessary code to handle the specific requirements of each type, such as converting between internal representations and external formats like JSON or XML. This not only reduces the amount of manual coding but also ensures consistency and correctness across different data types.

Reflection, with its capability to inspect and manipulate program elements at runtime, provides a powerful tool for creating dynamic and adaptable applications. One advanced use of reflection is in implementing dynamic scripting or plugin systems. In such systems, the application can load and execute external scripts or modules at runtime, based on user input or configuration files. By using reflection, the application can examine the available modules, determine their interfaces, and invoke their functionalities without needing to know the details at compile time.

For example, imagine developing a plugin-based architecture where different modules can be dynamically loaded to extend the application's functionality. Reflection allows you to inspect the classes or functions provided by each plugin and determine how to integrate them into the main application. This capability is particularly valuable in scenarios where the exact set of plugins or extensions is not known ahead of time, and the application needs to remain flexible and extensible.

Custom macros extend the metaprogramming capabilities further by allowing developers to create new language constructs or modify existing ones. Macros operate by transforming the abstract syntax tree (AST) of the program during compilation, which enables complex code transformations that go beyond what templates can achieve. This feature is instrumental in creating domain-specific languages (DSLs) or implementing custom language constructs that simplify specific programming tasks.

A practical example of custom macros is the creation of a DSL for defining and executing business rules. Suppose you are developing an application that requires a set of rules to be defined and evaluated dynamically. By using macros, you can introduce a new syntax for specifying these rules, which is then transformed into the necessary code for evaluation. This approach not only makes the rules more readable and maintainable but also allows for more expressive and domain-specific programming.

Another advanced application of custom macros is in implementing code analysis and transformation tools. Macros can be used to perform complex code transformations, such as automatically generating boilerplate code, enforcing coding standards, or even performing static analysis to detect potential issues. For instance, you could create a macro that automatically generates logging code for specific functions, ensuring that all critical operations are adequately logged without manually inserting logging statements throughout your codebase.

Combining these advanced techniques—code generation, reflection, and custom macros—provides a robust toolkit for developing sophisticated and flexible software solutions. By effectively employing these metaprogramming features, you can create code that is not only more adaptable and reusable but also easier to maintain and extend. These techniques enable developers to tackle complex programming challenges with greater efficiency and precision, resulting in more powerful and dynamic applications.

As we continue to explore the depths of Nim's metaprogramming capabilities, it becomes clear that mastering these techniques can significantly impact the way you approach software development. Whether it's through automating repetitive tasks, enabling runtime adaptability, or extending the language to fit specific needs, the power of metaprogramming in Nim offers a wealth of possibilities for creating advanced and flexible code structures.

Expanding on advanced metaprogramming techniques in Nim, it's crucial to delve into more intricate applications of reflection, code generation, and custom macros to fully grasp their potential in practical scenarios. These techniques not only enhance code flexibility and reusability but also contribute to creating more maintainable and sophisticated systems.

To illustrate the power of reflection, consider the scenario of developing a dynamic configuration system. In many applications, configurations may vary based on deployment environments or user preferences, necessitating a mechanism to adapt configurations at runtime. By utilizing reflection, you can design a system that inspects and applies configuration settings dynamically. This involves creating a structure where configurations are loaded from external sources, such as JSON files or databases, and then mapped to application components using reflection.

For instance, if you have a class representing a server configuration, you can use reflection to identify the properties of this class and update them based on the loaded configuration data. This approach allows for flexible and extensible configuration management, where changes in configuration files do not require recompilation of the application. Moreover, you can implement validation and error-checking mechanisms to ensure that the configurations are correctly applied, leveraging reflection to dynamically inspect and enforce rules based on the defined schema.

Code generation, on the other hand, can be used to automate the creation of repetitive or boilerplate code, reducing the risk of errors and improving consistency. Consider a scenario where you need to implement various data access objects (DAOs) for different entities in your application. Manually writing each DAO class can be tedious and error-prone. Instead, you can create a code generation template that automatically generates DAO classes based on entity definitions.

In this process, you define a generic template that takes entity metadata as input and produces the necessary DAO code. This metadata might include information about the entity's fields, their types, and any required CRUD operations. The template generates the corresponding methods for each operation, ensuring that the generated code adheres to the required conventions and integrates seamlessly with the rest of your application. This approach not only speeds up development but also ensures that the generated code remains consistent with the specifications.

Custom macros further enhance metaprogramming capabilities by enabling developers to define new syntactic constructs or modify existing ones. These macros can be employed to create domain-specific languages (DSLs) tailored to particular problem domains, making code more expressive and easier to understand. For example, if you are developing a domain-specific language for defining mathematical expressions, you can create a macro that allows you to write expressions in a more natural and intuitive way.

The macro would transform these expressions into equivalent code that performs the required computations. This approach simplifies the process of defining complex expressions and ensures that they are evaluated correctly. Additionally, macros can be used to implement custom annotations or attributes that affect how code is processed or executed, providing a powerful means of extending the language to better fit specific needs.

Another advanced application of macros is in generating boilerplate code for common patterns. For instance, if your application uses a particular design pattern extensively, such as the observer pattern or the factory pattern, you can create a macro that automatically generates the necessary code for implementing this pattern. This can significantly reduce the amount of repetitive code you need to write and maintain, ensuring that the pattern is applied consistently throughout your codebase.

Additionally, macros can be used for performing code analysis and enforcing coding standards. For example, you might create a macro that scans your code for specific patterns or practices and generates warnings or errors if they are not followed. This can help ensure that your code adheres to established guidelines and improve overall code quality. Macros can also be employed to integrate static analysis tools or other code quality checks into your development workflow.

Combining these advanced techniques allows for a high degree of flexibility and efficiency in software development. By leveraging reflection, code generation, and custom macros, you can create code that is not only more adaptable and reusable but also easier to maintain and extend. These metaprogramming features empower developers to tackle complex problems with greater ease and precision, resulting in more robust and dynamic applications.

The ability to generate code dynamically, inspect and modify program elements at runtime, and create custom language constructs provides a powerful toolkit for addressing a wide range of programming challenges. Mastering these advanced metaprogramming techniques in Nim can lead to more sophisticated and effective solutions, enabling you to build applications that are both powerful and adaptable to changing requirements.

Managing Dependencies and Versioning

Effective dependency management is fundamental to ensuring the stability and reliability of software projects. In the realm of Nim, this entails not only managing the libraries and frameworks your project relies on but also handling versioning issues that can impact your project's build and runtime behavior. Through a careful approach to dependency management, you can mitigate risks associated with library updates, avoid conflicts, and maintain a consistent development environment.

One of the first steps in managing dependencies effectively is understanding how to specify and control library versions. In Nim, this is commonly handled through the use of the Nim package manager, Nimble. Nimble allows developers to define and manage dependencies in a `nimble` file, which includes specifications for library versions, compatibility constraints, and other metadata. By specifying precise version constraints for each dependency, you can ensure that your project uses compatible versions that have been tested together.

Version constraints are critical for avoiding conflicts between dependencies. In Nim, you can use version constraints to specify the exact version of a library or a range of acceptable versions. For example, you might specify that your project requires version `1.2.3` of a library, or any version within the range `1.2.x`. This flexibility allows you to balance between using the latest features and maintaining compatibility with other parts of your project.

Managing conflicts between dependencies can be particularly challenging when different libraries require different versions of the same dependency. In such cases, you need to carefully assess the compatibility of the required versions and consider whether it's feasible to update or adjust the versions to align with the needs of all libraries involved. This might involve contacting the maintainers of the conflicting libraries to discuss possible solutions or considering alternative libraries that offer similar functionality but with compatible dependencies.

Dependency management also involves monitoring and updating libraries as new versions are released. Regularly updating your dependencies can help you take advantage of bug fixes, performance improvements, and new features. However, it's important to approach updates with caution. Before updating a dependency, you should review the release notes and changelogs to understand what changes have been made and how they might affect your project. Automated tools and continuous integration systems can assist in testing your project against updated dependencies to ensure that changes do not introduce regressions or new issues.

Versioning issues extend beyond just managing library dependencies. They also encompass versioning your own project and its releases. Effective versioning practices involve clearly defining how versions are incremented based on changes made to the project. Semantic versioning is a widely adopted approach where versions are incremented based on major, minor, and patch changes. A major version increment signifies breaking changes, a minor version increment indicates backward-compatible enhancements, and a patch version increment represents backward-compatible bug fixes.

Implementing semantic versioning requires maintaining a consistent versioning scheme and clearly documenting the changes associated with each version. This documentation, often found in release notes or changelogs, helps users and developers understand what has changed between versions and make informed decisions about when to update. For larger projects, it's also important to have a versioning strategy that aligns with the project's release cycle and development practices.

In addition to version control, managing the build and deployment process is another aspect of dependency management. Build systems and continuous integration (CI) tools can automate the process of fetching, building, and testing dependencies, ensuring that your project is always built with the correct versions. CI tools can be configured to run tests and checks whenever changes are made to the project's dependencies, providing early feedback on potential issues.

Another key practice is isolating dependencies to avoid conflicts and ensure reproducibility. Tools such as Nim's `nimble` can create isolated environments for your project, where dependencies are installed and managed separately from other projects. This isolation helps prevent version conflicts and ensures that each project has access to the specific versions of dependencies it requires.

Handling dependencies and versioning also involves being prepared for scenarios where dependencies are no longer maintained or supported. In such cases, you may need to evaluate alternative libraries, update your project's code to work with new dependencies, or even contribute to the maintenance of the existing library. Engaging with the community and staying informed about the status of the libraries you depend on can help you anticipate and address such issues proactively.

By adopting these practices and strategies, you can effectively manage dependencies and versioning in Nim, ensuring that your projects remain stable, reliable, and maintainable. Proper dependency management not only helps you avoid common pitfalls but also contributes to a more streamlined and efficient development process.

To manage dependencies effectively in Nim, it is essential to understand how to navigate the Nim ecosystem's specific tools and conventions. Nimble, the package manager for Nim, plays a pivotal role in this process. Nimble simplifies the installation, updating, and removal of packages, providing a centralized mechanism for managing dependencies. This tool also supports specifying dependencies in a project's `nimble` file, which defines the required libraries and their versions.

The `nimble` file is crucial for maintaining consistency across different environments. It allows you to specify exact versions or version ranges for each dependency, which helps in ensuring that the project remains compatible with the versions of libraries it was designed to work with. When specifying versions, it is important to distinguish between exact versions, which lock the dependency to a specific version, and version ranges, which allow for flexibility while still maintaining compatibility.

Handling version conflicts is a common challenge in dependency management. This occurs when different libraries or modules require different versions of the same dependency. In such cases, resolving conflicts often involves analyzing the dependencies' requirements and determining if there is a compatible version that satisfies all constraints. If no compatible version is available, you might need to consider alternatives or workarounds. It is also beneficial to keep an eye on updates and changes in the libraries you depend on, as newer versions might resolve such conflicts or offer improved compatibility.

Another important aspect of dependency management is the use of dependency management tools that facilitate versioning and conflict resolution. Nimble's dependency resolution mechanism attempts to find a version of each library that satisfies all constraints specified by the project's dependencies. However, manual intervention might be necessary when automatic resolution does not yield satisfactory results. In such cases, understanding the dependency tree and the interdependencies between libraries can provide insight into the underlying issues.

Moreover, it is important to have a strategy for managing development and production environments. In a development environment, you might want to use the latest versions of libraries to take advantage of new features and improvements. Conversely, in a production environment, stability and consistency are paramount. Therefore, it is advisable to lock dependencies to specific versions that have been tested and verified. This ensures that your production environment remains stable and that any issues encountered in production are not caused by unexpected changes in dependencies.

When dealing with versioning issues, adopting semantic versioning practices can be highly beneficial. Semantic versioning involves incrementing version numbers based on the type of changes introduced. This convention helps in communicating the nature of changes to users and developers. For instance, a major version increment signifies breaking changes, a minor version increment indicates backward-compatible new features, and a patch version increment represents backward-compatible bug fixes. By adhering to semantic versioning, you can better manage expectations and ensure that updates do not inadvertently introduce compatibility issues.

Furthermore, integrating continuous integration (CI) and continuous deployment (CD) practices into your development workflow can significantly enhance dependency management. CI systems can be configured to automatically fetch and build dependencies, run tests, and verify that changes do not break the project. CD practices, on the other hand, ensure that updates are smoothly transitioned from development to production environments. Both CI and CD systems can help catch issues early in the development cycle, reducing the risk of encountering dependency-related problems in production.

To mitigate the risks associated with outdated or unsupported dependencies, it is important to regularly review and update your dependencies. This involves monitoring for new releases, bug fixes, and security updates. Automated tools and services that track dependencies and alert you to updates can be invaluable in this regard. By staying proactive about updating dependencies, you can address potential issues before they impact your project.

In cases where dependencies are no longer maintained or supported, you may need to evaluate alternative libraries or frameworks. This involves researching and testing new options to determine if they meet the project's requirements and are compatible with the existing codebase. Contributing to the maintenance of existing libraries or engaging with the community to advocate for continued support can also be effective strategies.

In conclusion, managing dependencies and versioning in Nim requires a comprehensive approach that includes using tools like Nimble, resolving conflicts, adhering to versioning conventions, and integrating CI/CD practices. By adopting these practices and staying proactive in managing your dependencies, you can ensure the stability, compatibility, and maintainability of your Nim projects. Effective dependency management not only simplifies development but also contributes to the long-term success of your projects by preventing and addressing potential issues.

Addressing dependency management in Nim involves not just technical execution but also strategic planning. An essential practice is to utilize Nim's built-in tools and community standards to ensure that your project's dependencies are handled efficiently and predictably.

One effective strategy is to utilize version pinning within your `nimble` file. Pinning specific versions of dependencies can provide a reliable and consistent development environment, reducing the risk of unexpected changes that might disrupt the project. By specifying exact versions, you ensure that every developer and build environment uses the same set of libraries, thereby avoiding discrepancies that can arise from version updates. This practice is particularly important in large projects with multiple contributors, where consistency across environments is crucial.

However, pinning versions is not a one-size-fits-all solution. There are scenarios where allowing for minor version updates while pinning major versions can be beneficial. For instance, minor version updates often include bug fixes and small improvements that do not introduce breaking changes. Allowing such updates can help keep your project up-to-date with improvements and security patches without risking major disruptions.

When managing dependencies, another key consideration is the resolution of dependency conflicts. These conflicts typically occur when different libraries require different versions of the same dependency. To address this, I often start by analyzing the dependency graph to understand which libraries are causing the conflict and what versions they require. Tools like Nimble offer commands to visualize and troubleshoot dependency trees, which can be invaluable in pinpointing and resolving such issues.

In cases where conflicts cannot be resolved by simply adjusting version constraints, more involved solutions may be necessary. This might include refactoring parts of your codebase to reduce reliance on conflicting libraries or contributing to the upstream projects to resolve compatibility issues. Contributing back to the libraries you depend on not only benefits your project but also supports the broader community.

In addition to handling conflicts, managing dependency updates is a critical aspect of maintaining a healthy project. Regularly reviewing and updating dependencies ensures that your project benefits from the latest improvements and security patches. Automated tools and services that monitor dependencies for updates can assist in this process. For instance, GitHub's Dependabot can automatically open pull requests to update dependencies, allowing you to review and merge changes without manually tracking updates.

Another effective approach for managing dependencies involves using dependency locks. Nimble supports creating a lock file that captures the exact versions of all dependencies at a given point in time. This lock file can be committed to version control, ensuring that everyone working on the project uses the same set of library versions. Lock files are particularly useful in CI/CD pipelines where consistent build environments are necessary for reliable testing and deployment.

Dealing with versioning issues also involves understanding and implementing semantic versioning principles. Semantic versioning provides a structured way to communicate the nature of changes between different versions of a library. By adhering to semantic versioning, libraries can signal whether updates include breaking changes, new features, or bug fixes. This practice helps in setting expectations and planning for updates in a way that minimizes disruption.

Furthermore, engaging with the Nim community can offer additional support and resources for managing dependencies. Community forums, mailing lists, and discussion groups often provide insights and solutions for common dependency management challenges. By participating in these communities, you can share your experiences, seek advice, and learn from others who have faced similar issues.

Finally, effective dependency management also includes handling deprecated or abandoned libraries. If a library you depend on is no longer maintained, it is essential to evaluate alternatives that can provide similar functionality. Researching and testing new libraries requires careful consideration of compatibility and support to ensure that any transition does not introduce new issues. In some cases, you might need to take over the maintenance of a library or collaborate with others to keep it updated.

In conclusion, managing dependencies and versioning in Nim is a multifaceted task that involves careful planning, ongoing maintenance, and community engagement. By utilizing tools like Nimble, pinning versions, handling conflicts, and adhering to semantic versioning practices, you can ensure that your project's dependencies are managed effectively. Regular updates, proactive conflict resolution, and engagement with the community further contribute to a stable and reliable project environment. Through these practices, you can maintain the stability and integrity of your Nim projects, facilitating successful development and deployment.

CHAPTER 32:

In dealing with database integration, it's essential to understand the specific requirements and capabilities of each database system to ensure effective use of Nim's features. For relational databases, apart from basic CRUD (Create, Read, Update, Delete) operations, complex queries and database schema management are integral aspects. Handling these tasks efficiently in Nim involves leveraging its robust database libraries and understanding their advanced features.

For relational databases such as PostgreSQL and MySQL, managing complex queries involves constructing SQL statements that may include joins, subqueries, and aggregations. Nim's database drivers, like `db_postgres` and `db_mysql`, provide comprehensive support for executing such queries. You can execute complex queries using the `execute` function, which allows you to run SQL commands and handle results within your Nim application. When dealing with results from complex queries, Nim's database libraries often provide data access methods that allow you to fetch results in various formats, such as rows or result sets.

For instance, handling results from a multi-join query might require iterating over rows and processing columns. Nim's built-in types and libraries can be used to parse and manipulate these results efficiently. When processing query results, it's crucial to ensure that the data is correctly mapped to the appropriate Nim types to avoid type mismatches and ensure accurate data handling.

In addition to query execution, schema management in

relational databases often involves creating and modifying database structures, such as tables and indexes. Nim's database drivers usually provide functions for executing DDL (Data Definition Language) statements that allow you to manage database schema elements. For example, creating a new table might involve executing a `CREATE TABLE` SQL statement through the driver, and modifying an existing schema could involve `ALTER TABLE` commands.

Database schema changes can be challenging, especially when dealing with production systems. Therefore, implementing a robust migration strategy is crucial. This strategy involves scripting schema changes and applying them systematically across development, testing, and production environments. Tools and libraries that support database migrations can be helpful in automating this process and ensuring consistency.

Turning to NoSQL databases, the integration approach differs significantly from relational databases due to their schema-less nature and document-oriented structure. When working with NoSQL databases like MongoDB, the focus is on document manipulation rather than relational data management. The `mongo_nim` library facilitates interaction with MongoDB by providing methods for performing CRUD operations on documents and collections.

In MongoDB, for instance, data is stored in collections of documents, which are analogous to rows in relational databases but can have varying structures. This flexibility requires a different approach to querying and data manipulation. For example, inserting a document into a MongoDB collection involves creating a document object and using the `insert` function provided by the `mongo_nim` library. Querying documents involves constructing queries in JSON format and using the appropriate methods to execute them.

The document-oriented nature of MongoDB means that queries can be more flexible, allowing for complex filtering and aggregation directly within the database. Nim's `mongo_nim` library supports a range of query capabilities, including filtering, sorting, and projecting specific fields. Understanding how to construct efficient queries in MongoDB is crucial for optimizing performance and ensuring that the application retrieves the necessary data efficiently.

Handling schema changes in NoSQL databases also differs from relational databases. Since NoSQL databases like MongoDB allow for schema-less documents, changes to the data structure can be made more dynamically. However, managing these changes still requires careful consideration to maintain data consistency and application stability. Implementing validation rules and migration strategies for document structures can help manage schema evolution effectively.

When integrating databases with Nim, it's essential to address performance considerations and ensure that database interactions do not become a bottleneck in your application. Techniques such as indexing are critical for optimizing query performance. Both relational and NoSQL databases support indexing to improve the speed of data retrieval operations. Creating appropriate indexes on frequently queried fields can significantly enhance the performance of your database interactions.

Connection management is another crucial aspect of database integration. Efficient handling of database connections is vital for maintaining application performance and resource utilization. Connection pooling is a common practice that involves reusing a pool of pre-established connections to reduce the overhead of establishing new connections frequently. Nim's database libraries often provide support for connection pooling or allow for custom implementation to manage connections effectively.

Error handling and logging are integral to managing database interactions. Implementing robust error handling mechanisms ensures that your application can gracefully handle issues such as connection failures, query errors, and data integrity problems. Comprehensive logging of database operations helps in diagnosing issues and understanding application behavior, providing valuable insights for troubleshooting and optimization.

In summary, integrating Nim with various database systems involves leveraging the appropriate database drivers, understanding the specific interaction models of relational and NoSQL databases, and implementing best practices for query execution, schema management, and performance optimization. By effectively using Nim's database libraries and addressing aspects such as connection management, error handling, and logging, you can build applications that interact with databases seamlessly and efficiently.

When integrating Nim with databases, attention to the nuances of each database type ensures efficient and effective data management. Having explored the interaction with both relational and NoSQL databases, it is crucial to delve deeper into some advanced practices and considerations that impact real-world applications.

In relational databases, the execution of transactions is an important aspect of maintaining data integrity and consistency. Transactions allow multiple operations to be performed as a single unit of work, which either completes entirely or rolls back if any part fails. In Nim, managing transactions involves using the `beginTransaction`, `commit`, and `rollback` functions provided by the database libraries. Transactions are essential for operations that require atomicity, such as transferring funds between accounts or updating multiple related records. Ensuring that transactions are handled correctly can prevent data anomalies and ensure consistency in concurrent environments.

For instance, when performing a transaction in a Nim application interfacing with PostgreSQL, you might start a transaction with `beginTransaction()`, execute several queries, and then commit the transaction if all operations succeed. If an error occurs during the transaction, invoking `rollback()` ensures that none of the changes are applied, maintaining the database's integrity. Proper exception handling around transaction operations is essential to manage errors and ensure that the application can respond appropriately.

Another advanced topic in relational database integration is the use of stored procedures and triggers. Stored procedures are precompiled SQL statements stored in the database, which can be executed as a single call. They are useful for encapsulating complex business logic and improving performance by reducing the need to send multiple queries from the application. Nim's database libraries typically allow executing stored procedures by calling the appropriate function and passing necessary parameters.

Triggers are database mechanisms that automatically execute predefined actions in response to specific events, such as insertions, updates, or deletions. They are useful for enforcing data integrity rules or automatically updating related records. While integrating Nim with databases, understanding how to define and manage triggers ensures that your application can leverage these powerful features effectively.

In the realm of NoSQL databases, managing and querying data involves different strategies compared to relational systems. One important consideration is schema design, particularly for document-oriented databases like MongoDB. Unlike relational databases, where schema changes can be managed through migrations, document databases allow for flexible and evolving document structures. However, this flexibility also requires careful planning to ensure that queries remain efficient and data consistency is maintained.

Designing effective indexes in NoSQL databases is crucial for optimizing query performance. Indexes are structures that improve the speed of data retrieval operations. For MongoDB, you can create indexes on fields that are frequently queried or used in sorting operations. The `createIndex` function in the `mongo_nim` library facilitates index creation. Proper index design helps in reducing query execution time and improving overall application performance. Monitoring and analyzing query performance can help identify opportunities for adding or modifying indexes to enhance efficiency.

Handling large volumes of data in NoSQL databases involves strategies for data partitioning and sharding. Sharding distributes data across multiple servers or nodes to balance the load and improve performance. For instance, in MongoDB, sharding can be implemented by specifying a shard key that determines how data is distributed across shards. Understanding sharding strategies and configuring them appropriately ensures that the database can scale horizontally to handle increased data loads.

Another advanced consideration in NoSQL database integration is managing data consistency and replication. Many NoSQL databases provide mechanisms for data replication to ensure availability and fault tolerance. For example, MongoDB uses replica sets to provide redundancy and high availability. Each replica set consists of a primary node that handles write operations and one or more secondary nodes that replicate the data from the primary. Configuring replication and understanding its impact on data consistency and availability is crucial for designing resilient applications.

Security is a critical aspect of database integration, regardless of the database type. Implementing secure database connections involves using encryption protocols such as TLS/SSL to protect data in transit. Both relational and NoSQL databases support encrypted connections, which should be configured to prevent unauthorized access to sensitive information. Additionally, applying the principle of least privilege by creating and managing database users with appropriate access levels helps in minimizing security risks.

Another security practice is regularly updating and patching database systems to address vulnerabilities and apply security fixes. Database vendors frequently release updates that include security enhancements, and keeping your database system up to date is essential for maintaining a secure environment.

Finally, monitoring and auditing database activity is crucial for detecting and responding to potential issues. Implementing logging and monitoring solutions helps in tracking database performance, identifying bottlenecks, and detecting anomalies. Many database systems provide built-in tools or third-party integrations for monitoring and auditing, allowing you to gain insights into database operations and make data-driven decisions for optimization.

By addressing these advanced practices and considerations, you can ensure that your Nim applications interact with databases effectively and securely. Understanding the intricacies of transaction management, schema design, indexing, sharding, replication, and security is essential for building robust and high-performing database-integrated applications.

CHAPTER 33:

In contemplating the trajectory of Nim's development, it's imperative to address how the language's future features and capabilities might intersect with broader technological trends and community needs. One of the prominent areas under consideration is the expansion of Nim's support for concurrent and parallel programming. As computational tasks increasingly demand multi-threaded and distributed processing capabilities, Nim's ability to efficiently handle concurrency will become more critical. Future advancements in this domain might involve enhanced support for asynchronous programming models, better abstractions for parallel execution, and more sophisticated concurrency primitives. These improvements would not only address current challenges in high-performance computing but also position Nim as a robust option for developing complex, scalable systems.

Another crucial aspect of Nim's future evolution is its integration with modern development practices and tools. The rise of DevOps and continuous integration/continuous deployment (CI/CD) methodologies has transformed software development workflows. To align with these practices, Nim might benefit from more seamless integration with popular CI/CD tools, improved package management systems, and better support for containerization technologies like Docker. By enhancing its ecosystem to facilitate these modern practices, Nim can better support developers in deploying and managing applications efficiently throughout their lifecycle.

In parallel, the advancement of Nim's tooling ecosystem is essential for maintaining developer productivity and engagement. As the language matures, there is an opportunity to refine and expand the available development tools, such as integrated development environments (IDEs), debuggers, and profilers. Improved tooling can significantly enhance the development experience, making it easier to write, test, and optimize Nim code. Investments in this area might include creating more feature-rich IDE plugins, enhancing debugging capabilities, and developing advanced performance profiling tools. These enhancements would contribute to a more streamlined development process and empower developers to build higher-quality applications more effectively.

The future of Nim also involves exploring new domains and applications where the language can make a significant impact. One promising area is systems programming, where Nim's low-level capabilities and efficient execution are particularly well-suited. As systems programming becomes increasingly complex, with growing demands for high performance and reliability, Nim's features could be further refined to address these challenges. This might involve improving support for systems-level programming constructs, optimizing low-level memory management, and providing more comprehensive abstractions for system interactions. By advancing in this space, Nim could solidify its position as a valuable tool for developing critical systems and infrastructure.

Moreover, Nim's role in the broader programming landscape could be influenced by its ability to interface with emerging technologies and paradigms. For instance, as machine learning and artificial intelligence (AI) continue to advance, integrating Nim with popular machine learning frameworks and libraries could open new avenues for its application. Future developments might focus on creating bindings or extensions for widely-used AI libraries, enhancing support for data processing and analysis, and facilitating the development of machine learning models directly in Nim. These capabilities would expand Nim's reach into cutting-edge technological areas and provide developers with new tools for tackling complex data-driven challenges.

The community's role in shaping Nim's future cannot be overstated. As the language evolves, the feedback, contributions, and support from the Nim community are pivotal in guiding its development. Active engagement from users, contributors, and advocates helps identify areas for improvement, propose new features, and drive the language's growth. Future directions for Nim may involve fostering a more inclusive and collaborative community, encouraging contributions from diverse perspectives, and expanding outreach efforts to attract new users and contributors. A thriving community not only supports the language's development but also ensures its continued relevance and vitality.

In summary, the future of Nim is characterized by exciting potential and opportunities for growth. As the language evolves, it will likely address emerging needs in concurrency, tooling, development practices, systems programming, and integration with new technologies. By focusing on these areas and leveraging the collective efforts of its community, Nim can continue to advance as a powerful and versatile language, capable of meeting the demands of modern software development and making meaningful contributions to the field.

As we delve into the potential future directions for Nim, it's essential to consider how advancements in language design could enhance its functionality and appeal. One critical area of focus is the improvement of language ergonomics. Enhancing Nim's syntax and usability to better align with modern programming practices could significantly impact developer adoption and productivity. This might involve streamlining language constructs, refining error handling mechanisms, and introducing more intuitive abstractions that simplify common programming tasks. By making the language more accessible and user-friendly, Nim could attract a broader audience and foster a more vibrant development community.

In addition to language ergonomics, the integration of Nim with emerging paradigms in software development represents a key area for future exploration. For instance, the rise of edge computing and the Internet of Things (IoT) necessitates robust support for distributed systems and resource-constrained environments. Nim's potential to excel in these domains hinges on its ability to offer efficient, lightweight, and scalable solutions. Future development efforts might focus on optimizing Nim's performance in such contexts, developing specialized libraries for IoT and edge computing, and enhancing its support for distributed computing frameworks. By addressing these needs, Nim could become a preferred choice for building applications that operate in increasingly decentralized and heterogeneous environments.

The integration of Nim with modern web technologies also presents a promising avenue for growth. As web applications continue to evolve, the demand for languages that can seamlessly interface with web technologies and frameworks is increasing. Nim's potential in this area might involve improving its capabilities for web development, including better support for web frameworks, enhanced tools for frontend and backend integration, and more robust mechanisms for handling web-specific tasks such as asynchronous processing and network communication. By bridging the gap between Nim and contemporary web technologies, the language could become a more versatile tool for developing a wide range of web applications and services.

Another important consideration is the evolution of Nim's ecosystem and its relationship with other programming languages and tools. As the software development landscape becomes increasingly interconnected, the ability of Nim to interoperate with other languages and systems will be crucial. This might involve developing better foreign function interfaces (FFIs) to facilitate integration with libraries and frameworks written in other languages, as well as creating more comprehensive tooling to support cross-language development workflows. By enhancing its interoperability, Nim can leverage existing technologies and ecosystems, making it a more flexible and valuable tool for developers working in diverse environments.

Furthermore, addressing challenges related to security and reliability will be essential as Nim continues to grow and mature. As applications become more complex and security threats more sophisticated, it is vital for programming languages to provide robust mechanisms for ensuring code safety and reliability. Future developments in Nim might focus on enhancing its security features, such as improving its support for secure coding practices, integrating advanced static analysis tools, and providing more comprehensive mechanisms for runtime safety and error handling. By prioritizing these aspects, Nim can better support the development of secure and reliable software, which is increasingly critical in today's digital landscape.

The potential for Nim to make significant contributions to the fields of scientific computing and data analysis is also worth exploring. As data-driven applications become more prevalent, the need for efficient and effective tools for handling large datasets, performing complex calculations, and visualizing results is growing. Nim's strengths in performance and low-level control could be leveraged to develop powerful libraries and tools for scientific computing and data analysis.

This might involve creating specialized libraries for numerical computations, data manipulation, and visualization, as well as enhancing Nim's support for parallel and distributed computing to handle large-scale data processing tasks.

Finally, fostering a strong and engaged community will be critical to Nim's future success. The development and adoption of any programming language are heavily influenced by its community of users, contributors, and advocates. Efforts to grow and support the Nim community might include initiatives to encourage more contributions, provide better resources and support for new users, and organize events and collaborations that bring together developers and enthusiasts. A thriving community not only contributes to the language's growth but also ensures its continued relevance and innovation.

In summary, the future directions for Nim are shaped by a combination of language enhancements, integration with emerging technologies, and community engagement. By focusing on improving language ergonomics, supporting new paradigms, expanding its ecosystem, addressing security and reliability challenges, and fostering a vibrant community, Nim has the potential to evolve into a powerful and versatile tool that meets the needs of modern software development and makes significant contributions to various fields.

Security Best Practices

When it comes to systems programming, ensuring the security of your code is paramount. Writing secure code in Nim involves understanding and applying a range of best practices that address common vulnerabilities, implement secure coding techniques, and employ strategies to protect applications from various security threats. The focus here is on how to leverage Nim's features effectively while mitigating risks and enhancing overall security.

The foundation of secure coding in Nim begins with understanding and addressing common vulnerabilities that can compromise the integrity of an application. Buffer overflow vulnerabilities, for instance, remain a significant concern in systems programming. Nim's memory safety features, such as bounds checking and automatic memory management, are designed to help prevent such vulnerabilities. However, developers must still be vigilant, particularly when interfacing with lower-level code or external libraries that may not adhere to the same safety practices. It is essential to validate and sanitize inputs rigorously to prevent buffer overflow attacks and other related issues.

Another critical aspect of security is managing user input. Input validation is crucial to prevent injection attacks, such as SQL injection or command injection. Nim's standard library provides mechanisms for safe handling of inputs, but it is up to the developer to implement these mechanisms correctly. Use parameterized queries when interacting with databases to avoid SQL injection vulnerabilities, and carefully validate and sanitize all user inputs to prevent malicious data from being processed by your application.

In addition to input validation, understanding and applying principles of least privilege is essential for securing your code. The principle of least privilege dictates that each component of a system should have only the minimum level of access necessary to perform its function. This principle should be applied both in terms of user permissions and in the design of the code itself. For example, limit the scope of variables and functions to only what is necessary for their intended purpose, and avoid using overly broad permissions that could potentially expose your system to attacks.

Secure coding practices also involve safeguarding against race conditions and concurrency issues. In Nim, which supports concurrent and parallel programming, it is important to manage access to shared resources carefully to avoid race conditions that could lead to security vulnerabilities. Employ synchronization mechanisms, such as mutexes or locks, to ensure that concurrent operations do not interfere with each other and that shared data remains consistent and secure.

Error handling is another critical area where security best practices must be applied. Proper error handling ensures that exceptions and errors do not expose sensitive information or disrupt the normal operation of the application. Nim's exception handling mechanisms should be used to manage errors gracefully and securely. Avoid exposing detailed error messages or stack traces to end users, as these can provide attackers with valuable information about the internal workings of your application. Instead, log errors internally and provide generic error messages to users.

Security best practices also extend to managing dependencies and third-party libraries. When incorporating external libraries into your Nim projects, it is crucial to evaluate their security and maintainability. Regularly update dependencies to incorporate security patches and fixes, and be cautious of libraries that are no longer actively maintained or have known vulnerabilities. Nim's package management tools can help manage dependencies, but developers should remain proactive in monitoring and addressing potential security issues related to third-party code.

Another important consideration is ensuring secure communication and data handling. When dealing with sensitive data, such as user credentials or personal information, it is essential to use strong encryption techniques. Nim's standard library includes support for cryptographic functions, but developers should follow best practices for encryption, such as using established and secure algorithms and properly managing cryptographic keys. Additionally, ensure that data transmitted over networks is protected using secure protocols, such as HTTPS, to prevent interception and tampering.

Finally, implementing comprehensive security testing and auditing practices is vital for identifying and addressing potential vulnerabilities in your code. Regular security testing, including static and dynamic analysis, penetration testing, and code reviews, can help uncover security issues that may not be immediately apparent. Nim's tooling and third-party security tools can assist in this process, but a proactive approach to security testing and code auditing is essential for maintaining a secure application.

In conclusion, writing secure code in Nim involves a combination of understanding common vulnerabilities, applying secure coding techniques, and implementing strategies to protect against security threats. By focusing on areas such as input validation, least privilege, concurrency management, error handling, dependency management, secure communication, and security testing, developers can significantly enhance the security of their Nim applications. Adhering to these best practices ensures that your code is robust, resilient, and better equipped to handle the evolving landscape of security threats.

In continuing the exploration of secure coding practices within Nim, it becomes evident that handling sensitive data with care is paramount. One fundamental principle here is data protection, which encompasses both data at rest and data in transit. For data at rest, encryption plays a critical role. Nim offers libraries that support encryption algorithms, but selecting a robust and up-to-date algorithm is essential. Implementing proper key management practices is equally important; this includes securely storing and handling encryption keys to prevent unauthorized access. Similarly, when dealing with data in transit, such as during network communications, employing secure protocols like TLS ensures that data cannot be intercepted or tampered with. It's imperative to configure these protocols correctly and keep them updated to mitigate vulnerabilities.

Additionally, implementing secure authentication mechanisms is a cornerstone of application security. Authentication verifies the identity of users or systems attempting to access your application. In Nim, leveraging established libraries and frameworks that provide secure authentication methods is advisable. For instance, incorporating multi-factor authentication (MFA) adds an extra layer of security beyond mere username and password combinations. It is also essential to handle authentication data, such as passwords, with care—using hashing and salting techniques to protect against password breaches. Password storage should employ algorithms designed for security, such as bcrypt or Argon2, rather than relying on simple hashing functions like MD5 or SHA-1.

Authorization, which determines the permissions granted to authenticated users, is another critical aspect. After verifying the identity, it is crucial to enforce appropriate access controls based on user roles and privileges. In Nim, implementing role-based access control (RBAC) or attribute-based access control (ABAC) can help manage and enforce these permissions effectively. Each user or role should have the minimum necessary permissions to perform their tasks, adhering to the principle of least privilege. Regularly reviewing and updating access control policies helps prevent privilege escalation and unauthorized access.

Another significant area to address is session management. Secure session handling prevents unauthorized access to user sessions and protects against session hijacking or fixation attacks. Nim's libraries for session management should be used to create secure session identifiers, enforce session expiration, and use secure cookies for session tracking. Ensuring that sessions are invalidated upon logout and implementing secure mechanisms for regenerating session tokens are also essential practices.

When integrating third-party services or libraries into your Nim application, it is crucial to assess their security implications. While leveraging existing libraries can expedite development, they may introduce security risks if not properly vetted. Regularly updating these dependencies to incorporate security patches and fixes is vital. Moreover, scrutinizing the security practices of the third-party services and libraries, such as their handling of sensitive data and adherence to security standards, helps ensure that they do not undermine the security of your application.

Another aspect of maintaining application security involves monitoring and logging. Comprehensive logging practices allow for tracking of application behavior and detection of potential security incidents. Nim provides mechanisms for logging, but it is important to configure logging to capture relevant security events without exposing sensitive information. Implementing real-time monitoring and alerting systems can help detect and respond to suspicious activities promptly. Regularly reviewing logs and conducting security audits further enhances the ability to identify and address security issues proactively.

In the realm of secure coding practices, considering the implications of deployment and configuration is also crucial. Ensuring that your application is deployed in a secure environment involves configuring servers and infrastructure with security best practices. This includes using secure configurations for web servers, databases, and other components, as well as employing firewalls and intrusion detection systems. Secure deployment practices also involve managing software updates and patches to address vulnerabilities and applying security hardening techniques to minimize the attack surface.

Moreover, security is not a one-time effort but an ongoing process. Regular security assessments, including vulnerability scanning and penetration testing, help identify potential weaknesses in your application. Nim's ecosystem, combined with various security tools, can assist in performing these assessments. Staying informed about emerging security threats and trends, and continuously adapting your security practices, ensures that your application remains resilient against evolving threats.

Finally, fostering a culture of security awareness within your development team is essential. Training and educating team members about secure coding practices, potential security risks, and best practices for safeguarding applications contribute to building a security-conscious development environment. Encouraging a proactive approach to security and incorporating security considerations throughout the development lifecycle helps in creating robust and secure applications.

In summary, applying security best practices in Nim involves a multifaceted approach, addressing areas such as data protection, authentication, authorization, session management, dependency security, monitoring, and deployment. By focusing on these areas and maintaining a vigilant and proactive stance, developers can significantly enhance the security of their Nim applications and safeguard them against a wide range of threats.

In continuing to delve into secure coding practices within Nim, it's crucial to address the handling of user input and output, as improper handling can lead to significant vulnerabilities. Validating and sanitizing user input is essential to prevent common attacks such as SQL injection, cross-site scripting (XSS), and command injection. When dealing with inputs, it's important to define strict validation rules and use predefined methods and libraries that help enforce these rules. For instance, if your application interacts with databases, using parameterized queries or prepared statements is a best practice to mitigate SQL injection risks. In the context of web applications, escaping output to ensure that user-generated content does not introduce malicious code is imperative.

Equally important is understanding and managing the security of your application's communication channels. This involves using secure protocols for data exchange, such as HTTPS for web traffic. Nim provides various libraries that support secure communication, but configuring these libraries properly is crucial. Enforcing encryption for data in transit not only protects against eavesdropping but also ensures data integrity and authenticity. When using HTTPS, ensure that you're not just relying on the default configurations but also verifying certificates and enforcing strong cipher suites to bolster security.

Another significant aspect is the implementation of proper error handling and exception management. While it might seem like a less critical concern compared to other security measures, improper error handling can reveal sensitive information or provide attackers with clues about potential vulnerabilities. It is essential to handle exceptions in a way that does not expose stack traces or internal logic to end users. Custom error pages should be used to display user-friendly messages while logging detailed error information securely on the server. This approach helps in diagnosing issues without compromising the security of the application.

One area often overlooked in secure coding is the use of secure coding patterns and principles. Adopting coding standards and best practices tailored for security can greatly reduce vulnerabilities. For example, implementing coding practices that minimize the use of unsafe functions, avoid hardcoding sensitive information, and ensure proper access control helps in maintaining secure codebases. Nim's capabilities can be harnessed to implement these practices, ensuring that the language's features are used effectively to adhere to security guidelines.

Addressing the security of APIs is another crucial area. APIs often serve as the interface between different components or systems, making them a potential target for attacks. Implementing strong authentication and authorization mechanisms for APIs is vital. This includes using API keys, OAuth tokens, or JWTs (JSON Web Tokens) to control access and ensure that only authorized entities can interact with the API. Furthermore, securing API endpoints by validating and sanitizing inputs, enforcing rate limits, and monitoring API usage can help protect against abuse and unauthorized access.

When considering the integration of third-party services or libraries, the potential security implications must be thoroughly evaluated. Although incorporating these external components can accelerate development, it's crucial to vet them carefully. Ensure that third-party libraries are from reputable sources, have been reviewed for security vulnerabilities, and are regularly updated. Relying on outdated or unverified libraries can introduce risks, so maintaining an updated inventory of dependencies and monitoring their security advisories is essential.

Additionally, secure configuration management is a critical aspect of maintaining application security. Misconfigured servers, databases, or other infrastructure components can expose vulnerabilities. It's important to follow security best practices for configuring these components, including disabling unnecessary services, enforcing strong authentication mechanisms, and applying least privilege principles. Regularly reviewing and updating configurations in response to new security findings helps in minimizing risks.

The practice of secure coding also extends to software development lifecycle management. Incorporating security testing and reviews at various stages of the development process is essential. This includes conducting static and dynamic analysis, performing code reviews with a focus on security, and integrating security testing tools into the continuous integration/continuous deployment (CI/CD) pipelines. Automating security tests and incorporating them into the build process helps in identifying and addressing vulnerabilities early in the development cycle.

Furthermore, fostering a culture of security awareness among development teams contributes significantly to maintaining secure code. Training developers on secure coding practices, common vulnerabilities, and the latest security threats ensures that security considerations are integral to the development process. Encouraging developers to stay informed about emerging security trends and best practices helps in proactively addressing potential risks and adapting to new threats.

In conclusion, maintaining a secure application in Nim requires a comprehensive approach that encompasses input validation, secure communication, proper error handling, adherence to secure coding practices, API security, careful management of third-party components, secure configuration, and integration of security testing throughout the development lifecycle. By implementing these practices diligently and continuously adapting to evolving security threats, developers can build robust and secure applications that effectively safeguard against a wide range of security risks.

CHAPTER 34:

Expanding on the practice of creating and using Nim bindings, it's crucial to delve into more complex scenarios that involve integrating Nim with both C and C++ libraries, particularly when dealing with advanced features such as class methods, templates, or complex data structures. The intricacies involved in these scenarios often necessitate a deeper understanding of both Nim's foreign function interface (FFI) capabilities and the external library's API.

When integrating Nim with C libraries, handling complex data structures can pose significant challenges. For instance, if a C library exposes a structure with nested fields or pointers to other structures, one must accurately replicate these structures in Nim. Consider a C library that provides a function for manipulating a custom data structure. The C definition might look something like this:

```c
// complex_struct.h
typedef struct {
  int id;
  char name;
} ComplexStruct;

void initialize(ComplexStruct cs);
void updateName(ComplexStruct cs, const char name);
```

To bind this in Nim, one must define a corresponding Nim structure and correctly manage the memory and data interactions:

```nim
complex_struct.nim
import ffi

type
 ComplexStruct object
  id: cint
  name: cstring

proc initialize(cs: ptr ComplexStruct) {.importc: "initialize()".}
proc updateName(cs: ptr ComplexStruct, name: cstring) {.importc: "updateName(, )".}
```

Here, the `ComplexStruct` type is defined in Nim to match the C structure. The `importc` pragma is used to declare the external functions, and the `ptr` keyword is used to denote pointers, reflecting the original C function signatures. It is imperative to manage memory allocation and deallocation carefully, particularly with pointers and dynamically allocated memory. Nim's garbage collector does not automatically manage memory allocated by C, so manual intervention is required.

Integrating with C++ libraries introduces additional complexity due to C++'s object-oriented features, including classes and templates. A typical C++ library may define classes and methods with varying access specifiers and inheritance hierarchies. Binding C++ classes to Nim often involves using C wrappers to simplify the interface. For instance, if a C++ library provides a class with multiple methods:

```cpp
// cpp_library.h
class MyClass {
public:
```

```cpp
  MyClass();
  void doSomething();
  int getValue() const;
private:
  int value;
};
```

Creating a C-compatible wrapper might be necessary to expose this functionality to Nim:

```cpp
// cpp_wrapper.cpp
extern "C" {
  MyClass createMyClass() { return new MyClass(); }
  void destroyMyClass(MyClass obj) { delete obj; }
  void doSomething(MyClass obj) { obj->doSomething(); }
  int getValue(MyClass obj) { return obj->getValue(); }
}
```

The corresponding Nim bindings for this wrapper would be:

```nim
cpp_library.nim
import ffi

type
 MyClass object
   ptr: ptr object

proc    createMyClass():    ptr    MyClass    {.importcpp:
"createMyClass()".}
proc    destroyMyClass(obj:    ptr    MyClass)    {.importcpp:
"destroyMyClass()".}
proc    doSomething(obj:    ptr    MyClass)    {.importcpp:
"doSomething()".}
proc getValue(obj: ptr MyClass): cint {.importcpp: "getValue()".}
```

` ` `

In this scenario, Nim interacts with the C++ library through the C wrapper functions, abstracting the complexities of C++ features. This approach not only simplifies the Nim bindings but also ensures better maintainability and clarity.

Additionally, integrating Nim with external libraries often requires handling various build and link-time configurations. Dependencies must be correctly specified, and the build system must be configured to include the necessary header files and link against the appropriate libraries. Nim's build system supports passing custom flags to the C compiler and linker using the `--passC:` and `--passL:` options. For example, linking against a specific library might involve:

```bash
nim c --passL:"-lmyexternal" my_program.nim
```

This command instructs the linker to include `libmyexternal` during the linking phase. Proper configuration ensures that all dependencies are correctly resolved, and the external libraries are correctly linked into the final executable.

Testing and debugging bindings involve unique challenges, particularly when dealing with memory issues and undefined behavior. Utilizing tools such as Valgrind or AddressSanitizer can help detect and diagnose memory-related problems. Thorough testing, including unit tests for each binding and integration tests for the overall system, is essential to verify the correctness and stability of the integration.

In summary, creating and using Nim bindings requires careful attention to detail in replicating foreign function interfaces, managing memory and resources, and handling complex data types and class structures. By employing strategies such as using C wrappers for C++ libraries, configuring build systems accurately, and employing rigorous testing practices, developers can leverage Nim's capabilities to integrate seamlessly with external libraries and tools, enhancing the language's utility and versatility in various application domains.

Integrating Nim with external libraries often involves dealing with various challenges related to data type conversion, error handling, and maintaining compatibility across different platforms. As we delve deeper into practical examples of setting up and using bindings, it's essential to explore these aspects thoroughly.

One significant challenge when creating bindings is converting between Nim and the foreign language's data types. For example, when working with a C library that uses complex data types such as structs with pointers, it is crucial to ensure that Nim's representations align correctly with those in C. Consider a scenario where a C library provides a function that operates on a structure containing a dynamically allocated array:

```c
// dynamic_array.h
typedef struct {
    int array;
    size_t size;
} DynamicArray;

void initializeArray(DynamicArray da, size_t size);
void setValue(DynamicArray da, size_t index, int value);
int getValue(DynamicArray da, size_t index);
void freeArray(DynamicArray da);
```

To create Nim bindings for this C library, we need to carefully handle the dynamic memory and ensure that Nim can interact with these structures appropriately. The corresponding Nim code might look like this:

```nim
dynamic_array.nim
import ffi

type
  DynamicArray object
    array: ptr cint
    size: cuint

proc initializeArray(da: ptr DynamicArray, size: cuint)
{.importc: "initializeArray(, )".}
proc setValue(da: ptr DynamicArray, index: cuint, value: cint)
{.importc: "setValue(, , )".}
proc getValue(da: ptr DynamicArray, index: cuint): cint
{.importc: "getValue(, )".}
proc freeArray(da: ptr DynamicArray) {.importc:
"freeArray()".}
```

Here, `ptr cint` and `ptr DynamicArray` are used to represent pointers, while `cuint` and `cint` correspond to C's `size_t` and `int`, respectively. Handling memory management correctly is critical to avoid leaks and ensure that memory allocated by C is properly freed when no longer needed.

Error handling is another critical aspect when interfacing Nim with external libraries. Many C libraries use error codes or specific conventions to report issues, and Nim must be able to handle these effectively. Suppose the C library function returns an integer error code; the Nim binding could use a custom error handling mechanism:

```c
// example.h
```

```
int performOperation(int param);
` ` `
```

In Nim, you could define a procedure to handle the operation and check for errors:

```nim
example.nim
import ffi

proc performOperation(param: cint): cint {.importc: "performOperation()".}

proc safePerformOperation(param: cint): int
 let result performOperation(param)
 if result ! 0:
   raise newException(ValueError, "Operation failed with error code: " & $result)
 result
```

In this case, `safePerformOperation` wraps the C function and raises an exception if an error occurs, making it easier to handle errors in a Nim-like fashion.

Maintaining compatibility across different platforms requires careful consideration of compiler-specific details and ABI (Application Binary Interface) variations. For instance, differences in calling conventions, data alignment, and size of fundamental types can affect how Nim interacts with C or C++ libraries. Testing on multiple platforms is essential to ensure that bindings work consistently. Nim's ability to use conditional compilation can assist in handling platform-specific variations:

```nim
when defined(windows):
 const
  LIB_EXT ".dll"
```

```
else:
 const
  LIB_EXT ".so"
```

```
proc loadLibrary(libName: cstring): ptr Lib {.importc: "dlopen(,
RTLD_LAZY)".}
```

In this snippet, `when defined(windows)` is used to set the appropriate library file extension based on the operating system. Nim provides several tools to manage such cross-platform concerns and ensure that bindings remain functional across different environments.

Another crucial aspect is managing the build process for projects that include bindings. Ensuring that the build system correctly includes necessary header files and links against the appropriate libraries is essential for successful integration. For larger projects, it might be beneficial to use build tools like CMake or Ninja in conjunction with Nim's build system. Configuring these tools to handle complex build requirements can streamline the development process and facilitate easier maintenance.

For example, to integrate a C++ library using CMake, one would typically create a `CMakeLists.txt` file to configure the build:

```cmake
cmake_minimum_required(VERSION 3.10)
project(MyProject)

add_library(mylib STATIC mylib.cpp)
target_include_directories(mylib          PUBLIC          $
{CMAKE_CURRENT_SOURCE_DIR})

add_executable(myapp main.cpp)
target_link_libraries(myapp mylib)
```

This configuration ensures that the C++ source files are compiled into a static library and linked with the executable. Integrating this with Nim involves specifying appropriate flags and linking options in Nim's build configuration.

In summary, creating and using Nim bindings involves meticulous attention to data type conversions, error handling, and cross-platform compatibility. By effectively managing these aspects and leveraging tools for building and linking, developers can successfully integrate Nim with a wide range of external libraries and tools, enhancing the language's flexibility and applicability in various domains.

CHAPTER 35:

When approaching performance analysis, it is vital to recognize that benchmarking and profiling are not isolated activities but integral parts of a holistic strategy for optimizing application performance. Each technique provides different insights and complements one another in identifying and addressing performance issues.

To benchmark effectively, one must design tests that accurately reflect real-world usage scenarios. This involves setting up test cases that simulate typical workloads and usage patterns. For instance, if you are developing a web server in Nim, benchmarks should measure how the server performs under various loads, such as handling multiple simultaneous connections or processing a high volume of requests per second. This helps gauge the server's ability to scale and its responsiveness under stress.

When writing benchmarks, I focus on isolating the code segments of interest to ensure that the measurements are not influenced by external factors. It is also crucial to use a representative sample size to avoid skewed results. For example, if I am benchmarking a sorting algorithm, I ensure that the input data size and distribution are consistent across test runs. Additionally, running benchmarks multiple times and taking the average of the results can help mitigate the effects of transient system states, such as background processes affecting performance.

In Nim, the `benchmark` module can be particularly useful for such tasks. This module provides facilities for measuring the execution time of code blocks. It is also designed to be simple and straightforward, allowing developers to focus on writing effective benchmarks without dealing with complex configurations. Here is an example demonstrating how to set up a benchmark to evaluate the performance of a custom sorting function:

```nim
import benchmark

proc customSort(arr: var seq[int])
  A sample sorting algorithm
  for i in 0..<arr.high:
   for j in i+1..arr.high:
    if arr[i] > arr[j]:
     swap(arr[i], arr[j])

var data: seq[int] @[5, 3, 8, 6, 2]

benchmark "Sorting performance" do:
  customSort(data)
```

In this example, `customSort` is the function being benchmarked, and the `benchmark` block measures its execution time. It is beneficial to include various test cases with different data sizes and characteristics to assess how the sorting algorithm performs under diverse conditions.

Profiling, on the other hand, provides a broader view of application performance by examining how time and resources are allocated across different parts of the application. Profiling tools collect detailed information about function calls, memory allocations, and other runtime metrics. This data helps developers identify which parts of the code are consuming the most resources and where optimization efforts should be focused.

To profile a Nim application effectively, I use tools such as `gprof` and `Valgrind`. The `gprof` tool, for example, helps in generating a profile of program execution by collecting statistics about function call frequency and execution time. By analyzing the resulting profile data, I can determine which functions are the most time-consuming and prioritize them for optimization.

Using `Valgrind` with its `Callgrind` tool provides more detailed insights into the performance of an application. `Callgrind` generates a call graph that visualizes the relationships between functions and shows how much time is spent in each function. This information can be instrumental in identifying performance bottlenecks and understanding the impact of function calls on overall performance. To use `Callgrind`, I run the application with `Valgrind` and analyze the output with a visualization tool such as `KCacheGrind`. This allows me to see which functions are called most frequently and which consume the most CPU time.

When interpreting profiling results, I focus on several key metrics. CPU time tells me how much processor time is spent in each function, while memory usage metrics reveal how much memory is allocated and freed during execution. High CPU usage in specific functions may indicate inefficient algorithms or excessive computation, while high memory usage can signal memory leaks or suboptimal memory management practices.

In addition to using profiling tools, optimizing performance often involves revisiting and refactoring code to improve efficiency. For instance, if a profiling report indicates that a particular function is consuming an excessive amount of CPU time, I might consider optimizing the algorithm used in that function or reducing the frequency of its calls. Code refactoring can include techniques such as loop unrolling, caching results of expensive computations, or parallelizing tasks to make better use of multi-core processors.

It is also important to consider the trade-offs between different optimization strategies. While optimizing for speed might reduce execution time, it could increase memory usage or make the code more complex. Conversely, optimizing for memory efficiency might impact performance negatively. Balancing these trade-offs requires a careful evaluation of application requirements and performance goals.

Benchmarking and profiling should be seen as ongoing processes rather than one-time tasks. As applications evolve and new features are added, performance characteristics can change. Regular benchmarking and profiling help ensure that performance remains within acceptable limits and that new changes do not introduce regressions or new performance issues.

In conclusion, effective performance benchmarking and profiling involve a combination of measuring specific code segments under realistic conditions, analyzing detailed performance data, and applying optimization strategies based on the insights gained. By systematically applying these techniques, I can ensure that Nim applications are optimized for performance, providing users with efficient and responsive experiences.

When delving into the specifics of performance optimization, it is crucial to understand the nuances of interpreting the results derived from benchmarking and profiling. Analyzing these results not only provides insights into the efficiency of code but also helps in identifying potential bottlenecks that could be mitigated for better performance.

Profiling data often reveals which parts of the code are consuming the most resources, be it CPU time, memory, or other system resources. In Nim, as in other languages, the primary objective is to utilize this data to guide optimizations. For example, a common scenario I encounter is a function that appears to be a significant performance bottleneck. The profiling results might show that this function is called very frequently or that it consumes a substantial amount of CPU time. Understanding the root cause involves examining the function's implementation and its interactions with other parts of the code.

One method to optimize a frequently called function is to minimize the work done within it. This could involve reducing the complexity of algorithms, eliminating redundant calculations, or employing more efficient data structures. For instance, if a function is performing multiple lookups in a list, switching to a hash table could significantly improve lookup times. Refactoring the function to use more efficient algorithms or data structures based on the profiling results can lead to substantial performance improvements.

Another crucial aspect of performance optimization is memory management. Profiling tools often provide detailed information about memory usage, including allocations and deallocations. High memory usage or frequent allocation and deallocation of memory can indicate inefficiencies. In Nim, memory management is generally handled automatically, but developers can still impact performance by managing memory allocations wisely. For instance, reusing memory buffers or pools can reduce the overhead associated with frequent memory allocations and deallocations.

In scenarios where high memory usage is detected, analyzing the data for memory leaks is essential. Memory leaks occur when allocated memory is not properly deallocated, leading to increased memory consumption over time. Profiling tools can help identify such leaks by showing patterns of increasing memory usage. Addressing memory leaks involves ensuring that all allocated memory is properly released once it is no longer needed. This might require reviewing code to ensure that memory deallocation is handled correctly, particularly in complex data structures or long-running processes.

Performance optimization also extends to the use of concurrency and parallelism. Profiling data can reveal whether the application is effectively utilizing multi-core processors. If certain parts of the code are identified as being executed serially, introducing parallelism could improve performance. Nim's concurrency model supports various approaches, including threads and asynchronous programming. Implementing parallelism involves ensuring that tasks are appropriately divided and that shared resources are managed to avoid race conditions and other concurrency issues.

Beyond optimizing individual functions or components, it is important to consider the overall architecture and design of the application. Profiling results may indicate that the application's design introduces performance bottlenecks. For example, an application that relies heavily on synchronous I/O operations might experience delays if I/O operations are not optimized or if they are blocking other critical processes. In such cases, adopting asynchronous I/O or optimizing I/O patterns can lead to improved performance.

Furthermore, it is essential to recognize the trade-offs between performance improvements and code maintainability. While optimizing code for performance is crucial, it should not come at the expense of code readability and maintainability. Complex optimizations can make code harder to understand and maintain. Striking a balance between performance and code quality involves making informed decisions about where to apply optimizations and ensuring that changes are well-documented.

Regular performance testing and monitoring are key to maintaining optimal performance over time. As applications evolve and new features are added, the performance characteristics can change. Continuous benchmarking and profiling help ensure that performance remains within acceptable limits and that new changes do not introduce regressions. Implementing automated performance tests as part of the development workflow can help catch performance issues early and ensure that optimizations are effective.

In conclusion, the process of performance benchmarking and profiling is integral to developing efficient applications. By meticulously analyzing benchmarking data and profiling results, developers can identify performance bottlenecks, optimize critical code paths, and make informed decisions about architecture and design. This iterative process of measurement, analysis, and optimization is essential for creating high-performance applications that meet user expectations and perform efficiently in real-world scenarios.

CHAPTER 36:

As we reflect on the key insights from our exploration of Nim, it's crucial to synthesize the knowledge gained and consider how it can be applied moving forward. The study of Nim's features and methodologies has provided a solid foundation for understanding and utilizing this versatile language. This reflection not only reinforces the core concepts but also highlights the opportunities for further growth and exploration.

One of the central themes of our discussion has been the emphasis on practical application. The examples and techniques provided throughout the book illustrate how to effectively implement Nim's features in real-world scenarios. This practical approach is intended to bridge the gap between theoretical knowledge and hands-on experience, which is essential for mastering any programming language. By applying these techniques to your projects, you can better understand Nim's strengths and leverage them to solve complex problems.

A significant portion of our focus has been on performance optimization and profiling. Understanding how to benchmark and profile Nim applications is key to ensuring that your code runs efficiently and effectively. The methodologies discussed for measuring performance, identifying bottlenecks, and optimizing code are invaluable skills for any developer. These practices not only help in refining your current projects but also in preparing you to tackle more demanding and resource-intensive applications in the future.

Security has also been a major area of concern. The exploration of common vulnerabilities and secure coding practices is crucial for developing robust and resilient software. As you continue to work with Nim, maintaining a strong focus on security will help safeguard your applications against potential threats. The techniques and best practices outlined are meant to serve as a foundation upon which you can build a more secure coding approach. It's essential to stay updated with the latest security trends and practices to continually enhance your security posture.

Another important aspect of our discussion has been the integration of Nim with other languages and systems. The ability to create and use bindings allows you to leverage existing libraries and tools from different programming environments. This interoperability can significantly extend the functionality of your Nim applications and facilitate the integration of diverse technologies. Mastering this skill opens up new possibilities for incorporating Nim into a broader array of projects and systems.

As you advance in your Nim journey, exploring advanced topics and staying engaged with the Nim community are crucial for continued growth. The Nim ecosystem is dynamic and ever-evolving, with new features and improvements being introduced regularly. Keeping up with these developments will not only enhance your understanding of the language but also enable you to take advantage of new functionalities and innovations.

Engagement with the Nim community is another valuable avenue for growth. Participating in forums, contributing to open-source projects, and collaborating with other developers can provide new perspectives and insights. The community is a rich resource for learning, networking, and sharing knowledge. It offers opportunities to discuss challenges, exchange ideas, and collaborate on projects, all of which can enhance your skills and broaden your understanding of Nim.

In addition to community involvement, pursuing further education and training can deepen your expertise. There are numerous resources available, including online courses, tutorials, and technical documentation, that can provide additional insights and skills. Continuous learning is essential for staying current with best practices and emerging trends in the field.

Practical experience remains one of the most effective ways to solidify your knowledge and skills. Working on personal or professional projects that challenge you to apply the concepts and techniques learned is invaluable. These projects provide an opportunity to experiment with new ideas, tackle complex problems, and gain hands-on experience with Nim's features and capabilities.

Furthermore, consider exploring niche areas of interest within Nim or related technologies. Whether it's delving into advanced metaprogramming techniques, experimenting with concurrency and parallelism, or investigating new frameworks and libraries, exploring specialized topics can provide new insights and enhance your overall expertise.

Ultimately, the journey with Nim is an ongoing process of learning, application, and exploration. By consolidating the knowledge gained, staying engaged with the community, seeking further education, and applying your skills to real-world projects, you will continue to grow as a Nim developer and make meaningful contributions to the field.

As you embark on the next steps of your Nim journey, embrace the opportunities for growth and development that lie ahead. The foundation laid through this exploration provides a strong starting point, and with continued curiosity and dedication, you can advance your expertise, tackle new challenges, and contribute to the evolving landscape of Nim programming.

Reflecting on the exploration of Nim, it is clear that the journey through this language has been both profound and enlightening. The principles and techniques discussed form a solid foundation for both immediate application and long-term development. As you move forward, applying these insights practically will be crucial in honing your skills and expanding your expertise.

The detailed examination of Nim's capabilities has underscored its versatility and power. Understanding the language's core features, from its elegant syntax to its robust standard library, has provided a comprehensive framework for building efficient and effective software. Leveraging these features in various contexts will enable you to address complex programming challenges with confidence and precision.

A key takeaway from our discussion is the importance of continuous learning and adaptation. The landscape of software development is constantly evolving, and staying abreast of new advancements in Nim and related technologies is essential. This involves not only keeping up with updates and new releases but also engaging with ongoing educational resources. Courses, tutorials, and community-driven content can provide fresh perspectives and reinforce your knowledge.

Practical experience remains paramount. As you apply the concepts covered, you will likely encounter real-world scenarios that test and expand your understanding. Whether through personal projects, professional assignments, or contributions to open-source initiatives, these hands-on experiences are invaluable. They offer opportunities to experiment with new ideas, refine techniques, and learn from both successes and challenges.

The emphasis on performance benchmarking and profiling has highlighted the critical role of optimizing application performance. Understanding how to measure and analyze performance metrics allows you to make informed decisions about code improvements and resource management. This approach ensures that your applications run efficiently and meet the high standards required for modern software.

Security best practices, another major focus, underscore the necessity of writing secure code. The exploration of common vulnerabilities and secure coding techniques provides a framework for protecting applications against threats. By integrating these practices into your development process, you can build robust and resilient software that safeguards both user data and system integrity.

The ability to create and use bindings to integrate Nim with other languages and tools has expanded your capabilities. This interoperability allows you to harness the strengths of various technologies and incorporate them into your Nim projects. Mastering this skill will enable you to work with a broader range of libraries and systems, enhancing the versatility and functionality of your applications.

Looking ahead, there are numerous avenues for further exploration. Advanced topics such as metaprogramming, concurrency, and domain-specific languages offer exciting opportunities for deepening your knowledge and pushing the boundaries of what you can achieve with Nim. Engaging with these areas will not only enhance your technical skills but also open doors to innovative solutions and advanced programming paradigms.

Staying engaged with the Nim community is another crucial aspect of ongoing development. The community serves as a rich resource for learning, collaboration, and networking. Participating in forums, attending conferences, and contributing to discussions will keep you connected with the latest trends and developments in the Nim ecosystem. This engagement fosters a collaborative environment where ideas are shared, challenges are addressed, and advancements are made.

In addition to community involvement, pursuing specialized interests or niche areas within Nim can further enrich your journey. Exploring specific libraries, frameworks, or applications of Nim can provide new insights and deepen your expertise in particular domains. This focused exploration can lead to more innovative and tailored solutions in your projects.

As you continue to advance in your Nim journey, maintaining a curious and proactive mindset will be essential. The evolving nature of technology means that there will always be new concepts to learn and new challenges to tackle. Embracing this continuous learning process will help you stay at the forefront of software development and contribute meaningfully to the Nim community and beyond.

Ultimately, the knowledge and skills acquired through this exploration of Nim are not endpoints but rather stepping stones in a broader journey of programming and development. By building on the foundation laid here, pursuing further learning, and actively engaging with the community, you will continue to grow as a developer and make significant contributions to the field.